remembering...A Town That Was

To order additional copies, please contact us.
BookSurge, LLC
www.booksurge.com
1-866-308-6235
orders@booksurge.com

remembering...A Town That Was

Myrna Miller Messer

2006

remembering...A Town That Was

About the Author

Myrna Messer was born and raised in Foxholm, North Dakota, a small Midwestern town that has slowly dwindled away. After graduating from high school, she attended Minot Business College in Minot, North Dakota, and then Minot State Teachers College earning an associate degree in elementary education. After teaching several years, she married Ray Messer and retired to raise four sons. The family moved around with The Boeing Company for fifteen years while working on the Minuteman Missile Program and then settled in Derby, Kansas. Myrna returned to college and earned a Bachelor's Degree from Wichita State University. Now retired from teaching, she enjoys spending time with her two granddaughters, writing and traveling with her husband.

***

Acknowledgements

A special thanks to my son Jim, whose unflagging encouragement, support and faith made writing this book possible, to our computer expert Greg Dye who came to our rescue so many times, and to my husband Ray who was with me every step of the way. I also thank my son Mike, Dr. Christopher K. Brooks, and Lacey Heilman who spent many hours editing my manuscript, and the rest of my family whose faith never wavered.

I want to acknowledge Girdell Patterson of Carpio, who generously shared historical information, and my friend Marilyn Goheen, who dug up pictures and brainstormed with me about our 4-H days. My sister-in-law Verlene Miller, long-time Foxholm resident and veteran of Miller's Bar, also deserves heart-felt appreciation for reviving memories that had been buried under the dust of time.

Recollections from my Foxholm friends were invaluable. Each added its own special flavor, which when blended together present a proper picture of the town we once knew.

To my precious granddaughters
Allie and Sofie

Preface

After my mother died, we found a small book among her things that I had given her for recording memories. She hadn't written much but what she had written is priceless to us. Suddenly it occurred to me that I know very little about my parents and grandparents and could kick myself for not asking questions and recording their stories—stories that could have created an awareness and understanding of what our ancestors were all about—stories that I could have passed down to my sons and their children. With this lesson in mind, I am telling my story as a gift to my children. I want to paint them a picture of my life so they will know who we are and whose we are. I want to preserve the memories of people I have loved and lost, to keep happy experiences fresh, and worthy perspectives documented long after their due-date has expired. I want them to live on in my children's memories.

The people I have chosen to include in my book were very important to me. They were honest, hardworking and strong with a sense of humor. They were good people who taught me, helped me, changed me, made me laugh and sometimes cry—all of which helped to mold me into what I am today. These humble people did not lack intelligence but opportunity. Each had infinite powers waiting for development and release.

Day One

It was the morning of June 22, 1933. Dr. Garrison entered St. Joseph's Hospital in Minot, North Dakota to make his rounds and was greeted by the news that Ella Miller had checked into the hospital and was asking for him. This expectant mother had come to see him the day before, confident that her time had come, even though it was a month before her due date. Garrison, being the professional that he was, assured her that it was a false alarm and told her to go back home.

Highly indignant, she did go back home but not without telling him, "I'll go, but I'll be back! I haven't had six kids for nothing!" True to her word, Mrs. Miller returned, and a red-faced Dr. Garrison delivered her baby girl that very same day. Ten days later, which was customary length of bed rest after giving birth, Mom took me home to join the family.

The Village of Foxholm, North Dakota

Main Street of Foxholm. The first building on the left was the St. John's Dance Hall which was used for St. Mary's church functions until the new church was built.

The village of Foxholm, which I knew so intimately, was once a thriving pioneer community that served the prairie homesteaders, many of whom had emigrated from Minnesota. It is nestled in the Des Lacs River Valley about seventeen miles northwest of Minot. Sadly, Foxholm, like many other small towns in the area, is now only a faint shadow of its former self.

The area around the Des Lacs River was settled in 1886. Burlington, the town that met the settlers' needs, had a post office which was established in early 1884 and received mail arriving by stage coach from Devil's Lake. Letters and messages, however, were most likely carried through the area before Burlington became an authorized post office. There would have been nothing official about such postal activities since there were no mail routes, postage stamps or collection schedules. They would have simply relied on travelers who were undoubtedly asked to carry a letter for a friend or family.

There is no single factor that has contributed more to the settlement and development of North Dakota than the railroads which connect the countryside it covers. As the railroads laid track across the prairies, stations and sidetracks had to be established in order to do business in the surrounding areas. On each sidetrack was space for a depot, grain elevators and a lumberyard, making it a logical place to plat a townsite.

In 1893, the Soo Line Railroad was built through the Souris River Valley en route to Portal, North Dakota. The heavy work was done with teams of horses, and each thirty-foot section of rail weighed 720 pounds. Materials were hauled forward at the railhead by the work train, and telegraph lines were placed at the same time.

About ten miles up the river from Burlington and beside the railroad tracks, a water tower, windmill and section house were built to accommodate the operation of the railroad. A sign post bearing the name of Foxholm was put up near the buildings, and thus began the trade center town that would become my hometown. (As I was researching, one source said that Foxholm was named for "Home of the Foxes." I don't know if that's true or not, but in 1893 it could have been an appropriate name.)

Shortly after the railroad came, the settlers who lived in the Mouse River Valley, along with their neighbors who lived in the Des Lacs River Valley, petitioned for a post office and their request was granted. Jens Glein, Bill Zinninger's grandfather, (Bill still lives near his grandfather's homestead.) was appointed as the first postmaster, and the post office was on his farm which was located about a quarter mile upriver from the station. At that time, the postmaster's salary was based on the number of stamp cancellations that went through the postal station.

Bill Zinninger, grandson of the first postmaster Jens Glien,and wife
Polly

The mail came by rail. I remember that the passinger train, carrying
our mail, came through at 12:20 every day. If there were no passengers to
let off, the mail bag was thrown on the platform and was then delivered
to the post office by our depot agent Bill Markus. Markus was our depot
agent all the while I was growing up. When he retired, he was replaced
by Otto Knecht, who was originally from Hurdsfield, North Dakota.

When the train reached Portal, it's north-bound destination, it
turned around and made its way back to Minot and points beyond,
returning to Foxholm at five o'clock p.m. If the train didn't have to stop
for passengers, it used the "mail-on-the-fly" technique. The depot agent
attached the mail bag to a hanger device beside the track. As the train
sped by, the clerk on the train raised a catcher arm, a type of grappling
hook, which snagged the hanging mail pouch.

Foxholm Soo Line depot which was located on the original Railroad
buildings site.

When I was a young girl, Frank Lambert was our post master, and the post office was in his grocery store. If the service window shade was pulled down, we knew that he was still distributing the mail to our boxes and wouldn't be available for other postal services. In the spring, one might be greeted as he or she entered the store by a barrage of peeping. It was a common practice to order baby chicks which came as would any package. I'm sure the Lamberts, who lived in back of the store, were more than happy when the addressee picked them up.

In 1894, the settlers scraped together their hard-earned money and loaned the community enough to build the first school, which was located on the Glein farm. (I knew this farm as the Zinninger farm.) Not only did they put up the money, but they donated all the labor. Unfortunately, the funds ran out before they finished the interior. To solve the problem, classes were held only during the summer months. Gradually, the building resumed, and in 1908 the school was completed, and the school term reached a full nine months. Gretha Peterson Hooke, an old-time pioneer and the first female born in Ward County, attended this one-room school. One of her school friends was Mary Glein Zinninger who was two grades behind Gretha. Gretha graduated from the eighth grade and went on to the normal school in Valley City where she earned a teaching certificate. She returned to her old school and became Mary Glein's eighth grade teacher. In 1909 a new larger school was built in the village. The vacated first school stood on the Zinninger farm until recently when Bill had it burned down to prevent further deterioration and vandalism.

In the spring of 1902, settlers began to migrate into the area and homestead in both river valleys. There was no bridge spanning the Des Lacs River, so those who needed to cross used a raft. This was the year of the killer March blizzard that raged across the large expanse of prairie, taking its toll on humans and animals alike. Homesteaders who had just arrived were caught with unfinished houses and inadequate shelters for their livestock. Before they could catch their breath, they were faced with another natural disaster. As the snow melted, the valleys became flooded with water. Once again, their homes and livestock were in jeopardy. Many of the newcomers had been warned about the horrors that awaited them on the desolate plains of the Dakotas, but they could not have been prepared for disasters such as these. Still, these courageous pioneers stayed and, through their hard work, transformed the virgin land into a modern community. Only the bravest, hardiest and most determined could have accomplished this momentous task. I am proud to say that my maternal grandparents were among those who did.

That spring the land on the west side of the railroad tracks, which was owned by Anton Larson, was surveyed for a town site. A store was built and opened by T. L. Simmons. Soon after, a hotel built by Mrs. Minnie Pearl was opened, and the little railroad town of Foxholm was on its way.

Main Street of Foxholm about 1900

Foxholm from the west side about 1900

Next, the land east of the railroad tracks, Peter Fugelso's homestead, was surveyed and became the future residential area of the town. Several years later, Mr. Fugelso donated three of these lots on which the first church in Foxholm, the Congregational Church, was built. It was a bungalow-type church with a large corner tower and solid oak pews and pulpit furniture to match. All the windows were of stained glass with memorial inscriptions. There was a finished basement that greatly helped meet the needs of the growing church community. The total cost of this church was $4200. Reverend U. T. Richmond was the acting pastor. The church building, now used for personal storage, still sits in the same location. Eventually, the schoolhouse that I attended was built just across the road from this church.

Foxholm State Bank and patrons Frank Schloer and friend.

Foxholm began to grow. By 1910 it boasted of three elevators, a hardware store, a bank, a livery stable, two mercantile stores, a meat market, a drug store, a lumberyard, a pool hall, a confectionery, a blacksmith shop, a barbershop and a larger hotel.

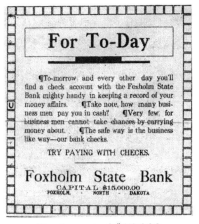

For To-Day

¶To-morrow, and every other day you'll find a check account with the Foxholm State Bank mighty handy in keeping a record of your money affairs.   ¶Take note, how many business men pay you in cash?   ¶Very few, for business men cannot take chances by carrying money about.   ¶The safe way is the business like way—our bank checks.

TRY PAYING WITH CHECKS.

Foxholm   State   Bank
CAPITAL $15,000.00
FOXHOLM   ·   NORTH   ·   DAKOTA

Bank capital $15,000

The grain elevators played an important role in our farming community. One of the early elevator managers was August Arnt who ran the Farmers Elevator. He and his family lived in one of the three cottages across the street from the Congregational Church. Jack Pritschet, a farmer in the Mouse River Valley, remembers hitching their horses, King and Blackie, to a farm wagon and hauling grain, which was loaded by hand, into Arnt's elevator. Sitting on top of the grain made the four-mile trip slow and hard for the young driver. Pulling a ton of grain up the hill near Baker's Bridge was a difficult job for the horses, and Jack had to stop midway to rest them. To prevent the heavy wooden-wheeled wagon from rolling back down, the brake had to be set. Going down the cemetery hill was just as arduous, and once again, Jack had to apply the brake lest the wagon overtake the horses. That was a big responsibility for a fourteen year old. Reaching his destination, Jack remembers unhooking one horse before driving into the elevator where the front end of the wagon was raised to allow it to empty. With the mission accomplished, the return trip was somewhat easier for both the team and driver, but rattling over the country road standing up couldn't have been much fun.

Jack Pritschet, local farmer

Feed-grinding mill near Foxholm

When Mr. Arnt retired due to ill health, his son Hank took over his job. It was at this time that my oldest brother Ralph was managing the Occident Elevator. Unlike today when the grain market can be checked on the computer at anytime of day, Ralph had to listen to the radio every day at noon to get the local price of grain, which was determined by the Minneapolis grain market. He and Edith were living with us at the time, and I remember times when Mom and Edith had to hustle to get his dinner on the table so he could be back to his office by twelve. Those were the mornings when Bonnie Bock visited, and they became absorbed in a hot pinochle game and forgot the time. I can still see

Bonnie dashing for the front door as Mom and Edith, giggling like two guilty kids, raced around the kitchen. Ralph knew them well enough to suspect they'd been up to something but would accept his canned soup or bologna sandwich without comment. Ralph's career as an elevator manager came to an end when he was drafted into the army during World War II and sent to California for his basic training.

The Foxholm News

A Continuation of The Carpio •Weekly News

Foxholm, Ward County, North Dakota, October 1, 1915.

Subscription $1.00 per year in ad

Some Special Bargains for Market Day Shoppers

GROCERIES

15 pounds of sugar	$1.00
6 bars Electric Spark soap	.25
7 bars Lenox soap	.25
3 cans standard corn	.25
3 packages of Jello	.25
1 33-oz can Gopher pork and beans	.15
4 packages Corn Flakes	.25
Regular 28c Nemo coffee, per lb.	.25

SHOES

FOOT SCHULZ CELEBRATED SHOES

1 lot Men's and Ladies' $4 shoes at $2.50
1 lot Men's and Ladies' $3.50 shoes at $2.00
1 lot of Ladies shoes at half price

DRY GOODS

5000 yards of Calico at 5 cents per yard
1 lot of Children's Hose at 5 cents a pair

Will Also Have Other Bargains Too Numerous to Mention

Extra Special We will give a 100-lb sack of Occident Flour FREE to party making largest cash purchase Market Day. **Extra Special**

F. W. LAMBERT, Foxholm, N. Dak.

Market Day Specials at Lambert's Mercantile
as advertised in The Foxholm News
Publisher, M.J. Pavlik
Subscription $1.00 per year in advance
October 1, 1915 issue

More Mercantile Fall Specials

F.W. Lambert's Mercantile, whose advertisements boasted of having cheap prices and complete, up-to-date stock, was the primary means of trade and commerce for Foxholm's rural community. The general store, which promised to compete with mail-order houses on everything, offered an enormous variety of articles: household items, groceries, hardware, farm equipment, bolts of cloth, colored thread, lace and ribbon, shoes, clothing, blankets, books, licorice whips, kerosene, wash boards and rat traps. They also handled harnesses which they hung on the walls and saddles and bridles that were draped over long wooden saw horses.

The majority of merchandise was displayed on shelves behind great wooden counters with barrels of nuts, apples and candies set in front of the counter. Unlike today's serve-yourself policy, Mr. and Mrs. Lambert assisted the customers with their purchases. A large ball of string and a huge roll of brown paper mounted on a metal frame with a sharp blade for cutting were used to wrap purchases.

Since money was scarce in the rural areas, an extension of credit was part of the business, and Mr. Lambert understood that he would be paid when the crop came in. It was also not unusual for a farmer to barter, and many bills were paid with a hog or fresh eggs.

Minot vs. Foxholm at Foxholm Sunday afternoon, July 25 : COME!

MARKET DAY AND CELEBRATION
FOXHOLM, TUESDAY, JULY 27, 1915

The Greatest Day Ever Held in Ward County Will Be Staged in Foxholm Next Tuesday--
The Gates Will Be Thrown Open and Keys Thrown in the River So That You
Can Have the Town to Yourself---Minot Band Will Be Here All Day
Long---Sport of All Kinds Are on the Program---Two Fast Base
Ball Games Will be Played--Big Bowery Dance--Royal
Good Time For Everybody

Arrangements have been completed for a rousing big market day and celebration to be staged in our fair village on Tuesday, July 27th. Our business men have united and are sparing no efforts towards making this day long to be remembered by people everywhere. The various committees appointed to look after the various details of the monster celebration are working tooth and nail so that nothing will be left undone that will tend to bring enjoyment and pleasure to the immense crowds that are sure to come to Foxholm on our First Annual Celebration and Market Day. A long list of varied sports are scheduled to take place during the day in which the girls, the boys, the fat and lean men, the ladies, in fact everybody will have an opportunity to show off their ability in running, jumping and divers forms of healthful amusements. Arrangements have been made to have the Minot Crack band of some twenty-five pieces here

for the auspicious occasions and they are under bonds to toot their horns all the long day, and mind you, the doings will start early on the morning of the 27th and keep on till after the wee, small hours of the next day, so bank on coming fully prepared to take in your share of the splendid things in store for you. Base Ball will be one of the chief sports on the programme and we understand that the teams of Carpio and Des Lacs, say nothing about our own boys, are getting loaded up for fair to capture the cash purse hung up for the sport, and judging from the silent activity going on the people can be certain of seeing some hair-raising stunts performed on the diamond. In the afternoon and evening a big bowery dance will be on for those who care to trip the light fantastic and we are told that after seeing and hearing what splendid music has been obtained to dispense the

sweet strains of melody, the people are already beginning to shake the toe so as to be in trim to enjoy the hop. Time is too short and space too precious to enumerate all the splendid amusements prepared for your entertainment, so take it for granted that you will miss a big time if you will not attend Foxholm's First Annual Market Day and Celebration. Forget your work for the day and come and spend a day of profit and enjoyment.

And, by the way, we almost forgot that our merchants are all making great preparations and stocking up with good bargains for the trade, so do not care to come for fun of which there will be bushels! make a long list of necessities to clothe and feed your families and come to take advantage of the splendid cuts that await the buying public. Any way see the large posters and come!

Market Day Celebration including baseball game between rivals
Minot and Foxholm.

The Lambert Store was still there when I was growing up, but the days of the small town mercantile stores were over. Thus, Lambert's sold only groceries and ice cream cones. Because the post office was still in the store, I was there a lot. I remember one day in particular. While walking out with our mail, I passed a bushel basket of beautiful, red ripe tomatoes. I loved tomatoes, and the temptation was too great; I reached down and took a nice big fat one. Suddenly I heard, "Uh, uh, uh." Mrs. Lambert just happened to be sitting in their darkened living room and caught me red-handed. I dropped that tomato like a hot potato and hurried from the store. I was terribly embarrassed and scared to death she would tell my parents. I lucked out; she didn't. I did, however, learn a good lesson; it was my first and last attempt at filching.

Ward County, one of the largest counties of North Dakota, lies almost entirely within the lignite area of western North Dakota. (The finding of lignite in the Dakota Region was reported by Lewis and Clark.) The discovery of coal was very important to the new settlers. Although it was sometimes difficult to burn, it was considerably better than the cow chips they were burning. Initially, the surface outcroppings were used for fuel, but this fuel was usually of a poor grade. As they dug deeper, rich veins of good lignite were found. As the area became more populated, commercial mining began.

Mine shaft at Foxholm

Underground coal mining opened in the Foxholm-Burlington area in the early 1900's giving another boost to the budding local economy. However welcome, it was a very dangerous operation.

To reach the coal vein, a shaft was usually dug into the side of the hill. The excavated dirt was used for a grade on which a tipple, an apparatus for emptying, was constructed. As the shaft deepened, it was timbered to prevent cave-ins. If the vein was adequate, side rooms were also excavated. The coal was loosened by blasting with dynamite or black powder. Narrow gauge tracks were laid for wooden cars that were loaded by hand and then pushed to the tipple where they were emptied by "tipping". As the mine deepened, mules or horses were used to pull the cars, which made the miner's job much easier. Once reloaded, the coal was hauled from the mine site by horse-drawn wagons.

Mule being used to pull coal cars out of the mine.

Foxholm Coal Mining

A highly successful mine called Tasker Coal Mine was located between Foxholm and Burlington at the junction of Highways 2 and 52. A boarding house and dance hall were built at this site.

Some of the coal was used to meet the needs of the surrounding community, and the rest was shipped out by rail. As many as four teams of men worked all day long as well as some nights loading the lignite into cars on the Soo Line siding.

Loading chutes at Foxholm Coal Mine

Sena Sartwell, a resident of Foxholm at one time, was one of the few women who worked in the mines. Sena didn't get paid, but with her help, her husband George was able to mine more tons in a week, which increased his paycheck. Slowly, during the 1920's, the coal mining industry declined, and gradually, all the mines were closed.

Several of these abandoned mines were located in the hills behind the Peterson farm where I lived as a little girl. Knowing the dangers of the old underground mines, Dad forbade my brothers Francis and Alvin to go anywhere near the area. In spite of Dad's warning, curiosity and a sense of adventure lured them to the abandoned mines where they discovered battered coal cars, rotted timbers and sections of rusty rails. Fortunately, they didn't end up on the bottom of an old mine shaft, as did some cows, but they did have interesting experiences that came to light years later.

On one of these exploring expeditions, they discovered an old Chevrolet car that was abandoned in a coulee. To hone their shooting skills with a .22 caliber single-shot rifle, they used its horn button as their target, competing, as usual, as they practiced.

In 1914, a fire destroyed Foxholm's three elevators and the depot.

Two of the elevators and the depot were rebuilt. Stockyards, holding pens for cattle that were shipped to market, were also built near the elevators. Hobos who rode the rails were frequent overnight guests in these stockyards. The town kids soon learned that, while some were friendly, others were mean and scary, which only added to the bums' mystique.

In later years, after trucking took the place of shipping by rail, we kids, recognizing a wonderful place to play, would congregate at the deserted stockyards. We'd walk, and even run, across the top of the pens, jump from one to another and swing on the gates. Each kid tried to be the most daring. We must have led the charmed lives of children because I don't remember anyone ever falling and breaking bones.

In 1922, a new school building constructed of dark Hebron brick, was built in town replacing the old one. This was my school, and I loved it. It was a magnificent structure and was considered to be one of the most modern school buildings in North Dakota. It had its own electric light plant and a complete water system.

Foxholm School dedicated in 1922

As reported by the Ward County Independent, the school was dedicated on November 29, 1922 "in an auspicious manner." A program given by the pupils was directed by the principal—Miss Anna Schwalier, Mrs. Stramer—the intermediate teacher, and Miss Tracy— the primary teacher. Several prestigious guest speakers attended the ceremony including Governor R.A. Nestos, Miss Minnie Nielson—State Superintendent of Public Instruction, and A.M. Waller—Ward County Superintendent of Schools. Short talks were also given by Ira Rush—the architect, Swen Olson—the contractor, Peter Fugelso—first clerk of the Foxholm School District, and Father Ott—priest at St. Mary's Catholic Church.

The school building was fifty-two by eighty feet. Entering either of the two entrances, one came upon two very wide fourteen-step stairways—one leading to the upper lever and the other to the basement level which housed the gymnasium, two bathrooms with connecting shower rooms, domestic science rooms, a janitor's room and a stage.

There were six rooms on the main floor and a spacious open cloakroom at each end of the hall that ran the length of the building. Coat hooks lined the opposite walls of the cloakrooms, and each had a large plate-glass window. Beneath each window was a good-sized steam-heat radiator. This was our favorite place to gather before school, especially on cold, blustery winter mornings. We'd huddle around the radiator that hissed and popped, trading confidences as we watched for schoolmates to arrive. After recess, we'd lay our wet mittens on the radiator, sending the smell of wet dogs floating down the halls. We were never allowed to turn the valve that regulated the heat, and if we did, we had the janitor, Johnny Haider, to reckon with. We were more afraid of him than we were of the principal. We all knew that it was a mortal sin to play on the gym floor with street shoes, and if he caught us at it, we'd better look out! Actually, though, I think he enjoyed his role at the school and the interaction he had with the kids. There was always someone in his janitor's room listening to one of his stories or just shooting the breeze with him. I can still see him lounging back in his chair with the radio playing, feet up, smoking and trying to keep a straight face as he teased. It didn't take long for us to realize that under his stern exterior lurked a practical joker. I remember the time he gave us a science lesson. He rigged up an electrical current that emitted a shock. One person took hold of a large iron vise, another held his hand, someone grabbed hold of the second kid and so on, making a human chain. Johnny would then press a button, and an electric shock would travel through the line, giving the last person a pretty good jolt. I ended up on the tail end more than once and took the shocks like a "man." There is no way that I would ever have let on that it hurt. I was too much of a tomboy.

Johnny Haider, school janitor

As the years passed, better roads and modern technology changed the complexion of the village. Some of the businesses survived, and a few new ones came in to replace the outmoded ones.

Fred Hjelm gave up blacksmithing and turned over the shop to Gorman Dahly. The majority of Dahy's business consisted of sharpening plow shoes, although he tackled all types of farm machine repairs. Gorman's son Will vividly recalls one of his visits to his dad's shop. The welding process was not yet used, and Gorman was forging together two short rods that he had heated to a molten red. He had just laid the completed rod on the ground when barefooted Will, not watching where he was going, turned and stepped squarely on it. The old saying, "once burned, twice wary" held true for Will. He assured me that it never happened again.

FRED HJELM

Foxholm, North Dakota

Blacksmithing
Horseshoeing

All Work Guaranteed First-
Class or No Pay

My story-telling Grandpa Hoerter used to fascinate me with his tales about his visits to the blacksmith shop. He made it sound mysterious and awesome, likening it to hell. He talked about the coals that sometimes were a tranquil blue, sometimes fiery red and sometimes white and how these coals became an inferno when the blacksmith fanned them with his bellows. Smoking his pipe, Grandpa would tell me how the blacksmith, with sweat running in rivulets, plunged the tip of the plowshare into the coals where they became white hot in a matter of minutes and how the powerful blacksmith with his bulging muscles shaped the metal by beating it with a heavy hand-held hammer. When he reached this point in the story, he'd tell in detail how the pounding on the metal created a shower of fearsome fiery sparks that reached the ceiling. I was mesmerized. To complete the process, the newly shaped metal, white hot from the forge, was plunged into water. Grandpa took great relish in describing how the hot steam shot up as it hit the water. His vivid description created a mental picture that I've never forgotten.

Another town survivor was the Cashman Hotel, which sat on the north end of our main street (Highway 52). It was an ornate old building with a very high, beautifully embossed tin ceiling and gleaming woodwork that always smelled of polish. An open oak stairway with carved newel posts wound its way up from the lobby to the guest rooms above. The lobby's walls were covered in flowered wallpaper that had accents of wine and gold and straight back chairs with curved ornate legs covered with matching wine-colored upholstery. Also in the lobby were a brown cowhide covered sofa and chair plus a small round table that matched the straight back chairs. An oak registration desk with a hand-held bell stood in the corner. I remember sneaking a look at the register, but we never dared touch the bell. My friend JoAnn and I would think up excuses to go into the hotel, and if we were lucky, we'd be invited in and offered a cookie. The swinging door that led into the kitchen from the dining room, which held the long, polished table and chairs that were used by the hotel guests, was always closed, but when she went to get the cookies, we'd get a glimpse of the kitchen with its hanging pots and pans. How grand it all seemed!

Like many of the businesses in town, the Cashman Hotel ran its course, and the doors were closed. All felt its closing, but Foxholm still had several businesses including my dad's bar and Joe Haider's service station. It also had the high school, which remained open until 1949 when, because of dwindling population, it was forced to consolidate with the Carpio School District.

The grade school continued to operate, but the attendance gradually waned until 1965 when there were only eight students remaining. The decision was obvious; the school that played such an important part in my life closed its doors one last time.

Vandalism flourished. Shades flapped from broken windows, and tattered, moldy text books and papers were strewn about the weathered floor. Battered desks once filled with lively students lay in a silent, twisted jumble. Downstairs, Johnny's gleaming gym floor was covered with a muddy slime that smelled of mold and rot. The time had come; the school building had to go.

Ruined desks litter the cloak room

Stairway to the main entrance now battered and beaten

The High School Room...blackboards gone, floors warped and
buckled, books and papers strewn about yielding to decay

I could have cried when I saw it being torn down. It felt like a personal violation. Visions of softball games, carnivals, spit wads, basketball and three-legged races flashed before my eyes. The once magnificent structure, the school that held so many wonderful memories, was gone forever.

Thanks to the farmers' business and the many fishermen who stopped in on their way to Lake Darling, the economy remained relatively steady, and the few remaining businesses continued to hold their own. Then, seemingly before our very eyes, Foxholm withered away to nothing but a hollow shell of its former robust, bustling community.

TEMPERANCE

LECTURE

Temperance Lecturer, Mr. P. J. Williams will speak in Carpio, Sunday, Aug. 22 at 11:00 a. m.; at Nazaret church at 2:00 p. m.; at Louie Pedersen's grove, Foxholm, at 4:00 p. m., and at Carpio at 8:00 p. m. Lecture at Carpio and Pedersen's will be in the English language.

Everybody Should Hear This Noted Temperance Lecturer

This took place in the same grove in which I played when we lived on the Peterson Place

Harvest Bee near Foxholm

Joe Clementich and Charles Liebel with an early threshing crew near Foxholm

History of St. Mary's Catholic Church

St. Mary's history goes back to 1883 when the first Catholic settlers, John Clouse and William Schneider, arrived by wagon from Devil's Lake and settled in the Mouse River Valley north of Burlington. Through their efforts, the first Catholic Church service was held sometime in 1885, and soon after, the first Mass was said at the Schneider home. The visiting priest's name was Father Cloud. From then on, Masses were held irregularly, sometimes at the Schneider home and other times at the Clouse home. These Masses, however erratic, provided sufficient evidence that there was a need to hold services at regular and stated times.

School house where Mass was first held in 1887

In 1887, this settlement became known as a station and was then named St. Mary's. A station was a designated location with a name but where no church had yet been built. This station was located on the Poepping farm that later became the site of the Harrington Ranch and then the Brooks Ranch. Today, it is where Highways 2 and 52 split, just north of Burlington. Priests came from Minot to serve the people. As the congregation grew, services were moved from individual homes to the Poepping School, which was located in St. Mary's School District. This schoolhouse was later moved to Lone Tree where it remains in its original state. My grandparents, John and Elizabeth Hoerter, were married in that school on May 14, 1889 in a double wedding ceremony with his sister, Eleanor, and Barney Schmitz.

FIRST DOUBLE WEDDING — May 14, 1889
Above: Mr. and Mrs. Bernard Schmitz
Left: Mr. and Mrs. John Hoerter

My Grandpa and Grandma Hoerter and Mr. and Mrs. Bernard Schmitz

In 1890, using the school building as a church, the station became a mission. Priests came from various places to conduct services. The community continued to grow as more Catholics moved into the area.

The first St. Mary's Church was built in 1890 on the George Peopping farm four miles north of Burlington for a total cost of nine hundred dollars. One hundred people now belonged to the congregation. The church was in use only a short time when tragedy struck. St. Mary's caught fire and burned to the ground. The cause of the fire was never determined. Some said lightning struck it, and others believe the source was the unattended candles that were lit on the altar. No one was present at the time of the fire.

Mr. Poepping provided violin music for church services

The people, once again, were without a place in which to worship. Recognizing the need, John Stammen volunteered his vacant residence that was located six miles north of where the church had been. Stammen eventually donated this building, which was located one-half mile from where Silver Bridge is today, to the church. Through the many talents and enthusiastic efforts of the congregation, the church was enlarged and remodeled. It was in this church that a young girl was tragically killed. Apparently, during a windstorm, the church door was blown open and was swinging back and forth. The Botz Family lived across the road from the church, and the mother, noticing the banging door, sent her daughter to close and lock it. The door had to be locked from the inside, and apparently, after locking it, the girl attempted to crawl out the window. The window fell across her neck, and unable to free herself, she died of strangulation.

At this time, a cemetery was also established next to the church, and the bodies buried near the Poepping station were exhumed and reburied in the new one.

The number of Catholics continued to grow. Immigrants from Prussia, Austria, Russia, West Holland and Stearns County, Minnesota moved into the area. St. Mary's community swelled in excess of 225 families, became incorporated and was established as a parish with a resident priest. The excited parishioners built their priest a 2½-story, wood-frame parish house which, at that time, was quite an impressive structure. The parish house was barely finished when they decided to make the village of Foxholm the center of their parish. The parishioners who lived north and east of the Heinen Bridge, now Silver Bridge, were, understandably, very unhappy about this decision. They thought that it would be entirely too far for them to travel with their horses and buggies, so they made the decision to build their own church, which they called St. Henry's. The site they chose was located four miles northeast of the present Lake Darling Dam. The church, a replica of the St. Henry's Church in Stearns County, was built in 1908 for the cost of $20,000. It was a beautiful structure with stained glass windows and solid oak pews that held about 250 people. It was served its entire life by the priests coming from St. Mary's in Foxholm.

Many of my ancestors are buried in this church's cemetery

Meanwhile, the St. Mary's people who did not join the St. Henry's group made plans to move the parish house to the site of the future church. They waited until fall when the ground was frozen to undertake this very difficult feat. It took dedication, determination and ingenuity to complete the task. The huge house was placed on planks and rollers and pulled by horses the entire five miles. To prevent the building from careening wildly down the steep hills they had to traverse, they hitched horses to the opposite side of the building to act as a brake system.

Parish house that was moved to Foxholm

With no church, St. Mary's functions were held in St John's Dance Hall on the main street of Foxholm. During this time, the parishioners were digging and building the church basement, which was also to serve as the church until the top half was completed. It took three years and twelve hundred dollars for them to complete the project. This facility was used for all church functions for the next seventeen years. My mother and father were married in this basement church. In 1927, under the leadership of Father Joseph Ott, St. Mary's Catholic Church was completed. The total cost was $18,700, and the church, which still stands, has a seating capacity of about 250 to three hundred, depending on the use of the choir loft. Its style and motif is Spanish. No one has ever been able to explain how a church of this style could make its way into a community that is almost entirely German. Seventy-five years later, this stately church is a tribute to the perseverance, dedication and sacrifices of the early parishioners and their Catholic faith.

Mom's First Communion Class at St. Henry's Church
St. Mary's Catholic Church

St. Mary's Catholic Church flanked by pine trees which were
Planted in 1928

St. Mary's Catholic Church in Foxholm has endured the passing of time and remains standing proudly, while all other businesses except one bar have succumbed to the times. Its Spanish style of architecture was unique in its locality and remains so today. St. Mary's and Father Kopp play a big part in my heritage. I was baptized, confirmed and married by him in this church that sits nestled in the Des Lacs River Valley.

Father Kopp

Father Anthony Kopp arrived in our parish the same year that I was born. In fact, I was the very first one whom he baptized in St. Mary's. Coincidentally, twenty-nine years later, my son, Jack, was the last one he baptized in this parish before retiring to the Memorial Hospital in Garrison, North Dakota where he served as chaplain until the time of his death in 1964.

Born in Russia on December 11, 1891, Father immigrated to the United States with his parents and settled near Harvey where he attended elementary school. He completed high school, college and theological studies at Assumption Abbey in Richardton, North Dakota. He finished his seminary studies at St. Paul Seminary and in 1917 was ordained a priest for the Diocese of Bismarck at St. Mary's Church in Richardton. Father served four parishes in the Diocese before being transferred to Foxholm in 1933.

Father, a small kind man, was a unique individual who fit right in to the German community of Foxholm. He spoke with a heavy German accent, and I later read that when he wrote his poetry and writings, he formulated the words in German and then wrote them in English, which sometimes made his writings hard to decipher. He heard Mom's confession in German, and when he left, I remember her saying that after going to confession in German for 64 years, she wasn't sure if she would know how to confess in English.

Father Kopp's sermons, today's homilies, were based on the Sunday's readings, and in these sermons, he never used the words "I" or "me" but always "the priest." I was very conscious of this but naively thought it must be theologically incorrect for a priest to refer specifically to himself while on the altar. Because I had never attended Mass in any other parish, I didn't realize until I moved to Crosby on my first teaching assignment and became a member of St. Patrick's Catholic Church that it was just Father's old German way of preaching.

As children, we attended catechism every other Saturday afternoon from two o'clock until four and every day for two weeks in the summer. The nuns, who came from Minot, were of the Benedictine Order, to whom my family has a special connection. They wore long black habits with black veils that completely covered their heads. Under their veils, they wore hood-like caps called coifs, which were white stiff bands that covered their foreheads, fit around their faces and extended down into the front of their robes like an old-fashioned dickey (detachable collar). That was before air conditioning, and the days of summer catechism could get plenty hot. I always wanted to ask if they shaved their heads to be more comfortable, but I wouldn't have dared. Such a personal question would have been disrespectful, and we were taught to respect the religious above all else. Each nun wore a large cross that hung from a chain around her neck and an oversized rosary, with its large crucifix, looped around her waist. The habit gave off an aura of reverence, which commanded respect.

As a text, we used the Baltimore Catechism, a book of questions and answers that was very difficult to understand. Each time we had class, we were assigned a number of questions for homework and were expected to learn the answers. It was hard and boring, but we diligently memorized every answer, and although we were able to recite them by heart, most of us had little understanding of what we were saying.

Although I disliked the catechism work, I loved the stories that the nuns told so well. I can still see Sister Anastasia; she was young and pretty with freckles scattered across her nose and a hint of devilment shining in her eyes. When she told us stories about the Old Testament, we could almost see the biblical characters. I also loved singing the old hymns. One of the sisters would play a small portable organ, which was set up in the church basement where we had class, and the other would line us up and direct the singing. "Mother Dearest, Mother Fairest" was one of my very favorites. "Holy God, We Praise Thy Name" was another. The rare times we sing these old songs during Mass today, I am flooded with these childhood memories, and for just a moment, I am back in that concrete church basement singing the hymns with those mystical nuns in their long black habits.

Little Angels (L.to R.) Rosie Greeman, ? Ahmann, Moudeen Pritschet and me

Making one's First Holy Communion was a special time, one that was conducted with great pomp and circumstance. During the two-week summer session, the nuns prepared for this occasion with great enthusiasm. All the communicants were dressed in white; the boys wore white shirts and pants, and the girls wore white dresses and veils. Each carried a white candle. When the children made their way to the communion rail, they were led by two "angels" of preschool age. I was an angel twice before I made my own First Communion. The nuns fashioned huge wings from wire, covered them with a gauzy material, and attached them to the angels who were dressed in long white dresses and halos. The procession was practiced several times so the children would know exactly when and where to kneel. (At that time, Catholics knelt before communion rails when receiving the sacrament.) During one practice, I fell asleep in the pew, and when I awoke, they were already standing in front of the altar. I ran down the aisle and was just in time to lead them back to the pew.

My First Holy Communion

As a reward for learning our lessons and sometimes just as a gift, the sisters gave us holy cards. I thought of them as being calling cards from heaven. They were similar to book marks in shape and depicted antique images of religious figures on one side and a short prayer on the other. They were beautiful, and I loved them.

I was nine years old when Father Kopp celebrated his twenty-fifth anniversary as a priest. The nuns, who had once again come to teach catechism, helped plan a big celebration for Father. It was decided that the parishioners would buy him a new chalice and present it to him during the special Mass that was attended by Bishop Ryan, senior clergy and priests from surrounding parishes. Since I was the first one Father baptized in our parish, I was chosen to carry the chalice and lead the procession into the church. I wore a white bridal gown and veil and carried the gold chalice on a white satin pillow. I remember sitting in the front pew and waiting for my signal from Sister. When she tapped on the pew with her ring, I was to go to the front, say my poem and present the chalice to Father. Sixty-three years have passed, but I can still hear that tapping and feel the surge of nervous excitement that ran through me as I made my way to the front of the church. I looked out at the sea of faces before me, then to Sister who gave me her nod, and I began,

"Jubilate, jubilate
Reverent Father loved and dear,
Five and twenty years of priesthood
Is our jubilant festive year."

I only remember this first verse, but on that special day, I recited it perfectly, much to the relief of my parents who were far more nervous than me.

Catherine Stockert, Father's cousin from Solen, North Dakota, was his live-in housekeeper. She was a lovely person, inside and out, and very capable of handling her job which included everything from cooking and cleaning to acting as hostess for visiting religious dignitaries. During the summer, my friend, JoAnn Bock, and I often walked down to visit her. When I think back, I realize that she must have been busy, but she always took time for us. Sometimes the three of us would sit on the back steps with a view of her beautiful flower garden and have lemonade and freshly baked cookies. She always had a story or two to tell us, and before we left, she'd cut each of us a bouquet of flowers to take home to our mothers.

When Catherine was in her late thirties or early forties, she married Roy Borgers, our confirmed-bachelor neighbor. She was a beautiful, radiant bride. She wore a lovely gown of evening blue satin fashioned with a full net overskirt and a matching blue veil that fell from a rhinestone-studded cap. Her bridal bouquet was made up of white star carnations with a gardenia in the center. At the conclusion of the wedding Mass, she laid a bouquet of colorful garden flowers on the Blessed Mother's side altar where she knelt in prayer while her soloist sang to the Blessed Virgin. It was a beautiful, touching moment, and I vowed that one day I would do the same. On June 30, 1958, my wedding day, I fulfilled that dream. I laid a red rose on that very same altar, and as I knelt in front of our Blessed Mother, my very dear Jewish friend, Franceen Glick, sang "Ave Maria."

I sang in the choir until I went to college. The entire Mass, with the exception of the sermon, Gospel and Epistle, was in Latin, as were many of the songs we sang.

The Requiem High Mass, which was the Mass for the dead, was a very solemn ceremony, full of ritual and heaviness. (In contrast, today's funeral Mass is a celebration of life, and instead of black vestments, the priest wears white.) I can still hear the somber music and smell the strong odor of incense that drifted upward into the choir loft.

As the funeral procession slowly entered the church, which was filled with black-clad mourners, Father began by intoning a soulful Latin prayer, which the choir answered with an equally somber Latin chant. The casket, which was covered with a black shroud, was sprinkled with holy water and immersed in the holy smoke of burning incense. During the Mass that followed, we sang the following chant many times: "Requiem aeteram dona eis..." begging the Lord to grant him eternal rest. The Requiem High Mass is one of my most poignant church memories.

St. Mary's Choir ...

Early St. Mary's Choir (L. to R.) Mike Schmitz, Fred "Dutch" Gorde, Julianna Haider, Ben Sauer, Leo Pritschet, Joe Haider, Andy Pritschet, Helen Burns, Teresa Haider, Margaret Lambert, Mae Gruber, Aloys Pritschet, Helen Lambert

One cannot talk about the St. Mary's choir and not think of Mae Gruber. She was a lifelong member, and although we had no official choir director, everyone knew that Mae, who had sung with several choir generations, was in charge. Tall, dignified and aloof, she exuded a self-imposed authority, much like that of an old-time schoolmistress. It was all business in her choir loft, and no one even could whisper without earning one of her famous over-the-glasses looks. Alvina Bock and I received several. Alvina had children my age and older than me, but it was she and I who were friends, and we couldn't go through an entire Mass without saying something to one another. Being the altos, we stood side by side, which made talking even more tempting. We laughed many times about those looks and swore, like naughty kids, that we didn't deserve a single one of them.

Alvina Bock

Mae, bless her heart, had been a good powerful soprano in her prime, but age taking its toll, caused her to sound a bit like a screech owl when she attempted to reach the high notes. This was especially noticeable and somewhat fitting during the funereal requiem Mass as her caterwauling added an extra dimension to the somberness of the occasion.

Mae took pride in her appearance. It was mandatory in those days that all women cover their heads during Mass. Many wore scarves, but Mae always wore a large black brimmed hat, which was tilted at a rakish angle nearly covering one eye. Unlike every other lady in town, she was never seen in old everyday clothes. She even changed into better clothes to walk uptown for the mail, and she was never seen without make-up.

I specifically remember Mae's mouth. It was unusually large, drooped at the corners and always painted a deep red, which emphasized its size. When she spoke, one's eye was drawn to over-sized lower teeth, which had loosened from age. Her once handsome face, with its distinctively high cheekbones, sagged at the jawline and sloped into a neck that revealed her many years.

Mrs. Gruber was not one to socialize with the neighbors unless given a special invitation, and seldom did she invite anyone to her home. This set her somewhat apart from the town's women who spontaneously visited back and forth. In an effort to include her, I once baked a cake, gathered up a few older ladies and took them to her house to celebrate her birthday. Clearly surprised and obviously pleased, she quickly removed her apron, fluffed up her hair and spent the afternoon basking in the limelight.

The Gruber house was one of the largest homes in town and the only one that was a Sears kit-house. It was ordered from the catalog and shipped in by rail, ready to be assembled. The kit included the entire house, with numbered parts, instruction booklets, paints, nails—everything that was needed except the wiring, plumbing and heating. The two-story house, with its rich hardwood floors and open porch that ran across the entire front of the house, was built on a large corner lot near the elevators. The Sears home, which I visited many times, has defied the ravages of time and proudly still sits on the corner lot. However, the three once thriving elevators and bustling train depot are now gone leaving only a gaping, weed-infested empty lot.

Mary Jane, Mae's daughter, was the church organist for many years. She was a tall, slim, striking young woman who verged on being a free spirit. I took piano lessons from her, and I can still see her long, slim fingers skimming over the keys and hear the soft jingle of the multitude of silver bangle bracelets she constantly wore. Mary Jane fell in love with a musician who was visiting Glick relatives in Foxholm and followed him to Chicago. St. Mary's was forced to find a new organist, but Mae continued to run the choir for the rest of her days. She died at age eighty-four and is buried beside her husband John in St. Mary's Cemetery.

Last remaining elevator. Picture taken shortly before it was burned down. Gruber's Sears home can be seen in the background.

The rectory (back) and the church as it looked in 1927.

Back view of St. Mary's rectory and church

Boniface Wimmer

Archabbot Boniface Wimmer, O.S.B. was the founder of the Benedictine Order in the United States. During his life in the nineteenth century, he was considered to be the greatest Catholic in America. He was also my great, great uncle.

Archabbot Wimmer was my Grandma Miller's uncle, and for as long as Dad could remember, his picture hung on the living room wall of the family home.

Sebastian Wimmer was born on January 14, 1809 in Thalmassing, Bavaria, which is very near and in the same Diocese as Regensburg, the oldest town in Bavaria. Cardinal Joseph Ratzinger, now known as Pope Benedict XV1, also hails from this Reagensburg Diocese. Both had ties to St. Benedict, the Patriarch of Western Monasticism and the Patron Saint of Europe.

St. Benedict's Rule titled "The Rule of St. Benedict" (or way of life) became the standard for almost all monastic life in the Western Church. Benedictine monks, who were the primary evangelists of their day and the foundation for Christian education for more than five hundred years, founded monasteries across Europe and the Holy Land.

Sebastian, the son of restaurant and bar owner Peter Wimmer, had thoughts of becoming a lawyer, but his meager inheritance after the death of his father forced him to give up the idea. A short time later, he won a scholarship, entered the seminary and was ordained a priest in 1831. The following year, in spite of thoughts by priests that he was a most unlikely candidate for monastic life, Father Sebastian was admitted to the Benedictine monastery in Metten, Bavaria, changing his baptismal name to Boniface. While at St. Michael's Priory, Boniface was made aware of the terrible plight of the German immigrants in America (which included my ancestors) and thus began his vision of taking the Benedictine Order to America. Consumed with the idea of spreading the Gospel and Christian education, Wimmer began his quest to become a missionary.

Father Wimmer's superiors thought he was crazy to even think of going to America, that only the extraordinary could do something like that. Known often to question and even oppose the judgments and decisions of his superiors, Father boldly and persistently petitioned Rome. Although his requests were repeatedly denied, Father Wimmer did not abandon his vision. In desperation, he appealed to Crown Prince Ludwig I who became his benefactor. Finally, Rome agreed and Father Wimmer was on his way to establishing a 1300-year-old Order in the new world.

On October 24, 1846, thirty-eight days after setting sail, Father Boniface, fourteen laymen and four students landed in New York. Upon his arrival, several priests tried to divert him from his monastic undertaking, which they said was not in accord with American ways. All of the Benedictines who had come to the United States before Father Wimmer had come as single missionaries. None had attempted to introduce monastic life to North America. Wimmer was not to be deterred and journeyed on to Latrobe, Pennsylvania where the small group of dedicated and determined monks settled and where St. Vincent Archabbey, the first Benedictine Monastery in the United States, still stands.

In order to construct a monastic foundation, Father Wimmer had to first build a physical plant to serve as headquarters for the life of prayer and work. His persistently followed plan, which was the Benedictine way, included purchasing land and working the soil. All the students were required to work in the fields. He believed that physical labor was good for them and was necessary for their survival. He often tucked the pectoral cross into his scapular and labored in the fields next to his monks. As a result, he was called "farmer abbot" in Rome. He gloried in the nickname saying that farmers were "the backbone of the nation."

Abbot Wimmer fought to stay self-sufficient and solvent by opening a brewery and selling St. Vincent's Beer to the Irish railroad gangs who were working nearby. This was considered scandalous by his Protestant neighbors. Bishop O'Conner of Pittsburgh, who had the ultimate authority over the monastery and who was a constant irritant to Father Wimmer, agreed with them and ordered that no more beer be sold. The monks quit selling to the public but kept the brewery for their personal use, but Bishop O'Conner was not satisfied. He wrote to clerics in Rome asking them to take to take the matter to the Pope. Father Wimmer, having supporters of his own in the Vatican, did not take this lying down. He petitioned Rome to have his monastery elevated to the rank of an abbey, which would make the monastery independent and free from the control of the bishop and therefore, enable them to continue their work as they saw fit.

As a result of his petition, Father Wimmer journeyed to Rome, and on June 19, 1855 was granted a private audience with Pope Pius IX. Being a non-conformist, my great, great uncle had the audacity to go before the Holy Father in the city of cleanly-shaven men with a long beard. Never seeing beards in Rome, some nuns were frightened by his shaggy appearance, people on the street gawked at him and Italian Cardinals raised their shaggy eyebrows. While in the Pope's presence, Father Wimmer referred to the beer controversy. In his straightforward and frank manner, he explained that the Bavarian monks, who were raised in an area famous for its beer, had nothing to drink but water. The Pope laughed heartily and said, "Yes, St. Paul wrote to Timothy to use a little wine for his stomach."

Father Wimmer's audience with the Pope was very successful. His monastery was elevated to an abbey, becoming the first independent Benedictine priory in the United States, and he was named the first Abbot of St. Vincent and irremovable pastor of the parish. As he was being dismissed, the Holy Father blessed him and said, "Long live Abbot Wimmer and his magnificent beard." The abbot never shaved again and encouraged his monks to do the same.

Not only had the community been elevated to the abbatial rank and given an abbot, it also was given the privilege of brewing beer for self-consumption (considered natural for Benedictine monasteries in Europe) plus wholesale distribution. As a result, the monks were free to operate other breweries in their effort to stay self-sufficient.

On December 29, 1883, the Holy See bestowed upon Boniface Wimmer the title of Archabbot for Life, and granted him the honor of wearing the cappa magna, the liturgical mantle worn by cardinals, bishops, privileged prelates and canons.

Archabbot Wimmer was an amazing man—deeply religious, deeply humane and charitable to all. He encountered formidable obstacles and hardships including disloyalty from some of his most talented and trusted monks and conflicts with the Benedictine nuns who joined them in St. Vincent. Through his extraordinary leadership, his ability to forgive, his undying faith and unfailing efforts to follow his motto, "Forward, always forward," he was able to overcome these difficulties and fulfill his dream of helping the poor German farmers in rural America. He did that and much, much more. Not only did he help the Germans, his evangelization efforts expanded to include Irish

Americans, African Americans and Native Americans. When he died, his small missionary band had grown into a large congregation with five abbeys (including St. John's Monastery in Collegeville, Minnesota) and two religious priorities with 152 missions and stations, including three bishops, four abbots, two priors, 220 priests and as many religious, and it was only the beginning. At present, the Benedictines have launched eighteen colleges and universities, all of which started with Archabbot's vision of preparing a sufficient number of priests to minister to the spiritual needs of the people.

Archabbot Boniface Wimmer, O.S.B.

Buffalo Bones

Wagon loads of Buffalo Bones on Main Street in Minot 1890

The earliest settlers of the Dakota Territory were awed by the countless buffalo that roamed the wild prairie in the 1880's. They were thrilled with the sight of the shaggy beasts which looked like "a huge black blanket as far as the eye could see" and were fascinated with the roaring of the bulls, which sounded like the continuous roll of a hundred drums that could be heard for miles. The over abundance of these animals and the warlike Indians who depended on them for their very existence were two obstacles that had to be overcome before the settlers could establish frontier homes. Prairie fires, drowning, stampedes and slaughtering by Indians killed many of the buffalo, but it was the hunters who exterminated them by the millions. In spite of the wicked, wanton and wasteful hunters, it took the building of the railroad to finally sound the death knoll for the buffalo.

In 1882, five thousand hunters and skinners invaded the Dakotas. The tremendous slaughter of the 1880's and 1890's had begun.

A typical hunting outfit consisted of four men: two hunters, a cook and the leader who provided the money, wagon, a team of horses and good guns. It was the leader's job to make arrangements with the tanner and meat packer. He also bought hides from other hunters who were on their own. The going price for a hide was twenty-five cents. On good days, they skinned eighty-five hides and on exceptional days, more. That was good pay when a dollar a day was a considered a good wage. After skinning, the hides were pegged down to dry and later stacked and hauled in wagons to the railroad yard where the buyer inspected and weighed them. Once he had been paid, the leader returned for another load.

Besides the hides, many of which were used to make highly coveted coats, a market was developed for buffalo meat, especially from younger bulls which produced the best meat. The tongue was considered to be a great delicacy, and to cut the cost of shipping, hunters would often take only that and leave the carcasses to rot on the prairie.

Buffalo were also killed for sport. The railroad set up enticing hunting excursions, which promised grand hunts on the plains. Huntsmen, including Teddy Roosevelt who made several trips to the Badlands, came from all parts of the country, as well as from abroad, some of whom were royalty. Many of the animals were shot without the hunters even getting off the train.

By 1884, after a few short years of slaughter, nearly all the buffalo had been annihilated. Only a few scattered groups remained and millions of bones.

Bleached bones whitened the landscape—leg bones, shoulder bones, ribs, backbones and skulls. Scattered all over the Dakota prairies, along the rivers, in valleys—everywhere—were the grisly reminders of the great buffalo herds that once were.

From the demise of the buffalo rose another big industry, the bone business. The sale of these bones—used for fertilizer, knife handles, combs, dice, buttons, bone china dishes, and even for the process of refining sugar—provided pocket money for most of the first settlers who came to this region in the 1880's. Settlers were paid between six and ten dollars per ton or given a receipt, called "buffalo bone money," which could be exchanged in stores for food and other necessities.

Grandpa Hoerter hauled buffalo bones in an oxen-drawn wagon to Devil's Lake, which was over one hundred miles away but was the nearest railroad point at that time. Sometimes, as the bones became less plentiful, it took him a week to find a wagonload and then another week to take them to the shipping point. The money he earned helped pay for staples. The average amount paid for a wagonload was fifteen dollars, which bought a goodly amount of groceries in those days. Flour was two dollars for one hundred pounds, and both sugar and coffee sold for a dollar for twenty-five pounds.

Shipment of these bones was the first contribution from northwest North Dakota to the manufacturing industries in the more established states. Although every town on the railroad served as a market for the bones, Minot, on the Great Northern Railway, was the leading concentration point. Old timers told of an amazing pile of bones near the Great Northern right-of-way, which represented seven thousand buffalo. It extended from Main Street eastward almost as far as to where Third Street is today. A spur track was built alongside the pile so the bones could be loaded directly into the railroad cars.

Buffalo Bones being loaded into railroad cars

A group of Roman Catholic half-breeds called Metis, offspring of French fur traders who married Indian women, traveled from the Turtle Mountain country near Pembina—the oldest settlement in the Northwest (1780) located where North Dakota and Minnesota come together at the Canadian border—to search the plains for buffalo bones. The bones were a godsend to the Indians who had depended on the buffalo for their subsistence. Following the animals' trails, they brought large quantities of bones to Minot in their unique carts called Red River Carts. Each cart was made entirely of wood with wheels sometimes six feet in diameter and a small body that rested on the axle and shafts. With an additional framework of buffalo skulls arranged around the top of the wagon box, each cart, drawn by a single pony, could carry six hundred to eight hundred pounds. No grease was used on the axles; consequently, they made a horrible screeching sound that could be heard miles away. As old-timer Joseph Kinsey Howard described it, "It was as if a thousand fingernails were drawn across a thousand panes of glass." One of these bone trains, which were drawn by oxen, was so long that when the first carts reached the Great Northern tracks in Minot, the last carts were still screeching on North Hill, north of the present Eighth Avenue.

Trails made by these Indians threaded their way near the present site of Mohall in Renville County and crossed the Mouse River near the site of the John Stammen homestead where Stammen, along with his wife and three sons, Henry, Phillip and Mike, settled. (Phillip was Ambrose's father, my sister Connie's father-in-law.) The Stammen Ranch later became the C.P. Ranch owned by Clarence and Ruth Parker, and later still, it became Eckert's E 7 Hereford Ranch.

The C.P. Ranch, known as "The Buffalo Ranch," which was located thirty-five miles northwest of Minot, was one of the only ranches in the state where a buffalo herd was maintained. I remember it as the home of my friend Marilyn Eckert, whose father George managed the ranch for the Parkers.

Clarence and Ruth Parker and George Eckert and son Donnie

The original buffalo, which for the Parkers were more of a hobby than a business, were shipped into Foxholm on the Soo Line Railway. Cowboys met the train and immediately set about getting the shaggy beasts into the stockyards. In spite of their prodding and poking, the buffalo refused to leave the rail car. Finally, frustrated and sweating, the cowboys would learn to step aside. When the prodding stopped, the buffalo, like docile sheep, filed quietly into the stockyards.

The Parkers never lived on the ranch but would occasionally spend the weekend in their cabin located on top of a hill overlooking the main house and ranch buildings. The view from the cabin was breathtaking. The Mouse River, rimmed with river-bottom woodlands, curved through the valley. Rolling hills covered with lush native grasses ran for miles on end, providing rich grazing land for buffalo roaming the prairie. Sunrises and sunsets painted the skies each morning and evening with a quiet yet magnificent radiance.

The Parker's cabin had a long, narrow kitchen, a big family room with a fireplace, two bedrooms and unique light fixtures throughout the cabin. Tucked away in the basement was a secret compartment for the storage of liquor, a holdover from the days of Prohibition. Behind the large cabin was a smaller log house that housed the outhouse and well.

Parker Ranch Cabin 1931

When the Parkers came, George's wife Kate always made sure they had fresh chicken and garden vegetables. Once the food was packed, it was Marilyn and her sister Joyce's job to deliver it. It was not an easy task for two little girls to tote the heavy basket up the hill, and Ruth always promised them a treat of candy or ice cream. Much to their dismay, the treats never materialized.

In the early days, the Parkers were known to have old-fashioned buffalo hunts. Wealthy eastern sportsmen who came by rail were given the royal treatment. In addition to the hunt, which the Parkers strove to make as authentic as possible, they were given the use of the cabin, including its infamous liquor cache.

Buffalo roaming on the Parker Ranch

The hunts are over; the buffalo are gone. Even their bones are gone. The view of the Mouse River is now that of Lake Darling. The Buffalo Ranch is deserted and the cabin is a lone sentry. The only things that haven't changed are the sunrises and sunsets. Each uniquely different and breathtakingly beautiful, they light up the sky with a splendor that is indescribable.

Parker Buffalo Ranch (E-7 Ranch)

Notorious "High Third"

When the people of my community and the surrounding area "went to town," Minot was their destination. In its earlier days, Minot was the major trade and transportation center in northern North Dakota and had earned the reputation, based on its volume of business, of being one of the most prosperous cities in the nation. A popular grain-shipping center, it had several grain elevators and two flour mills, one being the Russell-Miller Milling Company, maker of Occident flour. It also had a poultry plant and several creameries. I was very young when Dad and Mom had cream to sell, and the only memory I have is unloading the cream cans at White's Creamery and receiving an ice cream cone from Penny, one of the girls who worked there and who just happened to be sweet on my oldest brother. The production of ice cream was big business in all the creameries (Bridgemans' was the largest producer during my time.), and at one time, Ward County ranked second out of all North Dakota's counties in its production.

Saturday was a popular day for shopping, including lunch at Woolworth's and a beer or two (while the women shopped) at the North Main Tavern.

Woolworth's—with its warm, colorful atmosphere—was today's Wal-Mart except nothing was put on shelves or hung on racks. It was all displayed on top of the counters: cosmetics, fingernail polishes, glassware, women's nylon stockings, sewing notions and patterns, toys, oilcloth (used as kitchen tablecloths), Big Little Books—almost any small item you might find in anyone's home—and the saleswomen stood behind the counter and brought out the items one by one. I remember buying Tangee lipstick before I was actually old enough to wear makeup. It looked orange in the tube but was little more than pale pink Chapstick; it made me feel quite grown up.

Woolworth's lunch counter is the thing I remember best. (Except for some odd reason, I remember the store's wooden floors.) The lunch counter was a favorite place for shoppers to sit and have coffee, and Mom and I often had lunch there. It was located to the left as you entered the store and consisted of a long counter with red leather-backed swivel stools. Colorful signs announcing the ice cream sundae and soda specials hung on the wall, and several kinds of pie and cookies were displayed in a glass case on the back counter next to the large coffee urn. The waitresses wore starched uniforms and little tiara-style matching headpieces, and all were required to wear hairnets. It all looked so fancy to me, and when they cut my toasted tuna salad sandwich into three pieces, I was really impressed. I remember something else about Woolworth's lunch counter; there were always people standing behind us during the lunch hour waiting for an empty stool.

Once Dad gave up farming and bought the bar, my folks no longer went to town on Saturdays. Having only one car, Mom and I sometimes took the intrastate bus to Minot, which was convenient and cheap (forty-six cents). It stopped at the post office at eleven a.m. and returned at four o'clock on its return trip to the end-of-the-line at Crosby. Although the "dime store," as Woolworth's was called, had a little bit of everything, when it came to buying shoes, D&S Bootery was the only store that stocked my long and narrow size. Those were the days when shoe salesmen actually measured your feet, brought the shoes to you and put them on. D&S had an X-ray machine that you could stick your foot into to see if your new shoes were fitted properly. It was a popular and effective tool, but in the 1950's, health concerns caused the machines to be removed from the store.

Northwest Piano, located on south Main Street near the Uptown Nook, was also a favorite store of mine. One could buy pamphlets listing only the words of popular songs, which I really enjoyed, as well as sheet music. I often played the piano, strictly for my own entertainment, as we had no television or video games to entertain us.

Unlike the Minot I remember, which proclaimed itself as the "Magic City," the Minot of my parents' youth had the unique reputation of being the only North Dakota city with "organized vice."

During the U.S. Prohibition Days of 1920-1933, Minot was known from coast to coast as a wide-open city. With bootlegging, trafficking and commercializing with the pimps, prostitutes, pushers and hoodlums of the nation, Minot earned the nickname "Little Chicago," "Sin City" or "Crime Capitol of North Dakota."

During these days of Prohibition, bootleggers smuggled liquor from Canada into Minot. My dad told of sitting on the bank of the Mouse River near Minot on a Sunday afternoon and watching "rum-runners" as they whipped along at forty miles per hour on the frozen river in their high-speed cars. 1924 Dodge "High-Wheelers" seemed to be the bootlegging cars of choice. The cars, each of which could carry four hundred pounds of alcohol in the back seat under the floor, drove directly into the Stearns Building on South Broadway (today's I. Keating Furniture World), entering through a large freight door in back. In a few minutes, the emptied cars would reappear and roar back up the road to Canada where they were readied for another run. It was an easy and exciting way for the "runners" to make ten dollars for a one-day trip. It was also very dangerous, and the smugglers knew that the ones who got caught never talked about it. They were dead.

Most of the roads between Canada and Minot during the 1920's were not much more than prairie trails. It was not unusual for booze runners to get stuck, nor was it uncommon for farmers to pull them out with a team of horses and be paid in whiskey.

Much of the illegal booze ended up in the Leland Parker Hotel, which was well known by infamous gamblers and gunmen, including Diamond Jim Brady and Al Capone. (History tells us that Minot was a central hub of Al Capone's smuggling operations.) The bootleggers would drive up to the freight door of the hotel, onto the freight elevator and up to the floor where all the gambling took place. Minot's radio station, KLPM, was located on top of the Leland Parker, thus radio call letters LPM. It was the most modern and up-to-date station at the time with one hundred watts of power.

Leland Parker Bandstand during the age of orchestras

Nothing went better with Minot's notorious thirst for booze than gambling and prostitution. It was well known that whenever a pimp or prostitute was arrested elsewhere, his or her address book most likely contained Minot addresses.

Third Street, Minot's "Red Light District" had thriving bootlegging business during the days of prohibition. Dee Dee Govan's Parrot Inn and Saul Davis's Saul's Barbeque, both on Third Street, were the most notorious businesses in town.

Govan came to Minot in 1932 to join his aunt and uncle who owned the Parrot Inn. This café, which was later operated by Govan, was a favorite hangout for young people after Saturday night dances. Govan insisted over the years that it was not a "sporting place;" in fact, the only thing you got there was good food. (Chicken was one of its specialties. One could get half a fried chicken for a dollar and fifty cents and a good chicken dinner for only thirty-five cents. His barbequed ribs and potato salad were also famous.)

In spite of Govan's insistence, it was a well-known fact, that while patrons on the main floor were enjoying the famous fried chicken, gambling was the main attraction in the basement, with liquor flowing freely. Although Govan had been arrested numerous times for bootlegging liquor and, after Prohibition, selling without a license, he continued doing both. According to Govan and Davis, the reason they sold it illegally was because, being black, they were denied liquor licenses.

There were no Mexicans in Minot so "Dee Dee's Tamales" were a new welcome delight to local taste buds. People were known to make special trips to the Parrot Inn for Govan's tamales. My dad's brother, Uncle Butch, had many different business ventures, one of which was selling these new Mexican treats. He peddled them to different businesses, such as Dad's bar, and to any individuals he encountered along the way. My uncle's tales about his association with the well-known Third Street businessman would provide us with entertaining stories for years to come. Govan was also a regular customer of Dad's during the 1940's and 1950's, leaving the bar with several bottles of spirits and beer on each visit. Sociable, outgoing and a rare black man surrounded in a sea of German and Norwegian farmers, he always made a statement.

Along with the Parrot Inn, Govan also owned The Grill on Third Street. Both were well-known hot spots. Although they did not have reputations as brothels, according to Govan, there were twenty-five to thirty houses in town that leased flesh with one to three girls working in each. Conveniently, many of these houses were on his street. Few of these houses had business fronts; most were nondescript houses with porches. Every third house or so might have a rocking chair on the porch. If the porch light was on, there might be a girl, often very young, sitting in the chair, rocking away. It was said that the going rate for a prostitute on Third Street in 1932 was four dollars per fifteen minutes, jumping up to ten dollars for the same amount of time in the early 1960's.

Davis also insisted that his café was not a place of ill-repute although it was common knowledge that food was only a sideline. He readily admitted that he had been "not really arrested" forty-two times and that, more than once, he left Minot for Canada when there were warrants out for his arrest. He also said that he once hid in the back of an ambulance covered with a white sheet as the police were scouring the area for him. Still, Davis argued that the people in the Third Street area were respectable citizens—good people who would take care of each other—and that one could safely walk the streets day or night.

Davis had not planned to make Minot his home but later said, "The good Lord was looking out for me when he left me in Minot. Being left behind was the best thing that ever happened to me."

Born in Louisiana in 1901, Davis grew up playing baseball on the sandlots of Bayou country. As a teenager, he traveled to Arkansas where he joined the Arkansas Negro Baseball League. In the 1920's, Davis advanced to the original National Negro League and became a starter with the Birmingham Black Barons. From there, he advanced to the Chicago American Giants, fulfilling a life-long dream. When Davis's skills began to deteriorate, he barnstormed around Canada, baseball gear and uniform in his car trunk, showing up at tournaments where he asked teams if they needed a player. He played against many good players but refused to play against Satchel Paige. "Cause you can't do no good," he explained. "I was trying to make a reputation. I could beat the average players in these white clubs. But when you get with these Negroes you got to be careful, you know. They gonna try to show you up." Although Davis was reluctant to face Paige on the ball diamond, his admiration for the incredible pitcher grew into a life-long friendship, and Paige, over the years, visited Davis in Minot several times.

Paige had other North Dakota connections. In 1933, at the request of Bismarck's semi-pro baseball team for a strong black player, Abe Saperstein, America's largest booker of baseball games and founder of the Harlem Globetrotters, sent Paige to Bismarck, where he led the team to a national championship defeating their arch-rival, Jamestown, North Dakota.

In the late 1930's, Saperstein asked Davis to become the player manager of the Zulu Cannibal Giants, also known as the Zulu Grass Skirt Team, a traveling baseball team who, in order to appear like tribal savages, would don grass skirts and tribal war paint and hit with bats shaped like African war clubs. Even Jesse Owens, the great Olympic sprinter, traveled with the Zulus. Owens would take on the fastest runners that teams could come up with, and then, of course, he would leave them behind. Davis told the story about how he and Owens won $1,100 from some area farmers when Owens beat a local star in a footrace. Laughing, he said, "They thought Negroes in broken-down trucks were easy pickings."

The Zulus were big crowd pleasers throughout the Midwest and Canada. When the Grass Skirt Team broke up, they had been traveling in North Dakota. After playing a game in Minot, Davis, who liked his liquor, went on a drinking spree with three locals, and when he didn't show up at the designated time, they went on without him. Barnstorming teams never waited for anyone; everyone was expendable. Davis ended up spending the rest of his life in Minot.

Saul Davis had no intention of opening a café when he found himself stranded in the small city of Minot. (He had been living in Chicago at the time.) He said that he had done a little cooking in his days, and people liked his barbeque, so he decided to give it a try.

Davis's assimilation into the white community took time and patience. There were only fourteen other Negroes in Minot when Davis arrived, and racism, having drifted north, made the white community edgy and uncertain as to how to deal with them.

In the early 1940's, Davis bought a neighborhood house on Third Street Northeast and hired Ernest Haldi, my friend Millie's father, to remodel it. Before Haldi could finish it, the city of Minot stepped in and told Davis that Negroes could only live on Third Street Southeast. The house remained empty.

A young Saul Davis and Saul's Minot home ..almost

In spite of his rocky start, Davis was still quick to say that he never regretted spending his life in Minot. He spoke of his close friends, many of whom were important people, and about the good times they had. He was quoted as saying, "I never ran into such a bunch in all my life," referring to the diverse ancestries of people in Minot which included Greeks, Norwegians and Syrians, "but, I found they were some of the best people in the United States." Slowly, the community became aware that Davis, himself, fit into that category. In 1974, Davis, who was once regarded a renegade, was awarded a plaque by the city of Minot which reads, "To an outstanding athlete. We wish to recognize your unselfish contribution to baseball and the community of Minot."

Early city Fathers were insistent that Minot wasn't tough. A little liquor was sold on the side, maybe, but the violence in their town was "no different than what occurs in any ordinary controlled society." C.D. "Clink" Johnson, who was mayor from 1962 to 1970, recalled that a shot was fired once and that another time, a knife was pulled on someone, but because these incidents occurred on Third Street, they were blown out of proportion. He added that the activities on Third Street were not glamorous; "It was just actually a lot of people trying to make a living."

It wasn't only on Third Street that people were "trying to make a living." In 1924, a father and two sons opened a car dealership in downtown Minot. It was said that they drove big cars so they could haul whiskey from Canada. On one such alleged liquor run, the brothers' car stalled near Bottineau while being chased by revenue officers. The brothers fled on foot across a field, losing the car and liquor to the officers.

In their effort to rid the area of rampant bootlegging, revenue agents sometimes interfered with the law-abiding people's lives. The story goes that a well-to-do, long-time resident of Minot owned a luxurious black Buick sedan and that he and his family enjoyed Sunday afternoon rides north and west of the city. The joy rides were many times interrupted by federal liquor agents who suspected such a car to be involved in illegal happenings. Hijackers also thought that such a car might be carrying whiskey.

Dad and his farmer friends Dutch Gorde and Fred Ahmann were known to hoist a few while discussing the price of grain. On one of his trips to town, Dad bought a gallon of whiskey from a bootlegger but failed to get it home. He was hijacked on Maple Street near John Broten Lumber Company, and the whiskey was stolen.

Young men on the town (L. to R.) Dutch Gorde, Fred Ahmann, Dad

It was said that tunnels once used to move the illegal liquor run beneath the streets and buildings in downtown Minot, including the present I. Keating Furniture World building and the past Clarence Parker Hotel. Govan said that there were no tunnels that he knew of, but a cave-like room that supposedly hid a still and stored illegal liquor during Prohibition was discovered on Third Street when a speakeasy was demolished. An underground storage was also found under the Stern speakeasy when city officials were attempting to get property taxes out of the bootleggers. Some said that the tunnels running down Main Street were part of a central heating system for the downtown businesses. The jury on these underground tunnels is still out, so the mystery remains today.

The Leland-Parker Hotel Orchestra, Minot, N.D.

Besides the highly profitable liquor and prostitution traffic, an illicit drug trade existed in the city. In December of 1922, a series of opium raids were made on certain hotels, cafés, and other opium dens on infamous Third Street. In one house a thousand dollars worth of opium in the form of "decks" and "books" was confiscated. The street value of a "deck," which was one-third smaller than a "book," was one dollar. The drug raids went on for two years before most of the opium and cocaine traffic was ended. Chinese, some of whom were illegal immigrants, apparently handled these drugs. In 1924, Louis Lolling, a Chinese-American who had recently opened the popular American Café, was wrongfully arrested during an opium raid at the Dakota Hotel on South Main Street where he had gone to look for an employee who didn't show up for work. Although charges were soon dismissed, the café owner was so discouraged with Minot that he sold his new café and left town.

There were several reasons why vice crimes in Minot were able to flourish for such a long time. Prostitutes spent a lot of money downtown, and the merchants "wanted to see Third Street exist." It was said that downtown merchants, during an election for States Attorney, supplied campaign money to the candidate who was not interested in cleaning up

"High Third". Some of Minot's prominent businessmen were involved in the bootlegging activities. Years later, during a Memories of Minot panel discussion, Govan, explaining why no one was caught doing anything illegal during raids, revealed that a lot of people, including a well-known state official, had vested interest in the cafés and had received "cuts," special deals, for the activities in the Red Light District. Govan said that the police in those days took a cut and, in turn, made only tepid attempts to raid the establishments when public pressure demanded action.

In spite of many active attempts to abolish the activities on Third Street, all seemed to fizzle out, and the problems that had plagued Minot's Red Light District for over thirty years continued. Not until the area was brightly illuminated, making it easy to identify a person a block away, was progress to rid the area of these problems notable. Through the persistent efforts of the community "do-gooders" to increase law enforcement and to stop the deterioration of the buildings on Third Street, the demise of Minot's Red Light District became a reality. With this reality, Minot's unofficial nickname, "Little Chicago," was happily replaced with its official nickname, "Magic City."

Family History

Mom as a young lady and on her 98th birthday

My mother, Eleonora Elizabeth, whom everyone knew as Ella or Ma Miller, lived 104 happy, healthy, productive years. Up until the very end, her mind was alert and her sense of humor intact.

Mom was born on December 1, 1897 to John and Elizabeth Hoerter on my grandparents' homestead in the Mouse River Valley. There was no doctor available so a neighbor lady helped with the delivery and then stayed on to help with the housework for the ten days that Grandma was in bed.

Mom's grandmother, Anna Diederich, was born southwest of the Rhine River city of Koblenz in the village of Arbach, Prussia (Germany) on December 29, 1833. At age twenty-four, an old maid in those times, she married John Diederichs (no relation) who died five short years after their marriage. Less than six months later, widowed with two young sons, Stephen and Mathew, she married Mom's grandfather, Nick Hoerter, five years her junior and a resident of a near-by village where he was a student in a seminary. It is not known if he was studying for the priesthood or if he was just there for a good education.

The couple had six children including my grandfather, John, who was born on March 11, 1866 and Eleonora (Laura) who eventually married Barney Schmitz. In 1867 in search of a better life, the family sold their farm, boarded a tall masted ship and sailed for America. After two and a half weeks at sea, they landed in New York Harbor and made their way to Wisconsin where they lived several years before moving to Holdingford, Minnesota.

In 1888, my mother's father, John Hoerter, his parents and several of his siblings immigrated to Burlington, North Dakota (the Dakota Territory) where they homesteaded in the Mouse River Valley. In their later years, my maternal great-grandparents gave up farming and moved in with their daughter and son-in-law, Laura and Barney Schmitz, where they remained until they passed away—Anna at the age of eighty-one and Nick at the age of ninety-five.

Grandma and Grandpa Hoerter

Mom's mother, Elizabeth Duesch, was born on February 23, 1863 in Richmond, Minnesota, which is about twenty-two miles west of St. Cloud.

The country school that she and her siblings attended was several miles from their farm. Getting to school was not easy, and having to cross a river made it even more difficult. They had no problems crossing in the winter because the river was frozen solid, but crossing in the spring and fall was a different story. Spring thaws often caused the placid river to become a raging torrent, making crossing impossible, and in the fall, thin ice made crossing dangerous.

Most of the people in their rural community were Germans, as were the teachers. Often their accents were so heavy that they could not spell or pronounce the words correctly, which made it hard to keep the children's interest. Difficulty getting to school, the lack of interest and being needed on the family farm caused many students to quit school before finishing the eighth grade. Grandma Hoerter's brother Joseph was a good example of this; he didn't start school until he was past eight years old and quit when he was only twelve.

Lured by the abundance of rich farm land, Grandma Hoerter, her brother Joe, her sister Gertrude, and her father, my great-grandfather Nick, traveling by covered wagon, immigrated to Dakota Territory in 1885. Their friend, Joseph Clementich, and his son traveled with them. Among the bare essentials that were taken were one cow, four horses, feed for the livestock, a cast iron cook stove that was also used for heating, a hand-made cupboard, a table and four chairs, bedding, a food supply and a few cooking utensils. The furniture was shipped by rail as far as Devil's Lake, which was as far as the Great Northern Railroad went, and then freighted by covered wagon to Burlington where they homesteaded.

Mom's family arrived in Minot on May 30, Decoration Day. As they made camp, they witnessed a funeral that was in session. The man, a surveyor who was working in the area, drowned in the Mouse River. There was no clergy to take charge of the funeral, so Joseph Colton, the founder of Burlington, helped with the simple service and burial which took place near the Ole Spoklie cabin, just west of Minot. Ward County, of which Minot is now the county seat, was not yet organized at the time of their arrival.

Because the land had not yet been surveyed, Grandma and her family could not file their land claims via the Homestead Act and thus were forced to live as squatters for the first two years. At the completion of the surveying in 1887, the family filed for their land and became legitimate homesteaders.

The Homestead Act of 1862 provided free land to people who met the challenge of proving up, which often was very difficult to do. To prove up the 160 acres of land, the homesteader had to pay ten dollars to claim the land temporarily and a two-dollar commission to the land agent. The homesteader was required to build a house, make improvements and live on the land for five years. If the crops were poor, the homesteader might have to seek work in a nearby town to supplement the family's income, therefore making the requirement of actually living on the land for six months out of the year very difficult. When all the requirements were met, the homesteader paid a final six dollars and then received a patent that was signed by the President of the United States. Many times, the signed patent was framed and hung on the wall by the proud new landowner.

The first dwelling that Grandma Duesch's family built with the help of neighbors was a fourteen foot by sixteen foot frame shanty constructed from wood found in the nearby coulees. It had a shingled roof, wood floors (not dirt as many were), and double-boarded walls with paper lining the inside. There were two windows which offered a clear view of the lush river valley. Wood from the river banks and the nearby coulees and lignite coal from the Burlington mine were used for fuel.

Because of their isolation, homesteaders had to fend for themselves which many times created startling ingenuity. My great-grandmother's shanty was lit by the flame of a candle made my threading a string or cloth through a large button, twisting it tightly and dousing it in grease until it was the desired thickness. Early to bed, early to rise was a necessity, not a choice. She made soap using lard and lye which she got from draining water through a barrel of wood ashes, kept lard for baking (It made great pie crusts.), and sewed clothes for the entire family.

Some of their provisions were purchased in Burlington, but the prices were so high that they often freighted things in from Devil's Lake, or a couple of teams would make the wagon trip to Devil's Lake to pick up necessities. The trip, which was over one hundred miles, took at least a week round trip, but they felt it was worth it as flour was four dollars a hundred pounds at Burlington and only two dollars and fifty cents at Devil's Lake. Money was too scarce to buy much sugar or coffee the first few years. Many people used peas or barley for coffee.

The first year, they had fifteen acres of wheat, oats and Indian corn—just enough to feed their animals. After cutting the grain with a scythe, they bound and stacked the grain by hand. It was then threshed by "someone below Minot" who had a horse-powered threshing rig.

The drought of 1889 forced many settlers to let their land, which they had previously claimed, go. Grandma Duesch's brother, my Uncle Joe Deusch, was one of them. Having never married and thus having no family responsibilities, he bummed around the country working odd jobs for several years. Returning to Minot in 1922, he made his home in the Windsor Hotel where he lived for the remainder of his life.

My grandparents, John and Elizabeth Hoerter, married May 14, 1889, settling on grandmother's homestead near Burlington. During the following two years, the settlers became increasingly worried about a threat of an Indian uprising (the half-breeds from the Pembina area). In 1891, fearing attack, my grandparents and baby Nick, among others, hurried back to Holdingford, Minnesota. To feed his growing family, Grandpa operated a blacksmith shop. When the Indian trouble quieted, my grandparents and children, who now totaled three, moved back to North Dakota where they moved from Grandma's claim to my grandpa's claim in the Mouse River Valley.

My uncles, aunt and friends (L. to R.) Anna Hoerter Age 2, Joe Hoerter age 4, the Peopping brothers and Nick Hoerter age 6, (notice the hats) Photo taken in 1895

Mom was the middle child among seven children: Nick, Joe, Anna, Mom, Rose, Mary (Mayme), and Elizabeth. Nick, the oldest, was killed in a farming accident at age sixteen. It was April 1906, and Grandpa Hoerter, preparing for the spring planting, had purchased a wagonload of seed grain. With intentions of unloading the grain, Nick pulled the wagon up to the granary, which sat on a slight incline. To prevent the wagon from rolling forward, Nick bent down and put a rock under the front wheel. At that moment, the heavy, steel-reinforced wooden tongue of the wagon swung around knocking him to the ground. The wagon with its full load of grain lurched forward and struck Nick. A wheel ran over his head, killing him instantly. Grandma Hoerter, a frail woman who suffered from respiratory problems, never fully recovered from this terrible tragedy. Twelve years later, her youngest child, Elizabeth (Lizzie), died in the infamous Spanish Flu Pandemic of 1918. Her death left Grandma in an even more weakened state. Six years later she had a heart attack and died at the age of sixty-one. Her body, which was washed and dressed by neighbor ladies, was kept at home in a cool bedroom for two days until the priest arrived for the burial service, which took place in St. Henry's Catholic Church.

Mom grew up with her parents and siblings in a two-story log house which was built by my grandfather on his land just below the hill from the J.P. Sauer farm very near the Mouse River. There was one large room upstairs with two beds. Grandpa, also a carpenter, as most homesteaders had to be, made the wooden bedsteads from wood found along the river banks. The bed springs were made of ropes which were placed about six inches apart lengthwise and then crosswise. The mattresses were made of heavy ticking material stuffed with straw, which was changed every fall when fresh straw was available. Mom shared the bedroom with her four sisters. In the hot summer months, this caused many sister spats, but during the frigid winter months when it was so cold that they could see their breath, sleeping together was not only welcome but nearly a necessity. Even under a mound of feather ticks, they huddled together for warmth. Often, Grandpa had to get up during the night and fire up the stoves which he had let burn down.

The Hoerter Family—Mom 2nd from left in back row

My grandmother died before I was born. Only through Mom's stories do I know her. She was religious, superstitious (If a cat washed himself, company was coming.) and soft-hearted. She was also the disciplinarian of the family. As Mom put it, "Grandpa only gave a little tap on the head." Mom clearly remembered the only real slap that she ever got from her dad. It was during the spring, and the river was high. My grandparents were going to the neighbors', and because crossing the swollen river was dangerous, the kids were told that they had to stay at home. My four-year old mother begged to go, but my grandparents held firm. As they were traveling down the road, they turned to see Mom running after the buggy, screaming and crying at the top of her lungs. Grandpa stopped the buggy and picked her up but not without first giving her a good hard swat on the bottom. My mischievous mother, who was known to say, "Hollering doesn't hurt and a lickin' doesn't last long," felt that even though she got the slap, she had won the round.

Sundays were set aside for going to church, visiting and relaxing. Absolutely no work of any kind was done; my grandmother saw to it. Her favorite saying was, "What you do with your hands on Sunday, you take out with your nose on Monday." Even Sunday's dinner was cooked on Saturday and was always enough for unexpected visitors. Every Sunday, rain or shine, the family settled into the buggy for the six-mile trip to St. Henry's Catholic Church, which was located on the other side of the Mouse River. During the spring thaw, the river would rise over the narrow bridge which meant going many miles out of their way, but as far as my grandmother was concerned, that was no excuse for missing Mass. During Holy Week, they made four trips, attending services on Ash Wednesday, Holy Thursday, Good Friday and Easter Sunday. At Christmas, the entire family, bundled in fur robes with heated stones at their feet, traveled twelve miles in a horse-drawn sled, sometimes over three-foot snow drifts in twenty-below weather, to attend Midnight Mass.

Grandma was very afraid of storms. If there was a lightning storm at night, she would get all the children up and make them sit in the middle of the room. To her, most everything drew lightning. "Don't sit there, windows draw lightning." "Stay away from the stove; it draws lightning." "Don't go near the door, you'll be struck." Grandma's fear influenced her young children. If they saw as much as a dark cloud in the sky, they were scared to death. Obviously, Mom outgrew this irrational fear. The mother I knew was the one who kept her head in a time of crisis. How often she said, "It's not so bad."

Every fall, Grandma would take out her foot-powered Singer Sewing Machine and make each of the girls a new school dress made from colorful print calico, which sold for five cents a yard at the Mercantile

Store. They wore the same dress every day, changing it as soon as they got home from school, until it was worn out or outgrown, at which time it was passed on down to the next sister. They also could afford only one pair of shoes per person per year. Mom and her siblings went barefoot after school and all summer to make their shoes last, and still, many times they had to put cardboard in their shoes to cover holes in the soles. In the fall before school started, Grandpa lined up the kids and had each one stand on a sheet of paper so he could draw around their feet. Once he had the correct sizes, he set off for town on the annual shoe-buying spree. The kids were so tickled to have new shoes that even if they didn't really fit, they'd cram their feet in and wouldn't say a word. While reminiscing, Mom laughingly shook her head and said, "It's no wonder we had corns and calluses."

Mom's schoolmates identified by Mom on next page
(notice the bare feet)

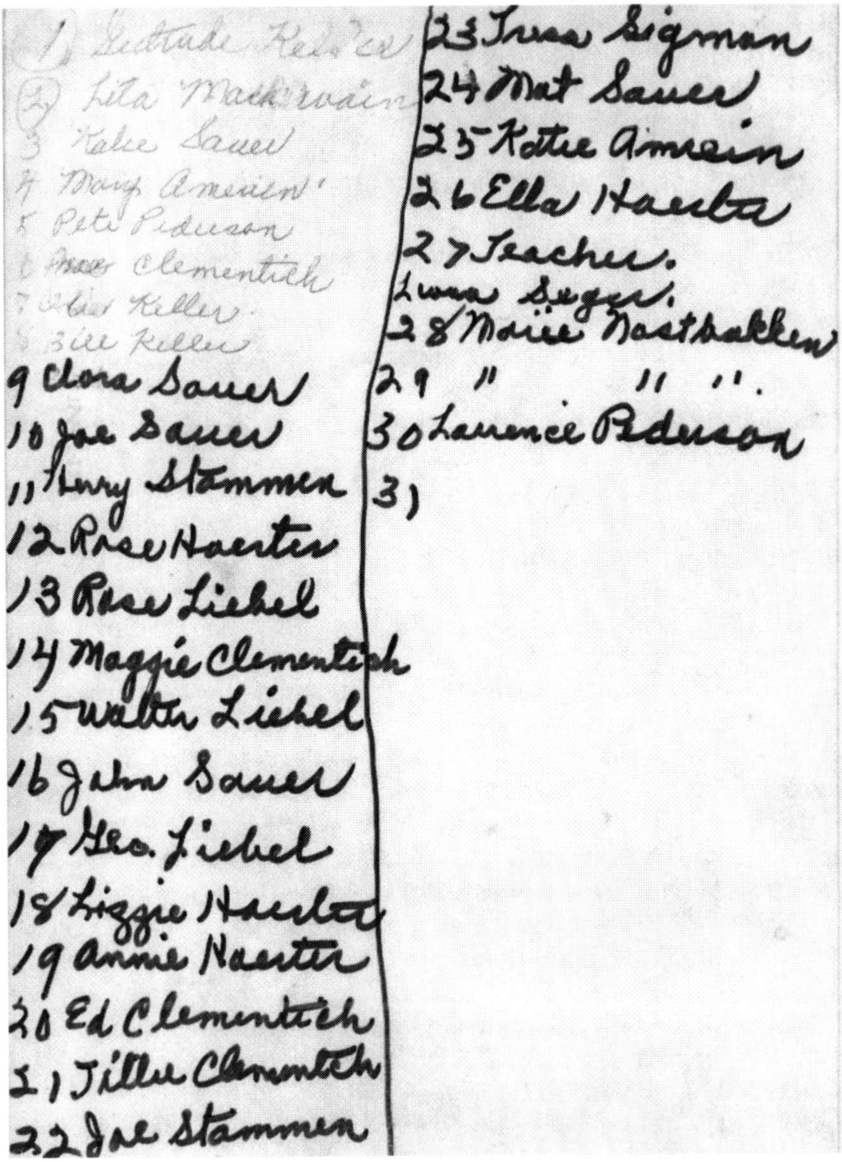

1) Gertrude Keller
2) Lila Mackiwain
3 Katie Sauer
4 Mary Amrein
5 Pete Piderson
6 Aner Clementich
7 ober Keller
8 Bill Keller
9 Clora Sauer
10 Joe Sauer
11 Henry Stammen
12 Rose Haerter
13 Rose Liebel
14 Maggie Clementich
15 Walter Liebel
16 John Sauer
17 Geo. Liebel
18 Lizzie Haerter
19 Annie Haerter
20 Ed Clementich
21 Tillie Clementich
22 Joe Stammen
23 Irma Sigman
24 Mat Sauer
25 Kottie Amrein
26 Ella Haerter
27 Teacher.
Irma Sigger.
28 Marie Nastbakken
29 "   "   ".
30 Laurence Piderson
31

Mom wrote the identifying names at age 102

Grandma, who had artistic talents, had long, curly, strawberry blonde hair. As she sat drawing and weaving her favorite wild flowers into intricate patterns, Mom would get the brush and play with her hair. Instead of sending her away, Grandma would sit patiently while Mom brushed and fussed and fashioned her hair into a mass of curls on top of her head. Unfortunately, neither Mom nor I, nor either of my sisters, were lucky enough to be blessed with Grandma's beautiful hair. We ended up with fine, thin, mousy brown, and we definitely had no curls. I did inherit her flair for drawing and originality, which I've used in creating specialty cakes for friends and family.

Childhood in the early 1900's was different than the sophisticated life of today's children. Having so little, it took much less to make the children happy. Mom and her sisters sat for hours in a playhouse that they made from stones making mud pies, which they decorated with seeds and pebbles and served on pieces of broken glass. Mom also remembered how tickled she and her sisters were to have the rope swing that Grandpa made and hung on a huge cottonwood limb. They also had a bicycle that Grandpa rode to do his job as county assessor. In the wintertime, neighbors gathered to ice skate on the Mouse River or to slide down the hills on a toboggan that Grandpa had made. Sometimes, Grandma made taffy. With buttered hands, she pulled and twisted and pulled some more until it resembled a long, glossy, golden rope. At other times she made popcorn which the kids gobbled down like hungry geese. It was simple, innocent fun, and they were happy.

When neighbors came to visit, children were expected to be seen and not heard. Many times the adults played cards, and sometimes they'd blow out the kerosene lamp and tell ghost stories by candlelight. Mom and her sisters would huddle in a dark corner and listen, wide-eyed, scared but mesmerized. Later they would be afraid to go out in the dark to the "backhouse" before going to bed. Wolves were never far away, and often times, they could hear them howling at night which heightened their fear. My aunt Rose was the nervous type, and my mother relished teasing her. After one night of scary stories, Mom said that she hid in the dark and jumped out when Rose came by on her trip before bed. Rose became hysterical and ran screaming into the house where she collapsed on the floor. My contrite mother was punished, and she said that it was the one time she felt she deserved it.

Chasing her petrified sister Mayme with angleworms was a different story. Mom still laughed eighty years later when the worm incidents were recalled while she and sister were reminiscing about old times. Aunt Mayme didn't think it was so funny, and for a few minutes, they were kids again, arguing about who did what to whom, each laying a little blame on the other.

One-room schools, once common fixtures throughout rural America, were usually located so that students lived within a walking distance of three or four miles. Mom's school was three miles away, and she and her siblings walked, weather permitting, every day. In the spring, knowing how much their mother loved them, they often stopped to pick delicate pale purple crocuses or blue bells which were tucked in among the prairie grasses or pink wild roses that grew profusely on the prairie. Their petals, smothered in cream and sugar, were a special after-school treat. At times they stopped to watch a herd of white-tailed deer jumping a fence or an antelope standing stock still, its tattooed neck like a message in unbreakable code. Sometimes, as they walked along the river, they found fish that were caught between stones in a beaver dam in the Mouse River. On such occasions, they had fresh northern pike for supper.

As a teacher, I have utmost respect for the one-room school teachers. Not only did they have to provide direct instruction in all school subjects, but they had to do so for eight different grade levels. This had to be a challenge and with few books and limited school supplies, even more so.

The role of the one-room school teacher required much more than teaching reading, writing and arithmetic. In my mother's time, it was the teacher's responsibility to fill kerosene lamps and see that the globes were washed and to haul in drinking water from the well and wood to start a fire in the pot-bellied stove. (Sometimes parents and older students helped with these chores.) The teacher also had to sweep and scrub the wooden floors and wash windows—all for twenty-five to thirty dollars a month. (In 1954, I earned $250 a month.) Teachers were also expected to set a good moral example—no drinking or smoking—and in some cases, their contracts stated that they could not marry. Married women might become pregnant and teaching children when "in the family way" was considered morally unacceptable. (During my first year of teaching, there was an unwritten dress code—no pants, not even slack suits—and teachers certainly were never seen drinking or dancing in a bar.)

Education in my parents' time was a privilege and was not designed to be fun and entertaining. Everything students learned was by memorization, and it was meant to be hard work. Paper was expensive; Mom and her schoolmates used individual slates and chalk. They also worked on large chalkboards, which were used by the teacher during her instruction. Discipline was strict, and there was no question as to who was in charge of the classroom. Rowdy students had to sit in the corner with their backs to the rest of the class. Sometimes serious misbehavior resulted in a "licking" given by the teacher. Henry Stammen, one of Mom's schoolmates and a master of pranks, spent a lot of time facing the corner. Mom laughed as she recalled the time he put a garter snake in the top drawer of the unsuspecting teacher's desk, which was located in clear view of every student. Imagine the chaos when she opened the drawer and out slithered an agitated snake. I don't know if Henry got the "licking," but Mom did say that his parents were called in and that he was unusually quiet for at least the next week.

Recess meant a time to run and have fun. Promptly at twelve o'clock, the students would eat their lunch brought in tin, one-gallon syrup pails and then hurry out to play. Softball, Crack the Whip and Pump Pump Pull Away were favorites for the older students and Drop the Hankie for the younger. In the winter, they all played Fox and Goose, skated on the river or went tobogganing on the nearby hill. With a twinkle in her eye, Mom went on to say that they sometimes pretended not to hear the bell when it rang. As punishment for being late, they had to make up the time after school. Sometime during the afternoon, one of the errant students would divert the teacher's attention while a cohort set the clock ahead. (Knowing my mother, she was probably the one who reset it.) When their allotted time was up, they innocently filed out at the regular dismissal time.

Many times, older boys didn't start school in the fall until after the harvesting was over, and in the spring, they had to leave school early to help get the crops planted, but regardless of age, they came to school when they could.

While there were definite challenges, there were also hidden benefits of the one-room school. Progressive education procedures of today, such as peer-group teaching, multi-age grouping and mainstreaming, occurred naturally. Children taught each other because the teacher was busy teaching someone else. A fourth grader could work at fifth grade level in one subject and on third-grade level in another, without the stigma associated with being left back or the pressures of being skipped ahead. A student with a learning disability could find his own level without being separated from other pupils and thus avoid being labeled as different, which can cause irreparable damage.

Not only was the school a center of learning, but it was also used as the township hall where people went to vote and as a place for neighbors to socialize. Box socials, a popular form of entertainment and a fun way to make money for the school, were held in the school. The women and girls would fill eye-catching baskets with appetizing foods such as fried chicken, fresh breads and cakes, and the men, both young and old, would bid on them. Whoever bid the highest got the basket and the privilege of eating with the one who brought it. Although the owner of the basket was supposed to be a surprise, Mom admitted that she and the girls would let the guys they were sweet on know which was theirs.

They also held whist parties at the school (similar to no-trump bridge) and dances. On the dance nights, men would move out the desks, and the fiddler's lively "Turkey in the Straw" would bring everyone to their feet. Grandma Hoerter didn't much approve of dancing, but Grandpa did. In fact, he taught Mom and my aunts how to dance. Uncle Joe played the violin, and he would take turns dancing his daughters around the kitchen table.

The end of the school year was celebrated with a picnic. All the parents came and everyone brought a dish to share. Ice cream freezers packed with ice that was dug out of the straw in someone's root cellar cranked out vanilla ice cream made from thick, rich cream, and there was always fresh-squeezed lemonade. Spirited games of softball and horseshoes filled the afternoon. At the conclusion of the day, the students and teacher went their separate ways. For most eighth graders, including my mother and father, it was the last year of their public education. Going on to high school involved determination and sacrifice which many were not willing or able to make. Those who did continue had to board in town with friends or relatives, as it would have been impossible to commute daily. This was still true when my oldest brother Ralph went to high school. He stayed with several different families in Foxholm during those four years, and for a short time, he even bunked with the janitor who had a room in the school. It was not easy.

Mom had her first job at age fourteen. She worked all summer as a companion for an elderly neighbor lady, which included doing household chores. Her pay check in the fall was a fat little pig. This was the same year that she received her favorite birthday present, soft pink cotton dress material from her godmother, Laura Schmitz. Mom was wearing the dress made from that material when she first saw my father, who at age sixteen had come from Albany, Minnesota to work with his uncle, Pete Miller. When she and her family entered St. Henry's Church for Sunday Mass, there he was standing on the floor register warming himself. Although he, with his dimples and fetching smile, caught her eye, her beautiful red-headed older sister Annie caught his. Barn dances were popular and although he'd ask Annie to go with him, he also extended the invitation to Mom who happily accepted. This greatly upset Annie. "Don't you dare come with us," she threatened. "Stay home where you belong," Of course, Mom ignored her.

Aunt Annie and Mom

After several of these threesome dates, Dad bypassed Annie and asked my mother to go with him. At this point, Mom turned to her sister, smiled sweetly and said, "Now you can stay home where you belong."

And that was the beginning of a lifelong romance; Mom and Dad married on September 26, 1915, and the beautiful red-headed Annie was her matron of honor.

Mom and Dad and 40 years later

Dad's brothers George, Norbert "Butch", Rupert

My grandfather Mike Miller (seated on the left) and friends

Harry

My brother Harry was ten years old when he was killed—two years before I was born. It was the hot, dry summer of 1931, and herding cattle was a must. My oldest siblings all took their turns. Many times, when it was Harry's turn, his friend went along to keep him company. The day he was killed was no different except that he and his friend, who was also ten, had snuck a .22-rifle out to shoot gophers while watching the cattle. During the course of the day, my brother squatted down behind a haystack. His friend was holding the gun when suddenly it went off, sending the bullet through the haystack and into Harry's abdomen, piercing his intestines. Not only was it a terrible tragedy for my family, it was terrible for the friend's family as well. I remember Mom saying that the boy's mother, her good friend, was too upset to even attend the funeral.

Harry was rushed to Minot where he immediately underwent surgery. His condition appeared to stabilize, and with the doctor's encouragement, Mom left his bedside and went home for much-needed rest. She would regret leaving for the rest of her days.

According to another patient, Harry somehow managed to get out of bed in the middle of the night and wander deliriously down the hall. The walking "tore everything open," as Mom put it. In today's world, Harry would have been in the Intensive Care Unit, and such a thing would not have happened, but it did happen, and the rudimentary medical techniques of the times could not save him. He passed away June 28, three days after he was injured.

My sister Connie was herding cattle when Harry's condition worsened. By the time she received word of his deterioration and made it to the hospital, he was already gone. Some seventy years later, a shadow of sorrow still clouds her eyes when remembering that terrible day.

Wakes, which could be incredibly difficult for the grieving family, were customary at that time, and thus, Harry's body was brought home the night before the funeral. How hard it must have been for my parents to see their young son lying in a casket in their very own bedroom. Dressed all in white—white short pants and shirt and long white stockings—and lying in a white casket with a spray of white lilies in his hands created a poignant picture of youth and innocence, an image that would linger a lifetime.

Stunned friends poured in bearing food and heartfelt sympathy. The body was never left unattended during the all-night prayer vigil. In the morning, Father Ott came to the house where he blessed the body before leading the funeral precession to St. Henry's Catholic Church for the Mass and burial in the family plot.

Harry

The Mike Stammen Place

"I had such fun today!" M.M.

When I was born, my family was renting a farm northeast of Foxholm known as The Mike Stammen Place. The house, which was later moved into Minot and in which my sister Connie still lives, was built on the side of a hill and had three levels of living space. I have a picture of myself sitting behind that house. I was about two years old and looked like a genuine Depression child minus the forlorn look—chubby cheeks smudged with dirt, soiled dress, baggy long black socks and well-worn, white high-top shoes. I also had the happiest, biggest grin you've ever seen. My sons tease me about my "Grapes of Wrath" appearance. I defend myself by reminding them that I lived on a farm during the Depression and played in the dirt because there was no grass. Actually, with the drought and subsequent money worries, our plight was somewhat similar to that of the "Grapes of Wrath".

I was born in the "Dirty Thirties," and times were tough. The stock market crash in 1929 began the financial woes of the farmers, and the severe drought that followed increased them a hundred-fold. Crops were poor at best, and pasture grass was nearly non-existent. To supplement the cattle feed, Dad raked together Russian thistles and sprinkled them with salt and molasses to make them more palatable. With no pasture grass, the cows had to be herded on the prairie and moved often so as not to damage the roots of what little grass there was.

My oldest siblings had the job of herding the cattle. Ralph, being the oldest, often helped Dad with the farm work, which left Connie, next in line, to do most of the herding.

Graduation Day Ralph (left rear) and friends

Herding cattle was a big responsibility. If they strayed onto an enticing grain field, there could be serious consequences, especially if the grain belonged to William Bock, Anselm's father. Connie found that out the hard way and learned in a hurry to be twice as vigilant when anywhere near his fields. Herding was done on horseback, as Connie usually did, or on foot. Either way, it was a tedious job. There were times when she fell asleep on the horse or while sitting on a big rock in the warm sun. Sometimes, she awoke to find the cows gone, and panic would send her scrambling in search of them. At times, when Connie herded on foot, our sister Evie, who was four years younger than her, would walk along. She was careful not to wear her red hat because someone teasingly told her that if she wore red, the bull would chase her.

Evie loved to play school. All the cows had names, and she made each one a report card, which included a grade for deportment. If one strayed too far while grazing, her grade went down. If she stayed within the boundaries, she earned a good grade for the day. As a reward for good behavior, Evie would make up a story which she told to the "students" who were quietly munching near by. All of these silly antics helped to lessen the boredom, so Connie was happy for her to tag along.

When the cows had eaten their fill and lay down to chew their cuds, it was time to round them up and head for home. The cows had a self-determined social order which they followed faithfully. When they headed for home, the same cow was always in the lead with the rest following in their designated order. The cattle stopped to water at a large spring that was surrounded by a four-foot-high wooden frame, which made it impossible for the cows to reach the water. This meant that the water had to be hauled out of the spring by hand, bucket by bucket, and poured into a stock tank. When one drew water for thirty to forty head of cattle, counting the calves, it was a tiring, backbreaking job. To make matters worse, Connie was afraid of frogs, and there were always a jillion of them near the water. Alvin, eight years younger than her, tagged along one day, and during the process of catching one of the frogs, fell headfirst into the deep water. Luckily, Connie was nearby and rescued him. After the dunking experience, he decided to leave the frogs alone and stick to snaring gophers.

Connie would tie her horse Prince to a fence post when she watered the cows. When it suited him, he'd slip out of his halter and run home leaving tired Connie to walk home behind the cows. Once home, the cows went directly into the barn and to their stanchions where they waited to be milked. Hay was pitched down from the haymow into the manger so the cows would be content during the milking which was done by hand—every day, twice a day, rain or shine, sleet or hail, hot or cold. Coleman lanterns were hung on a nail for the early morning and the dark winter evening milking. Mom did a lot of the milking. I can still see her with her head leaning on the cow's warm flank as she began the rhythmic "zzzzt, zzzzt, zzzzt" that eventually filled the pail. As she milked, the barn cats would line up for their expected bonus—a squirt of warm milk for each.

Mom was eighty-five when she milked her last cow, which just happened to belong to Question Mark from Question Mark and the Mysterians, who became famous with his 1960's hit "Ninety-Six Tears," and to his manager, Luverne Thompson. Luverne's fiancé had been transferred to the Minot Air Base, and they lived in the old Gorde house in Foxholm where Q, as Question Mark is known, attended St. Mary's Catholic Church. Luverne's elderly father Cecil was living with them, and since Cecil had grown up on a farm near Walhalla, North Dakota, they bought him an old Jersey milk cow, reminiscent of his childhood days, to give him something to do. Our son Jack, who still lives in Foxholm, became well-acquainted with Question Mark and Luverne, (Luverne was a carpet layer and taught Jack the trade.) and tells the story about the time Luverne and his dad went out of town for a couple days and left the milking to Q. Question Mark had never milked a cow in his life and had no desire to learn. Jack had never milked, either, but confidently got out the milk pail. After his chore was finished, Jack proudly showed his grandmother the milk, all of a quart in the bottom of the pail. Taking one look, Mom laughed, and back to the barn they went. Sitting on a three-legged stool, Mom remilked the cow, ending up with a brimming pail of milk. With a twinkle in her eye, Mom informed her two on-lookers that they'd better stick to singing and carpet laying because they'd never make it milking cows.

Question Mark "96 Tears"

North Dakota was nicknamed the "Flickertail State" and with good reason. Farmers called these little rodents gophers, which was a misnomer. Different from gophers, which are burrowing rodents who feed underground and are seldom seen, flickertails are ground squirrels that feed aboveground. During the early years before settlers broke the soil, the prairies were alive with these ground squirrels which could be seen scampering about or standing up like picket boards emitting their shrill mating calls. With each call note, their short little tails were flipped up and down in a farewell gesture as they disappeared down the burrow, hence the name flickertails.

Flickertails destroyed crops as they tenaciously tried to hold on to their original habitat. As grain fields spread over their range, they gathered to feast on the abundant new and wonderful food, eating the leaves and stems of the grain. They also dug up planted seed, eating the sprouts and kernels. They made burrows in the plowed ground or growing grain and bred hundreds of babies in the underground nests. To help eliminate the teeming pests, a bounty of five cents per tail was paid. My siblings and their friends made their spending money selling the tails.

Children of the dirty thirties Francis, Alvin (on the right) and me

Drowning was found to be one of the more effective ways of capturing the gophers. Ralph and Connie would load barrels of water on a stoneboat (a type of farm sled that was dragged by a horse and used for hauling heavy things), hitch it up to Birdie, and off they'd go in search of the gopher holes. As they poured in the water, the farm dog Teddy, alert and anxious, would stand next to the hole and wait for the gopher to emerge. As soon as the head appeared, "snap!" Teddy had it. Once they had caught the gopher, they'd cut off the tail and store it in a Prince Albert Tobacco can. To keep the tails from becoming putrid, they sprinkled them with salt.

While Birdie was used as a workhorse, Prince was used mostly for riding. He also knew a few tricks, which Alvin taught him. When touched in a certain place on his flank, he would kneel down, and when out herding, he would nip at an errant cow to turn it back to the herd. He was also mischievous and would occasionally bite anyone who stood in front of him. Dad told the story about the time a blowhard neighbor stopped at the farm and found Dad working on the corral. Just as the know-it-all bent over the fence to offer his unsolicited advice, Prince sauntered up behind him and playfully took a little nip. Startled, the man let out a yell and jumped a foot. It looked so comical that Dad couldn't help but laugh. It was the last straw for the nosy neighbor. He picked up his hat and left, rubbing his backside and muttering, "And he thinks it's funny. That damn horse ought to be shot!" Dad didn't shoot Prince; he sold him to the government during WWII, and he was shipped to Belgium and used by the military.

As a youngster, Evie was always on the delicate side and thus was excused from many of the farm chores that Connie did. Instead, she helped Mom in the house, which could be the reason she became such a good cook. Her cooking reputation began as a young child when she and Ida Gorde prepared a memorable dinner for their mothers—roast sparrows. Somehow they caught, cleaned and roasted the birds. The girls set the table, which Grandpa Hoerter had made for Evie, using Evie's little blue-flowered china dishes, and served the mothers in grand style. Connie remembers how cute the tiny roasted sparrows looked, all golden brown with their toothpick legs sticking straight up in the air.

While living on the Stammen Place, my siblings attended Stammen School District #26 which was located one mile east of the Heinen Bridge. Ms. Clara Zeltinger was Alvin's first grade teacher, and coincidentally years later, she, then Mrs. Ahmann, was Alvin's daughter Debi's first grade teacher.

Small rural schools often needed to offer housing to the usually low-paid teachers in order to make it economically feasible for them to move to the area to teach. Also, with the uncertainty of the weather and the conditions of the rural roads, it allowed them the convenience of staying right next to the school. The Stammen School District offered such housing to their teachers.

On the mild spring and fall days, my siblings walked to school, although, on occasion, Ralph and Connie rode on horseback. Connie smiled as she recalled how she used to dawdle as she tied up her horse so that she could miss a few minutes of school. Also, she had the excuse that she had to "check on her horse" during the day, which afforded her a few more stolen minutes. Times may change but kids never do.

Yuly School Students and transportation—Ralph (back row 2nd from left), Harry (first row 2nd from left), Connie (1st row middle}, Alice, Orrie and Bob Huizenga (future Huizenga Band members) are among the group

During the cold North Dakota winters, the kids rode a school bus that was driven by Ray Stammen. The bus was a horse-drawn wooden wagon box on sled runners with built-in wooden benches, a round coal stove heater in the middle and a canvas top. It was the driver's job, of course, to build the fire in the heater before starting his daily run.

All the kids took their sleds to school. Sometimes the bigger boys would hitch onto the back of the bus which was much more fun than riding inside. It was never too cold for sledding. Every recess and noon hour found all the kids sliding down the hill behind the school. With all the wet wool mittens that were spread out near the coal heater, the classroom constantly smelled like wet dogs.

For lunch, many of the kids would bring a big potato that they put into the ash pan of the heater. The more ingenious ones put theirs into a baking powder can, which was just the right size to accommodate a good-sized potato. Dad would go to the school early in the morning to build a fire for the teacher, and at the same time, would put potatoes in for my brothers and sisters. When twelve o'clock rolled around, they'd blow off the ashes and enjoy a hot lunch.

Eventually, roads and transportation improved, and with the population dwindling, small rural schools were forced to consolidate. The Stammen School was one such victim. When its doors closed, the teacherage was sold and moved to Foxholm where it became a private dwelling.

My first family picture 1933

It was customary for the neighbors to get together in the fall and butcher hogs for the winter's use. It was hard, messy work, but there were always stories and laughs that made the task seem easier. As you would suspect, Mom did her best to keep things lively.

It was Dad's job to stick the pigs. The hogs were then dipped in scalding water that was heated in a big black butchering kettle, which was suspended over an open fire. (That big kettle sat in our yard for as long as I can remember.) After the gutting and while the men were cutting up the hogs, the women, equipped with table knives, scraped the intestines which were used in the sausage making process. Once scraped, the intestines were soaked in salt water and then attached to the sausage-stuffer, which filled the casings with the ground, seasoned meat.

During one of these butchering sessions, Mom and her practical joke cohort, Fronnie DeGree, collected several eyeballs and slipped them into a friend's apron pocket. Years later, Mom and Fronnie were still laughing at their friend's reaction. Imagine reaching into your pocket and pulling out a handful of pig eyeballs. Needless to say, that butchering session was anything but dull.

Dad always saved the brains, which were considered a delicacy, and would fry them for breakfast the next morning. Breakfast was a big meal at our house during those days, and steak or pork chops were often paired with eggs.

The rings of sausage and the hams were hung in the smoke house for the final processing. After a sufficient length of time, the meat was stored in the granary where it was suspended from the rafters, safe from all interested varmints. To preserve side pork, uncured bacon, Mom fried it and put it layer by layer into a big crock. In between the layers of the meat, Mom poured fat, which congealed and thus preserved the meat. It was then stored in the cool root cellar. The bony pieces of pork were supposed to be eaten first because they didn't preserve as well. When Mom and Dad went to town and my sister or brother cooked, they'd sneak into the side pork, knowing they'd be caught, but doing it anyway because it was so much easier to prepare.

Another get-ready-for-winter project was putting up the vegetables that were raised in the garden. Mom, with the help of my sisters, Connie and Evie, canned everything but the tuber vegetables, which were stored in a root cellar. The carrots were put into large containers of sand that kept them firm and crisp. Lizards loved the cool, dark, dampness of the cellar, and one always had to watch where he stepped. There was no light in the cellar, so the person going in either opened the door wide or took a lantern. Connie often got the job of going to the root cellar for Mom. One day instead of a potato, she got a hold of a lizard, which technically was a salamander but everyone always called them "lizards." She had to go back to that root cellar many more times, and she swears to this day that, because of this, she did penance for every sin she ever was to commit for the rest of her life.

During these hard times, Mom raised turkeys and sold them for a few pennies. She also sold eggs. A few chickens were hatched by brood hens that sat on eggs in their nests until they hatched, but most of the eggs were hatched in an incubator. Chicken eggs took two weeks to hatch, and turkey eggs took three weeks. The eggs had to be turned every day. During the incubation period, Mom candled the eggs to see if they were fertile. She held the egg over a candle and looked at it through a tube or piece of rolled up paper. If not fertile, the eggs were removed and fed to the baby chicks. My brother Alvin laughed as he recalled how he and Francis once put a chicken hawk egg in the incubator along with the other eggs and actually hatched a bird of prey that loves to attack farmyard chickens. There among the fluffy yellow baby chicks was this dark brown scraggly bird with big yellow eyes. Seeing as chicken hawks are normally hunted and killed, not raised, Mom saw that it was a one time venture.

Farmers always kept a few horses even though they used tractors for most of the farming. To protect the horses from the harsh north winds, Dad built a three-sided shelter with a straw roof, which some straggler hens chose to use as a nest. Consequently, whoever had the job of gathering eggs had to be agile enough to climb up on the roof.

Along with the turkeys and eggs, Mom also sold cream. It wasn't much but it helped to buy the hundred-pound sacks of flour and the large bags of sugar that they purchased in the fall and stored away for winter. They also always managed to buy a big box of apples before winter set in. With these staples, plus our vegetables and meat, the family never went hungry.

Mom, all dressed up and ready to go. Dad and I, Alvin and Francis

I was only three when we moved off this farm. My one memory of our time spent there was the time Mom bundled me up in my snowsuit and

I headed off to the barn where Ralph was milking cows. I was walking the same pathway that the cows used, and suddenly, my little short leg went down into one of the holes made by a cow's foot. While I was struggling to get out, a belligerent old rooster taking advantage of my vulnerable state jumped on my head and began to scratch and peck. Petrified, I screamed bloody murder, which brought Ralph on the run. The sight and sound of that big mad rooster with its wild flapping wings and sharp claws made a lasting impression on me. To this day, I'm leery of walking through a farmyard where roosters are running loose.

Family group, Mom, Aunt Rose Trudell and George,
Grandma Miller and me

"Sweethearts" Johnny Ahmann and I

Bundled up for an outing with Dad

The Arnold Place

Searching for better conditions during the hard times of the Depression, my dad moved our family from the farm where I was born to another that our family, referencing the family who had lived there, called the Arnold Place.

My oldest sister Connie and her new husband, Ambrose Stammen, lived in a farmhouse just over the hill from us. During the fall, Ambrose pitched bundles with threshing crews which meant that Connie spent long days by herself. Having no children and only a small house to keep up, she often had time on her hands. One afternoon, she decided that she'd drive their Model A Ford Coupe down to our house. There was only one problem—she had never driven a car. Confident, Connie thought, "How hard can it be?" and climbed behind the wheel. Driver's licenses were not yet required, but on the cow paths we called roads, it wouldn't have mattered anyway.

Starting the motor was relatively easy. It was shifting and keeping it running that caused the problems. After several tries, Connie finally managed to shift it into gear without killing the motor. When she let out the clutch, the car bucked forward, and she was back to square one. Again she stepped on the starter button and again the motor roared to life. She shifted gears, slowly let out the clutch and pushed down on the gas pedal. The car shot forward narrowly missing a tree. Thinking a little practice might be helpful, she inched her way to the garden area. She had only driven a few feet when a rabbit hopped out in front of her. Swerving to miss it, she mowed down several potato plants. After making it around the garden twice without mishap, she was ready for the road, or so she thought. Starting out slowly, she was soon cruising along at twenty miles an hour. Suddenly, a pothole loomed before her. She cranked the wheel but it was too late; she hit it square on. The Model A bounced up and slammed back down. Shaking like a leaf, Connie managed to get herself and the car under control and continued on down the road. The hill was her next challenge. Clutching the steering wheel, she pushed down on the accelerator. Slowly, the car began to climb. Reaching the top, she breathed a sigh of relief…until she looked down. Riding the brakes, she began the descent. A few nerve-wracking minutes later, the Model A, with a smug Connie at the wheel, rolled to a stop in front of our house. "How hard could it be?" Indeed.

My brothers, Francis and Alvin, and their friend, Will Dahle, spent a lot of summer days meandering barefooted along the river where they skipped rocks and hunted for things that interest ten-year-old boys. During their ramblings, they discovered huge frogs on the riverbank. One of them (most likely Francis, as he was always the cook) came up with the bright idea of catching them and having a frog leg fry. That was the beginning of their great summer culinary adventures. Whenever they could sneak away from the chores of the day, the boys would grab a frying pan, load up on butter and head for the river. The unsuspecting frogs never had a chance. One hop and they were history. The boys built a bonfire, cut off the legs and fried them in butter. With the lingering aroma of the frog legs mingling with the scent of sun-dried pastures, they'd plop down on the riverbank and dream up their next Huckleberry Finn adventure.

My best and most vivid memory while living on the Arnold Place is my 4th birthday. Dad surprised me with a tiny black and white puppy. I was so excited and so happy, and the wriggling pup appeared to feel the same. Thus began our happy fifteen years together.

My 4th birthday party

Toots was part terrier, part bulldog, and I'm convinced, part human. Being the only child at home and with no neighbor kids my age, she became the playmate I longed for. Toots and I played house. I remember dressing her up in one of my baby bonnets and a little pink dress. (I can't believe how patient she was!) The dress was a good fit, but the bonnet covered everything but a flash of her eyes and her nose. After settling her in my doll buggy, I put on Mom's old black hat, which fit me about like Toots' hat fit her, and her high-heeled shoes, and "clomp, clomp, clomp," around the house we'd go. Eventually, Toots would decide that enough was enough, and with one leap she was gone—bonnet, dress and all.

Myrna and playmates (Toots escaped)

Tug-of-war was even more fun. It was a loud, boisterous game that we played until I was quite big. I would give her the signal by shaking my pant leg. That was all the encouragement Toots needed. She'd grab hold and pull me all over the floor, growling noisily and shaking her head like a high-speed windshield wiper. The harder she shook, the more I'd giggle and laugh. Round and round we'd go. Just so much of this noise and Mom would holler, "Quit with that dog!" Occasionally, her tugging ripped the seam of my pant leg, sometimes half way up to the crotch. Then we were in trouble. Not serious trouble, however, as Mom was quite tolerant when it came to my dog and me. Maybe after seven kids, she just gave up fretting about the small stuff. At any rate, she'd sew up the seam, and things would be pretty quiet for the next day or so.

I often wonder how my parents ever survived raising my two youngest brothers. Being their sister nearly did me in. They, like the Katzenjammer Kids (old cartoon characters), were masters of mischief and never backed down from a fight. If there was any excitement in the vicinity, one could count on them being in the middle of it.

While living on this farm, Francis and Alvin, who were two years apart in age, attended a country grade school that was located near the Zinninger farmstead. There were nine students, with boys outnumbering the girls five to four. Miss Aarseth, a local young woman, was their unsuspecting teacher. True to form, my brothers made life interesting for her. (She probably quit teaching.)

In the winter, Francis and Alvin sometimes skated to school on the Des Lacs River (about three miles). At one point, they had to cross a beaver's dam which was piled high with sharp sticks and rocks. Although the beavers work at night, my brothers occasionally came upon one nibbling on a branch, which the beaver held in his fore feet. At their approach, the ever-vigilant beaver would slap his black paddle-like tail and quickly disappear under the water. My brothers could have gone around the dam but that would have been too easy. They chose to crawl over instead. Even with bib overalls and long underwear padding their knees and mittens on their hands, it was not a comfortable crossing. They also had to be careful of their footing because there was open water around the dam and wet clothes in twenty-degree weather were not something to merely shrug off. Getting over the dam, however, was no problem for them. They learned the technique quickly. It was their interest in the beaver, whose pelt was worth money, which sometimes got them in trouble. If they dawdled at the dam, which they were known to do, and were late for school, they had to answer to my dad as well as their teacher.

Like flickertails, gophers remained on the North Dakota Prairie's "Most Wanted List," and the bounty of five cents per tail was still being offered. The nickels added up, so catching them became a favorite sport for the area's young people, Francis and Alvin included. Snaring the rodent was one way of catching them. A snare, made from cord, was carefully laid over the hole, and when the gopher stuck his head out, the cord was quickly jerked, snaring the gopher. To use this method, one had to be patient and quick. My brothers were quick but not always patient, so while one waited at the hole to pull the snare, the other one hunted them with a .22-rifle. To double their profits, they cut the larger tails in two. Their scheme was never uncovered.

Occasionally, Francis, the older of the two, would sneak Dad's twelve-gauge double-barrel shotgun with a broken-off stock and take it to school. He'd hide it in the woodpile so he could hunt gophers during recess. A few times, he got up and left the schoolroom, followed by all the boys, to pursue one that he saw running through the schoolyard. (I have to wonder what the teacher was doing all this time.)

Andrew Nelson lived very near the school, and somehow, my brothers found out that he kept shotgun shells hidden, for safety's sake, in the granary. The two of them would sneak into the granary and take shells for their gopher hunting. On one of these raiding sprees, Alvin was bitten by Nelson's large farm dog and bore the scars forever. (He showed them to me when we were reminiscing for this book.) No doubt he had to do some fast talking when they got home that evening.

Every afternoon at four o'clock, school was dismissed, and the teacher was free to leave. Before leaving, she banked the pot-bellied coal stove (during the cold season), adjusted the window shades, gathered up her papers and made sure that the padlock on the door was secured. After unlocking the school each morning, Miss Aarseth would take the key but naively leave the lock hanging on the door. One afternoon as my brothers left the school, temptation was too great; they snapped the padlock, locking their teacher inside. For some reason, she was unable to get out through a window and had to crawl through the coal chute, which, of course, was completely saturated with black coal dust. Oddly, the incident never got home to my parents, and it was never mentioned in the classroom, but after that, the padlock, as well as the key, was always removed when the door was unlocked.

Crows were a constant problem for the farmers during the dry years. Hungry, they would pull up young cornstalks to eat the seed kernel attached to the roots. Scarecrows were used in an attempt to scare them away, but the crows' persistence made them ineffective. Seeking a solution, crow-shooting contests were held in some areas with prizes given to the ones who came in with the most crow heads. A bounty was also offered for their eggs. While walking home from school one day, Francis and Alvin decided to make themselves a little money. They veered off their regular path in search of the eggs and wound up walking in the ditch along the highway. As they were searching, they spotted a magpie on a nearby fence post. Never missing a chance to prove who had the better aim, they each picked up a rock and fired away. One errant rock sailed right past the magpie and hit a car that was traveling on the highway, shattering a window and just missing the driver who happened to be Ward County's Superintendent of Schools, A.M. Waller, who had been out visiting area schools. That was one day the boys didn't have to walk home from school.

These two brothers of mine were as thick as thieves but still had their regular fights. Fistfights were common, but one day, when they were still quite little, they topped the fisticuffs with a rotten turkey egg fight. The turkeys hid their nests in the weeds, and when Mom wanted some for hatching, she'd send the boys out with a pail to hunt for them. One time they found a huge nest of rotten eggs, and for whatever reason, they got into a fight and pelted each other with the eggs. They came home with putrid rotten eggs all over—running down their faces, matted in their hair and splattered all over their overalls. Mom wasn't home, and it fell to Connie to bathe them. It was an unforgettable task, one that Connie talks about yet today. Another time, Alvin threw a rock at Francis, who retaliated with a brass gas faucet from the farm gas barrel. He hit Alvin smack in the mouth, knocking out one of his front teeth. Dad rushed him into Minot to our dentist, Dr. Robinson, but with dentistry in the mid-thirties being a far cry from the sophisticated technology of today, the tooth could not be saved. Alvin's teeth eventually grew together filling in the gap, but he was left with a constant reminder of his folly.

My brothers' rustic brawls and madcap pranks continued on into adulthood, creating fodder for the gossips, amusement for their friends, fits for my parents and total embarrassment for me.

When I was a senior in high school, Francis, who was still in the Marines, came home on leave. When he hit Minot, he made the rounds downtown, stopping at all his old haunts including the Buffalo Tap in the Leland Parker Hotel where he ran into his good friends, Bud Struckness and Sammy Norgaard from Hartland. As they exited the bar, Francis was spotted by the Minot Police and hauled to the police station. It seems he was wanted for a minor traffic violation, which he had failed to take care of before he left. Obviously, they let him go after he satisfied his debt because the three of them ended up that night on Highway 28 on their way to Hartland. There had been a heavy, wet spring snowstorm the night before, and, unbeknown to the tipsy trio, a portion of Highway 28 between Carpio and Berthold was still solidly blocked. Surveying their dilemma, they spotted a highway maintainer with an attached snowplow sitting along side the road. For some unknown reason, the road crew had left before the complete blockage was removed. It just so happened that all three of the guys were heavy equipment operators, which made for an easy solution. They would borrow the machine, open the highway and be on their way. In the process of carrying out their little plan, Sammy drove the maintainer into a slough, got out and never shut off the motor. With the motor running, its wheels kept churning and churning until the maintainer was buried so deeply that it took a caterpillar from Kenmare, thirty-six miles away, to pull it out. (The three had to pay for the use of the caterpillar.) The revelers finally got to Foxholm where they fell into bed only to be awakened the next morning by my very irate father. I don't know how the authorities found out who did the vandalizing, but the sheriff had come for the culprits. "Jesus Christ! In jail twice before you even made it home!" Dad bellowed. Today Francis and Buddy laugh when remembering, but at the time, they were at least smart enough to look contrite.

Buddy and Mom

Francis and Buddy (my fourth brother, as I call him) had many crazy adventures, but this one remains uppermost in their memories. Francis had been on an extended trip Out West, as a trip to the coastal states was often called, and the night he got back in town, he and his cohorts, including Buddy, rented the bridal suite in the Leland Parker Hotel. Later Buddy, a master of dry wit, said, "We had to have some place to sleep." As the evening and rollicking progressed, so did the noise, and before they knew it, a Minot cop was knocking at their door. This particular cop was a big man—at least six feet, four inches tall and three hundred pounds—and knew these young men well. (This cop was the same one who, while acting as a security cop at the American Legion Club, removed my slight five-foot, eight-inch banty rooster brother Alvin from a pending altercation by simply reaching in, picking him up, and holding him in the air, with feet dangling, until the spark was extinguished.) Soon, two more cops arrived, and now there were three city cops to investigate the complaint. Cordial as always, the boys invited them in for a little social drink in appreciation for the warning. Buddy laughs, remembering how their invitation evolved into a night spent in a bridal suite with three cops "supervising the festivities." At the peak of the evening, fueled with good cheer, Buddy donned the huge officer's uniform jacket whose sleeves hung down to Bud's fingertips and his hat that covered half of Bud's ears, strapped on his gun belt which sagged to his knees and walked down the halls, knocking on doors and calling out, "Quiet down in there!"

No matter how much fun they had or how long the night had been, these young party-hard guys never missed a day of work. A good work ethic was learned at the breast and stayed with them for a lifetime.

I did survive my brothers' embarrassing shenanigans, and perhaps they even prepared me for raising my own four sons. One thing is sure, my nieces and nephews didn't get away with a thing when they were growing up. Their fathers were always one step ahead of them. They had been there and done that.

The Peterson Place

The Depression continued. In a desperate attempt to keep the family's head above water, Dad moved us to another farm which was called The Peterson Place. It was a pretty location. The Des Lacs River, whose banks were dotted with native grasses and trees, meandered through the farmyard. Rolling hills stretched eastward from the river, providing good grazing land for the cattle. A grove of cottonwoods, most likely planted by the pioneer Petersons, surrounded the farm buildings, providing some shelter from the harsh Dakota winds.

A 4th of July Picnic gathering, Margaret Greeman and daughters,
Mary Greeman, Connie, Mom, Gertrude Sem, Julianna Gilday, and
me (leaning on the porch rail)

There were two houses on the farm. Hank and Tress Peterson and
family lived in one house, and we lived in the other, and just across the
river about a city block away, lived a third family, the Sems. There were
thirteen young people in all. After having no one but my dog Toots to
play with, I now had a slew of playmates.

Lowell Sem was four, a year younger than me, and his brother Jack
was a couple of years older. We were constant playmates. Summertime
found us outdoors all day long with only our imaginations to keep us
occupied. I remember making mud pies, smoothing and patting our
sculptures until we had them just so. Sometimes, we'd have a tea party
and would serve our "pies and cakes" on large rhubarb leaves, which
grew in abundance in the garden area. Occasionally, we'd each take a
big bite of the tart rhubarb and then see who could chew the longest
without puckering up. (I think three seconds was about the maximum
for any of us.) The faces we made, which were worthy of academy awards,
sent us into fits of giggling.

Pigweeds, which grew profusely near the riverbank, provided us
with endless fun. Our favorite thing was making the weed patch into an
"apartment building." The pigweeds stood about five feet tall (regular

skyscrapers to us) and had huge leaves and long thick roots. Pulling them was a tough job. Sometimes, it took all of us pulling together to get one of the tougher ones out. A sudden release found us on the ground sprayed with black dirt. Out of breath, we'd regroup and tackle the next one. Slowly the rooms and connecting hallways began to take shape. When our stomachs began to growl, we'd dust off the seats of our pants and head for the house. Many times it was the odor of fresh donuts that got our attention. (My mother's cake donuts were one of her specialties.) After refueling, we'd load up a fruit jar of Rawleigh's cherry nectar and a sack of warm doughnuts and trudge back to the pigweed patch where we'd spend the afternoon playing in our new pigweed palace.

Having few store-bought games and toys, we were forced to use our imaginations. Old tires, we discovered, were a lot of fun. We'd each take a tire and roll it down the road, and when we got it really rolling, we'd jump straddle it from behind and ride over it. We had to remember to keep running when our feet hit the ground, or we'd get bumped in the backside. Another thing we did was curl up inside the tire, and with someone pushing, we'd go rolling down the dirt road. Many times, we'd race. Always competitive, I would try my very best to keep my tire and rider in the lead, or if I was the one in the tire, try my best to stay there. Sometimes someone would fall out and get scraped up a bit, but most of the time, we hung in there. On one occasion, Jack had me rolling at a good speed when suddenly the tire swerved to one side, throwing me out. I rolled through a prickly brush pile and over a few rocks, and landed in a heap on the side of the road. The knees of my coveralls were shredded and blood ran down my legs, but no way was I about to cry in front of the boys, let alone give up. I dizzily scrambled back into the tire and the race went on.

Dad, as did most farmers, had chickens, milk cows and hogs, and consequently, even during those lean times, we always had plenty to eat.

Sows with babies are notorious for being mean, and the sow we had on the Peterson Place was one of the meanest. Bessie, a big, old, fat brood sow, and her latest litter were housed in the chicken coop. Knowing how mean she was, my parents warned us kids not to go anywhere near her and her babies, but the temptation to see those cute little pink pigs was too great. Lowell and I thought that if we climbed up on the chicken roosts, we'd be safe and would have a good view of the baby pigs. We were wrong. As soon as we put one foot onto the roosts, all hell broke loose; the old sow went berserk. She let out a loud, enraged squeal and lunged at us. Terrified, we scrambled for the highest roost. Lowell slipped, and as I grabbed for him, we both nearly fell into the pen. There we were, straddling the roosts with the mad sow, literally foaming at the mouth, directly below us. Luckily our moms were outside and heard our frantic screams. Mom grabbed a stick and diverted the crazed sow's attention, while Gertrude climbed up after us. Needless to say, we never had to be reminded not to go near that pig again. We had learned our lesson.

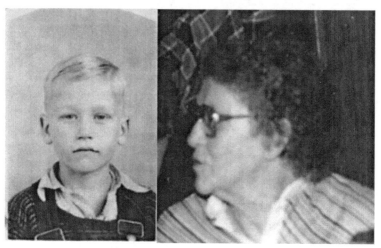

Lowell Sem and his mother Gertrude

At least once a week, Annie Lauinger and her children, Rose Mary and Frankie, would walk the mile and a half from town and spend the afternoon with us. I loved their visits. While Mom and Annie did their thing, we kids played in the pigweed palace or wherever our ramblings took us. I remember one such afternoon with utmost clarity.

It was a hot, muggy summer day. My friends and I were outside playing in the trees when suddenly, ominous black clouds filled the sky turning day into night. In a matter of minutes, large raindrops pelted the canopy of leaves above us, and a sudden blast of wind tearing through the branches sent them flying in all directions. Frightened, we ran toward the house and the sound of our mothers' calling voices. Just as they pulled us through the door, an angry roar filled the blackened sky. Wind and rain pounded the house. Windows rattled in their frames, and tree branches viciously slapped against them, threatening to shatter the panes. The fear I felt was indescribable.

Suddenly, the front door flew open! A blast of wind and rain poured into the living room. Terrified, we little ones huddled in a corner, too frightened to move. Using strength they didn't know they had, Mom and Annie fought to close the door, and then, with backs braced against it, they fought to keep it closed. Frankie started to cry, and I remember

Annie saying in a soothing voice, "Don't cry, Frankie. Pray." Trying to stifle his tears, five-year-old Frankie cried, "I'll pray; I'll pray. What should I pray?"

The horrifying sound of the driving wind and rain and the image of Mom and Annie pushing against the door were unforgettable. It seemed to last forever, but in reality, it only lasted a few minutes. The damage was extensive. The trunk of a big tree that stood right next to the house was twisted like a pretzel. A small building lay in scattered pieces; a piece of farm machinery was thrown against the barn, and tree limbs were everywhere.

The storm, a twister as it was called, was over, but the fear of wind stayed with me for many years.

The Des Lacs River provided us with endless fun. In the winter, we bundled up and went ice-skating. During the summer, we swam. I never really did learn to swim, but I was in the river with the rest of them, dog paddling around, stirring up the mud and tempting the bloodsuckers.

Francis and Alvin and the Peterson boys—Louie, Leon and Henry— dug a large cave in the riverbank which held our interest for a time, but their most memorable endeavor was the tree house they built in the cottonwoods that grew along the river. After scrounging for wood, they measured, sawed and hammered until they had a sturdy, two-story structure. Louie rummaged around at home and found an American flag, which they hung from the upper level.

The older boys spent hours in that tree house. Rarely would they let us younger kids climb up with them, but as soon as they weren't home, it was the first place we went. I loved that tree house. When we sat on the highest platform, all nestled in amid the branches, I was instantly in another world. It was the perfect place to create fantasies—to dream the wondrous dreams of innocent childhood.

During the summer months in North Dakota, daylight lingers well into the evening. We spent many of those long evenings playing games. The farmyard offered ideal hiding places for Run-Sheep-Run and an excellent setting for top-secret adventures.

On shivery dark nights, we'd gather in the dense grove of trees behind our house and tell ghost stories. A favorite spot was beneath a huge gnarled old oak tree that had a thick branch twisting down almost to the ground and rising again in the air. Only the light of the moon and stars illuminated the semi-circle in which we sat.

Louie Peterson was the best storyteller of all. He sat enthroned on a low stump and spoke in drowsy undertones as one does in the dark. Enthralled, we eagerly anticipated the big scare, yet we dared not to look over our shoulders for fear that we would see sinister figures lurking among the shadowy, tangled trees.

I remember one night in particular when we got together for a story-telling session. It was warm and muggy, and there was a full moon. It was very quiet; the silence was broken only by an occasional hoot of a screech owl or the lonesome howl of a coyote. Fireflies sparkled vividly in the darkest corner of the clearing. Louie sat on the stump, his words painting pictures of shivery apparitions. Suddenly, the moonlight faded, swallowed by dark clouds that hovered over the trees. At that moment, we heard a faint rustling sound, and a ghostly white form immerged from the darkness, groaning and shaking as it drifted towards us. I was petrified, too scared to move. Even the older kids sat transfixed, and then I heard my mother's familiar laugh.

Those wonderful, fun-filled days were before the age of television, video games and computers—days when children could be children. Allowed free rein to experiment with the world around them, childhood days were creative, imaginative, ingenious and highly active. I wonder—are the kids of today missing out?

The Struggle to Survive

The economic depression that began in the late 1920's and continued on into the 1930's brought about circumstances that maimed the small farmers. Misuse of land led to incredible devastation.

Overgrazing by cattle and sheep herds had stripped the plains of their cover, and land just blew away. With little grass, many farmers were forced to liquidate their livestock.

After World War I, patriotic zeal produced a surplus of wheat that couldn't be sold. Prices fell, and farmers were unable to meet their payments. Caught in a squeeze between the low prices for crops and high costs of their needs, desperate farmers intensified their efforts. They cultivated land that should have been allowed to lie fallow and then prayed for rain and a good crop. However, the drought continued. Hot winds yanked the moisture from the soil, turning fields into dust. Heartsick, farmers watched their crops and then their hopes wither and die. It is said that some ninety thousand fled the state. Some loaded a few possessions into a rattling car and headed out, some left everything and headed for the nearest highway, and many jumped a freight train. Some, like Andrew Arnold, our neighbor, chose madness.

In 1920, Andrew, a big, tall, raw-boned fellow, and Otto Olson opened a lignite coalmine on the north side of the valley on the Lewis Peterson land, which happened to be the farm that my dad rented years later. Coal was in demand, and for six years the mine prospered. Then tragedy struck. Otto was killed in an accident while working in the mine. His distraught partner dynamited the entrance, gave up the mining business and went into farming. Cattle were an important part of the local economy, and Andrew's herd was one of the finest.

Andrew had always stood out as being a little strange, but as time went on and the drought conditions worsened, his behavior turned bizarre.

At one point, he attempted to dig a coalmine on his farm by hand. Morning, noon and night he labored using nothing but a pick, shovel and wheelbarrow. His weathered face, etched with angular lines, always glistened with sweat that ran down in rivulets, which soaked his tattered sleeveless undershirt. His dirt-streaked bib overalls, which had once stretched snuggly across a barrel chest, now fell loosely from his shoulders. With hands that were callused and sore, he toiled on, looking for the illusive coal vein—and survival. The drought raged on, and the shattered man threw down his shovel; he had reached his breaking point.

Early Sunday morning, Andrew, dressed in his best Sunday attire, picked up a large knife and strode to the barn where he slit the throats of all his cattle. Stepping around the fallen animals, he torched the barn and left. Covered with the animals' blood, he drove his Model T Ford into town and burst into St. Mary's where my family was attending Mass. With a crazed look, he strode up and down the aisle, accusing members of the congregation of being sinful hypocrites and whores of Satan. While the stunned parishioners looked on, he made his way to the altar where he turned, and shouting God's name, condemned them all to a fiery hell. I don't know what happened to Andrew, but at that time, mentally deranged people were sent to Jamestown, where the state mental hospital was and still is still located, although now the facility has several additional functions.

Besides destroying the farm economy, the 1930's drought also began to affect the country's wildlife. The duck population fell to an all-time low. Alarmed conservationists took action. Jay N. "Ding" Darling, a flamboyant political cartoonist from Iowa, was instrumental in forming the Bureau of Biological Survey, which helped push the Duck Stamp Act through Congress in 1934. Proceeds collected from these stamps were allocated to buy and lease a waterfowl habitat. In 1935, our neighboring valley to the north, consisting of thirty-two thousand acres, was designated as The Upper Souris National Wildlife Refuge. This national refuge was established as a haven and breeding ground for migratory birds and other wildlife.

The Upper Souris Refuge straddles more than thirty-five miles of the picturesque Souris River Valley of north-central North Dakota. The Souris, also known as the Mouse River, is one of the few in the United States that flows north and eventually empties into the Hudson Bay. It originates in Weyburn, Saskatchewan, Canada, loops down into North Dakota near Sherwood, reentering Canada just west of the

International Peace Garden, a beautiful garden that commemorates the long-standing peaceful relationship between the United States and Canada.

The Refuge, which lies in the loop of the Souris River, is made up of rolling hills that are covered with mixed prairie grass and steep, brush-covered finger coulees that extend down to the river. In the spring, these coulees are alive with flowering Juneberry and chokecherry trees, their perfumes mingling with the heady scent of wild roses that grow among them. My Grandpa and Grandma Hoerter homesteaded in this valley, and Mom used to tell stories about their berry-picking outings in these very same coulees.

Two groups, the Civilian Conservation Corp and the Works Project Administration, hired a labor force, which included local men, to do the construction on this refuge. Dad, a skilled left-handed carpenter, was one of the locals hired to work on the dam which had the primary purpose of regulating the downstream water supply. The resulting Lake Darling was named in honor of the man whose efforts played such a large part in its making.

Lake Darling, with its northern pike, walleye and perch, became a popular fishing area, and being only seven miles from Foxholm, it was a boost to the town's economy. When Dad bought the bar in 1939, a large percentage of his business came from fishermen who stopped on their way to the lake. Many also stopped on their return to have a beer and to either brag about their catch or to bemoan that the big one got away. Dad ran "Biggest Fish of the Week" contests. He'd weigh the fish as they came in, and the names and weights were posted in a prominent place in the bar. The prize of the week, which was something like a six-pack or maybe even money, was always welcome but, as any fisherman knows, it was thrill of the catch and the resulting bragging rights that sent an angler back time and time again.

Al Schollmeyer of Minot and Dad.
A good catch!

Dad was an avid fisherman himself. He'd sneak away and head for the lake whenever he could sweet-talk my mother into tending bar for him. On one such afternoon, he and his fishing buddy, Art Buee, were out in the middle of the lake. As he cast out, he noticed a strangely familiar object bobbing in the water. As he looked more closely, he realized it was his billfold! Somehow it had slipped from his pocket and had fallen in. Between the two of them, they managed to maneuver the boat around and retrieve the wallet with everything intact; it was water logged, to be sure, but nothing was missing. Later, I found him at the ironing board pressing five hundred dollars worth of wet bills, the amount he regularly carried to cash checks and change bills.

Dad...gone fishin'

Fishing was Dad's passion. He was even "fishing" on his death bed—casting out while in a delirium of pain. His last words were, "I think I finally caught the big one." As I think back, I realize how little time he had to enjoy this sport that he loved so well. Owning a bar in such a small town forced him to be there all day, six days a week. Everything has its price.

Dad's Canadian fishing trip. "It doesn't get any better than this."

The economic benefits of this lake also sifted down to me. I sold minnows for bait at our Miller's Bar and Cafe from the time I was a teenager through my college years and the first four years of teaching. It was my summer job and quite lucrative. I had several minnow traps that I set along the banks of the Des Lacs River. These wire baskets, baited with stale bread, were made to trap the unsuspecting minnows as they wriggled around in quiet little pools that hovered on the fringe of the main river current.

I made my rounds in an old red rattletrap panel truck that rivaled that of the Beverly Hillbillies. Very early in the morning, I'd grab a peanut butter sandwich, don my baseball cap, load up a cream can full of cold water (to dump my minnows in) and a sack of bread, and off I'd go. Settled in my truck, I bounced up and down the riverbanks, water sloshing in the cream can, sometimes following a dirt trail and sometimes making my own. It's a wonder I never rolled into the water.

I loved everything about those cool early summer mornings: the gorgeous sunrises that filled the horizon with streaks of magnificent golds and reds, the dewy freshness, and the gentle quietness that was broken only by the singing of the birds as they welcomed the new day. Occasionally I'd see a meadowlark perched on a fencepost singing his song, showing his bright yellow breast and his black bow tie, as he waited for his mate. As I walked through the tall grasses to the river's edge, colorful butterflies flitted around my head. and gossamer spider webs, clinging to dewy bushes, shimmered in the morning sunlight. Sometimes I'd scare up a rabbit foraging for its morning meal, and once I came upon a sleek black muskrat chewing on a cattail. I don't know who was more startled, the muskrat or me. He quickly dove into the water, still holding the cattail between his teeth, and propelling himself with his strong webbed feet, he glided smoothly away, leaving a subtle rippling trail in his wake.

Tommy Gruber and "The Minnow Lady"

For a few summers, Tommy Gruber and I seined for minnows. We'd stand knee-deep in the river, mud squishing around our ankles, and sweep the water with the tightly woven fishing net stretched between us. It was hard work and not always pleasant. Many times, I came out of the water to find an ugly, black, jelly-like bloodsucker stuck to my leg. I hated them, and each time, I'd let out a little screech, which brought Tommy to my rescue. One tap with a lit cigarette and the blood-engorged leach would reluctantly loosen its grip. I still shutter when I think of them. Mosquitoes were also a big problem. For some reason, I was one of their favorite targets, and every bite I got, I kept for several miserable, itchy days. Rubbing alcohol was the only thing we had that brought any kind of relief, and I kept a big bottle on my nightstand. The quiet of the night was often broken by the sound of sloshing alcohol.

In the fall, I would give up my minnow business and return to my teaching position in Williston where my sister Evie and her family lived. Her husband Leonard loved playing practical jokes and was forever pulling something on someone.

I will never forget the night I went dancing at the American Legion Club. In those days, we dressed up when we went out for the evening, and that particular night I wore a chic black wool jersey formfitting sheath with a neckline that was cut very high in front and very low in back, and with it, I wore a gray iridescent brooch and matching earrings—several steps up from my teaching garb and a far cry from my minnow business attire. During the evening, I managed to attract the attention of a handsome, well-dressed, fabulous dancer, much to the envy of every single girl there. As we moved across the dance floor, I made a conscious effort to appear as sophisticated as he seemed to be.

While slowly swaying to the romantic "Unforgettable," there was a sudden tap on my shoulder, and a voice said, "Pardon me, Miss; aren't you the minnow lady?" (I had told my new acquaintance that I was a schoolteacher.) I glanced around and there was Leonard, who had had a few drinks by then, trying to look so innocent and so sincere. I chose to ignore him by pretending that I hadn't noticed his interruption, which could have been very possible with all the crowding and jostling on the dance floor. My partner and I danced on, smoothly doing the dip as we glided across the floor. Soon there was another tap on my shoulder, "Pardon me, Miss; aren't you the minnow lady? I swear, you look exactly like the lady who sold me minnows last summer." I was becoming more mortified by the minute, and thoughts like, "Go away, you fool" raced through my head. By now the intriguing dancer was beginning to look at me a little strangely. Finally, it was so obvious that I had to confess that he was my crazy brother-in-law and that indeed; selling minnows was my summer job. Laughing like a nut, Leonard shook his hand and danced away.

Leonard, my fun-loving brother-in-law

The building of the dam provided my sister Connie's first job. At barely fifteen, she worked for Frank and Annie Lyness who went into business feeding the 250 men who were living in barracks and trailer houses while working on the dam project.

The Lynesses moved into an old weather-beaten farmhouse that stood near where the old spillway was located. They removed a section of one wall to make an area big enough to accommodate a long dining table, fired up a big coal cooking range, hired several area girls and hung out their shingle. They charged by the month and fed in two shifts, the first one starting at four a.m. The baking was done at night to beat the heat and to make room for the cooks.

Bernice Black (who later married Paul Haider) and Alpha Olson (future wife of Walt Black who owned Walt's Place, Dad's competition in Foxholm) also worked for the Lynesses. They were paid four dollars a week plus their room and board.

The young waitresses...Bernice Black, my sister Connie, and Alpha Olson

Connie, Bernice and another young gal slept upstairs in a bedroom that had only one double-paned window, making it unbearably hot during the summer months. Moth-eaten screens did little to keep out pesky flies and hungry mosquitoes that reveled in tormenting them during the night.

There were three small beds. The bedsprings squeaked and threatened to poke through the lumpy mattresses, but at least each had her own. The heavy oak dresser, which had one long drawer and four small ones, had to be shared. (They drew straws for the long top drawer, and Connie won.) A kerosene lamp with a glass chimney, which was often streaked with black oily soot, sat in the middle of the dresser. Connie laughed as she recalled how they fussed about whose turn it was to wash that chimney. Ecru lace curtains, which skimmed the floor and colorful patchwork quilts brought by the girls added a touch of home. In one corner of the bedroom sat a wooden stand that held a white ceramic washbowl and a water pitcher. A bar on the side held the common towel and washcloth, and above it, hung a postage-stamp mirror. Pegs on a board that was attached to the wall were used in lieu of a closet. (Built-in closets were a rarity in those days.) A chamber pot that fit under the bed rounded out the necessary furnishings.

The girls took turns working the early breakfast shift. It was their job to wash all the utensils left by the bakers, who worked by light of gasoline lamps, before the cooks began breakfast. It was a dreaded job. Water had to be heated in the tin dishpans before they could attack the giant-sized pans with dried-on bits of dough that had been used for mixing the bread dough, and with such a large group, there was a lot of dough mixed. If the bakers were feeling charitable, they would help out before leaving by filling the dishpans and placing them on the coal range to warm.

A big breakfast for the men, who did hard manual labor, was a must. Hash, leftover ground up meat from the night before mixed with potatoes and onions, was a favorite. Pancakes, eggs, and biscuits and gravy were also regular fare. The food was served family-style but the serving bowls were small, the same size as those used for a family meal. Consequently, the girls literally had to run to keep them filled.

Cows were kept on the premises to provide fresh milk, cream and butter. They had no iceboxes; therefore, to keep from spoiling, these dairy products, along with other perishables, were kept in a root cellar that utilized the earth's naturally cool, stable temperatures. The cellar, a cave hollowed into the side of a hill, was framed and beamed across the top with logs to form a roof. The hard-packed dirt floor was covered with a walkway of boards. Shelves were added for more convenient storage. Large blocks of ice wrapped in gunnysacks were brought in to lower the temperature, enabling them to store the food for longer periods of time. Salamanders, who liked the dark dampness of the cellar, were frequent visitors.

Connie, being a farm girl and accustomed to using and cleaning a cream separator, got the job of taking care of the milk house. She was happy with this assignment as it gave her some time away from kitchen chores. "Furthermore," she reminisced, "cute guys were always milling around the area." She remembers the time she cut her finger while cleaning the separator. The male nurse on the construction site, who happened to be nice-looking and younger than most of the men, was called to attend to her injury. Connie, who is now eighty-seven years old, recalled how much extra time he had spent bandaging her finger. As she reminisced, her eyes twinkled, and a slightly naughty smile flickered across her face.

Mrs. Lyness was a very fussy taskmaster. Everything had to be done just so, without exception, and she was right there to make sure that it was. All the workmen washed up before eating. A long bench with many washbowls was set up near the entrance of the cookhouse, and the girls had to see that all the basins were filled with water and ready for use, and every night after supper, they had to wash by hand the towels that the men used. Water was heated on the stove, carried outside and poured into a washtub. Rinse water also had to be hauled, but this was taken from the water well, which was relatively close to the house. They had no washing machine, and all the hand towels had to be scrubbed on a washboard using homemade lye soap. It was not unusual to have to scrub until the girls' knuckles were nearly bleeding before the tightly woven cotton towels passed Mrs. Lyness's inspection. After rinsing, the laundry had to be wrung out and hung on the clothesline that stretched across the backyard. Most nights, it was ten or later before they finished their last chore of the day, and many times they were almost too tired to drag themselves upstairs to bed.

On Saturday afternoons, when the construction work had shut down for the weekend, the girls were on cleaning duty. They had to scrub the wooden floors and dining table until the boards were literally white. They also had to sweep the dirt floor of the root cellar and scrub the walkway boards which were also expected to be white. Even the crocks and jars had to be wiped off and arranged in an orderly fashion.

No matter how strenuous the week had been or how tired they were when it ended, the girls were always ready for a Saturday night barn dance. There was nothing like the sound of fiddles (and youth) to wash away fatigue, except, perhaps the thought of the guys who were waiting to whirl them around the dance floor, and maybe even to ask to take them home.

Dancing was an important and inexpensive form of entertainment during the Great Depression and in our rural community; entire families went to barn dances, many of which were held in Pat Galvin's barn which was just up the valley from the dam. Admission was usually five or ten cents, and the going rate for an orchestra (fiddles, guitar, banjo and maybe a mandolin) was between eight and ten dollars for the entire group.

The dancing was done in the hayloft, which was the upper story of the barn. A large group of dancers would cause the floor to move up and down, and one could actually see and feel it give to the beat of the music and the dancers' feet.

Certain areas were designated as a place for babies to sleep while their young parents danced. Children, including me, learned to dance at a very young age by hopping around among the dancers. Sometimes adults would dance with us, and then, we really felt grown-up and special. When the floor was cleared between dance sets (three songs), little boys would run and slide on the slick dance floor. Sometimes they'd slip and fall, but that was part of the fun.

There was always an intermission around midnight when the orchestra would take a break of about thirty minutes. As a moneymaker, groups such as Homemakers sold lunch, which usually consisted of a sandwich, a piece of cake or cookies and a pickle wrapped in a napkin, plus hot coffee.

These dances were the source of many entertaining stories that were repeated over and over. I can still hear Mom laughing as she told the story of one pleasingly plump mother of eight who lost her drawers on the dance floor. The elastic she had used to sew them broke, and her bloomers fell down around her ankles. She merely kicked them aside and kept on dancing to "Turkey in The Straw" (a lively circle two step) without missing a beat. A couple of young guys, who had been sampling the keg beer, picked them up and stretched them across two of the wall studs. On the back of the flour-sack bloomers was Occident's gold circle emblem with the words "Occident...Russell-Miller Milling Co," and below was written the slogan, "Costs More—Worth It."

One fall morning when Connie and Bernice were working the early breakfast shift, a man who was living in the trailer park came in and asked if his wife could stay there while he was working. She wasn't feeling well, and he didn't want to leave her alone for the day. Mrs. Lyness consented, and the ailing, heavy-set young woman was taken upstairs and given Connie's bed. It was an extra busy morning, and the woman upstairs was forgotten. Just as the noon meal was ready to be served, they were startled to hear the faint cry of a newborn baby. The "sick" woman had prematurely given birth—in the chamber pot! When her water broke, she did the natural thing; she sat on the pot. Moments later, the tiny infant was born. Quickly, the baby, who was as long as Connie's hand-span, was wrapped in a sterile dishtowel and carefully laid on a dinner plate. To transport the baby, he was placed in a shoebox on a bed of cotton batting, and the two of them were rushed to St. Joseph's Hospital in Minot. Mr. Lyness had called to alert them of the incoming emergency, and two nuns met them on the steps where they immediately baptized the baby. Miraculously, the little guy not only survived but also thrived under the loving care of the entire hospital staff. He was still too small to leave the hospital when the work at the dam shut down for the winter, so the parents left him and went back to their home in Minnesota. Several months later, the Johnsons returned for their little boy who had stolen the hearts of all the hospital staff. It was a happy but sad time when they said goodbye to their "miracle baby."

Twelve years later, the tall, handsome boy and his parents returned to Minot for a happy reunion with the hospital personnel who, with a wealth of love and prayers, had made this occasion possible.

I recently called and spoke with Bernice, Connie's co-worker who now lives in California. When I told her why I had called, her first reaction was, "My heavens, that was over seventy years ago." As we visited, long-forgotten memories slowly began to resurface. Starting as a mere trickle, they soon began to tumble forth, and as they did, I could feel that, just for a moment, she was once again young and invulnerable. At the end of our reminiscence, Bernice agreed with my sister when she said, "It was a memorable summer; we worked hard, but we had fun, too."

The drought dragged on, and families were continually looking for ways to make extra money.

Mom sold eggs and cream to bring in a few extra nickels for staples such as sugar, flour and coffee. She also planted large gardens and sewed clothes for the family, but still it was a constant struggle to make ends meet.

In the fall of the year, turkey breeders gathered up their fattened poultry and took them to market. They were sold to the Mandan Creamery in Minot where they were processed and shipped out to distribution centers. Dad and Connie had jobs at the creamery "picking turkeys," as it was called.

During this time, Dad stayed in town with Connie and her new husband, Ambrose. The twenty miles that he would have had to drive twice a day was not economically feasible. Every morning, Dad and

Connie would walk to the creamery where they took their respective places on the assembly line.

Hanging by their feet, the turkeys moved along a conveyor belt. Dad, wearing a long white coat jacket and rubber boots that were furnished by the creamery, stood beneath the unsuspecting turkeys and, as they came down the line, swiftly and efficiently stuck each one in the throat with a curved knife, sliced through the brain and cut back down, slitting its throat.

With blood running, they were moved along to a room where they were dipped in scalding water to loosen their feathers. The offensive stench of the hot, wet birds traveled straight through the cloth curtains, permeating the entire area. The scalding crew then sent the turkeys down to Connie and her co-workers who manually pulled out the feathers.

The workers were paid so much per turkey; therefore, speed was of the essence. (Each turkey was inspected so one had to be skilled as well as quick.) The white turkey's feathers were stubborn and harder to pull than of the dark, which slowed down the plucking process. This meant less money. Consequently, Connie remembers that everyone in the assembly line hoped their turkeys would be dark.

It wasn't a pleasant job, as many of them weren't, but times were hard, and people grasped for whatever jobs they could get to survive. Farming conditions remained critical, and with no relief in sight, Dad searched for a better way to keep his family going. In 1939, when he heard that John Gruber was selling his tavern in Foxholm, it was the chance he needed. He took a deep breath and with Mom at his side, made John an offer. With a handshake, the deal was made and Miller's Bar was born.]

Souris (Mouse) River downstream from Lake Darling

Miller's Bar

Miller's Bar

I got the call early in the morning; the bar was gone. For forty-six years, it had been an integral part of our lives, and in a matter of minutes, it was reduced to memories. On March 8, 1985, just as dawn was breaking, an electrical fire not only destroyed Miller's Bar, but completely erased all evidence that a once proud, thriving town had ever existed. Dad's bar was more than just a place to buy a beer. It was a social network that offered the comfort of familiarity in an atmosphere of good cheer, boisterous welcomes and bantering conversation. I was six years old when Dad gave up farming, made a verbal deal with John Gruber and became a tavern owner. Little did we know that Miller's Bar would become a landmark throughout the country.

Miller's Bar going up in flames

Millers Bar, a landmark throughout the country, is reduced to rubble. The dance hall remained standing.

Miller's Bar was located in downtown Foxholm. Our town consisted of one street, the only paved street in town—Highway 52, which meanders through the Des Lacs River Valley up through Kenmare and into Canada. The bar was a framed, flat-roofed, two-story building that stretched back to the icehouse, which was replaced with a dance hall when it was no longer needed. The high ceiling was covered with embossed tin panels, which spoke of the gentle elegance of that era. (Several years later, the ceiling was lowered, and the beautiful panels were forever hidden.) There was no electricity when Dad took over; hanging brass gas lamps provided light. Eventually, Dad installed a Delco thirty-two-volt DC power plant, which was used until REA reached the area.

Dad's bar (L. to R.)John Gruber, my brother Ralph, Dad, Mike Schmitz (his son Butchie in foreground), and "Boss" Stach (notice the Evan Cole Dance poster on wall)

Miller's Bar (L.to R.) Ralph, Dad, Paul Haider and my sister-in-law Edith

On the front door in Dad's handwriting was a sign that read: "No Minors or Indians Allowed." (It was not until 1955 that Indians were allowed in an establishment that sold alcohol.)

There were seven rooms above the bar, three on either side of the hall and one large one in front facing the main street. Being a soft touch for anyone in need, Dad was known to let men who needed a place to sleep stay in the upstairs rooms. Big Charlie, a huge, burly, redheaded, hard-drinking Polack, was one of the part time roomers. Charlie was known only as "Big Charlie." If he was ever asked what his full name was, he'd laugh and answer, "Charlie Wants-More-Whiskey."

During the crop-growing season, Big Charlie was a field hand for area farmers, Nick and Annie Clouse. He boarded at the farm, as itinerant hands often did, until the fall harvest was completed. During the winter months, he worked in the coalmines near Foxholm, and having nowhere else to stay, bunked above the bar. A colorful character, Big Charlie played the concertina, which is a similar to an accordion but smaller and with buttons instead of a keyboard. It was a beautiful instrument—a cherry red with intricate silver trim and bigger than most of its type. Not only did the rough, crusty old coal miner and field hand own such an impressive instrument, he played it very well. Polkas were his favorite, and his huge sausage-like fingers fairly flew over the buttons, making "The Beer Barrel Polka" a work of art. As he played, Dad's cheering patrons would buy him drinks, and the more whiskey he drank the more of a showman he became, sometimes swinging the concertina over his head or behind his back. He loved to imitate Whoopie John Wilfart, the famous polka king from New Ulm, Minnesota. While playing, Big Charlie would laughingly repeat the popular saying that was a natural play on Wilfart's name, "Whoopie John will fart, and his band will play."

Another couple, Joe and Cleo, rented rooms above the bar. All went well until Joe's adult stepson Ed, who turned out to be a little crazy, came to live with them. When people began to complain about Ed's strange behavior, Dad went up to have a talk with him. Just as Dad opened the door, a razor-sharp hunting knife came whizzing past his head; Ed was using the door as a target to practice his knife-throwing skills. The entire family was out immediately, and that was the last time Dad ever rented out the rooms.

Spanning one side of the bar room was a long, dark wood bar with a mirrored back bar flanked with shelves which held the bottles used for pouring drinks. There were no calls for fancy drinks such as margaritas, white Russians, or pink ladies, but "7-7's" (Seagram's and 7-Up) was a good seller, along with Tom Collins and whiskey sours. Shots of whiskey with a water chaser were common, and in the winter, there were a few calls for hot brandies and hot peppermint schnapps. These drinks were enjoyed, but the Germans in the community retained their love for beer. Along with bottles, Dad had draft beer on tap for many years. A few years later, the breweries came out with seven-ounce bottles called "ponies." Serious beer drinkers thought they were silly, but some really liked them. They were just the right size to quench one's thirst or for someone to imbibe who wasn't a real beer drinker. Dad drank them to quench his thirst. He'd reach into his walk-in cooler, grab a pony, tip his head back and down it in one swig.

Shooting the breeze in Dad's bar on a Saturday afternoon
Dick Musch (local farmer), M.O. Lee and Sy Engen (owners of
Foxholm's almost oil well), Scooter Taylor (driller on the oil rig) and
wife, and my brother Alvin. Behind bar, Dad and Bobby Hasledalen
from Carpio, self-appointed bartender.

Spaces on the back bar were saved for the clean glasses which rested mouth down on white towels. Between the glasses and the columns of displayed cigarettes, which were smoked without one thought of lung cancer or emphysema, was the nickel-plated, cast-iron National cash register. The till was small, ornate and beautiful. When a register key was pressed down, the amount of purchase popped up in the small window in the top of the register, a bell rang, and the cash drawer was thrown open.

Flashy beer signs, compliments of the beer companies, hung in prominent places, and a large attractive Budweiser wagon pulled by Clydesdales sat in a prominent place on top of the back bar. Fish plaques galore and fishing signs with proverbs such as Dad's favorite, "God does not deduct from man's allotted time that which he spends fishing," decorated the back bar.

A deer head with imposing antlers hung on the wall at the end of the bar. When Francis returned from the Marines, he took off his hat and hung it on one of the antlers where it remained throughout the years. One day, a couple of unsuccessful deer hunters stopped in for a beer on their way home from their hunt. Spotting the deer head, they impulsively wired their unused deer tags to the antlers and laughingly said, "We got our deer." It was the start of many more who got theirs the very same way, with some tagging the same deer two or three times. When the bar burned down, more people mentioned the loss of the deer head with all its tags than any other single item.

In the corner next to one of the large front windows stood the jukebox, which everyone incorrectly called the "jute box." With multicolored lights, bubble tubes and chrome, it was a welcome addition to the bar. For only a nickel, one could "Rock Around the Clock," or take a "Sentimental Journey" with Les Brown. The jukebox was owned by Fred Kaiser in Berthold, and Dad's was the only one that had to be converted from thirty-two-volt DC to 110 AC. David La Fountain, who worked for Kaiser and is now my niece Renee's brother-in-law, came around periodically and changed the seventy-eight rpm records, counted the money and gave Dad twenty-five percent of the take. I recently reminisced with David, and he recalled that Western music was the most popular, with Hank Williams's "Half As Much" being one of the favorites. He laughed remembering that he wasn't even old enough to be in the bar when he was working in them. The laws were on the books but weren't strictly enforced. In fact, in the first years that Dad owned the bar, he used to open the back door of the bar on Sundays after mass for the church-going farmers who enjoyed having a couple of beers with their neighbors to unwind after a hard, stressful week in the fields. John Cashman, the hotel owner who obviously disapproved of not keeping holy the Sabbath Day, turned Dad in several times. Each time, the sheriff would call and tell Dad that he was on the way, and by the time he got there, the bar would be innocently quiet and empty with the doors securely locked.

Before getting electricity, Dad had to rely on ice to keep his beer cool. Every winter, when the ice on the river became twelve to fifteen inches thick, Dad and some helpers cleared off the snow and scored the ice with a special tool. Once the ice was scored, they used a one-handed crosscut ice saw to cut the ice into cakes approximately three feet by eighteen inches. Using ice tongs, they loaded the ice and transported it to the icehouse where it was packed between layers of straw, which served as insulation. The ice, also used in the icebox at home, stayed frozen all summer.

The icehouse sometimes served another purpose. Old Charlie Kirklie, another hard-drinking drifter who roamed around the countryside in a buggy pulled by a big white stallion, was known to have body lice. None of the housewives would allow him to stay overnight in their homes, so he'd ride into Foxholm. Dad knew better than to bring lousy Charlie home to sleep, as he did with so many others, so he let him sleep in the icehouse, which really was pretty cozy compared to his open-air buggy.

During the days of the icehouse, the outhouse was located about a hundred feet from the bar's back door, which sometimes made it a challenging trip for a drinker in his cups. I remember one particular incident in which a tipsy straggler who had wandered in either didn't attempt the trek out back or waited too long thinking about it. After he left the bar, Mom came upon Dad fumigating the bar by swishing around a pail of burning rags.

Teenager Myrna wearing saddle shoes and rolled-up jeans. (old ice house and outhouse in background)

The bar had four wooden booths along the wall opposite the bar, which were eventually upgraded to four reddish-orange vinyl booths. Couples who were not regular customers usually sat in a booth, unlike the locals who bellied up to the bar to swap tales with my Dad or whoever happened to be sitting on the next stool. Occasionally, couples having a clandestine affair would come out from Minot. They were always booth customers, and although they came to the small town where they could be away from "eyes," they were as conspicuous as salesmen in white suits. Invariably someone would recognize one of them, and being the friendly lot that he was, would saunter over to say hello. So much for that couple's business!

Playing cards was a good way to pass the time, and since Foxholm was short on pastimes, the card table was often the hot spot of the bar. Blitz, a three-card draw and discard game, was popular, but whist was the all-time favorite. Many times, Mom and Dad would sit in and play while one of the regular customers would fill in behind the bar. It worked out perfectly.

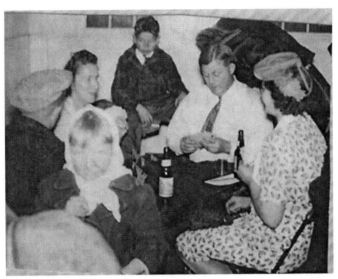

Mom and Dad playing whist with Charlie and Dorothy Limke from Carpio. (children, Larry and Ardella Limke)

Foxholm whist players built up over the years quite a reputation for themselves. Whist tournaments in the bar were popular during the winter months, and Foxholm was a mighty force. Of the towns who participated, Berthold and Tagus were two of their strongest opponents. Besides forfeiting their bragging rights, the losing team members had to buy the winning team's lunch, which the hosting bar served for a dollar per player at the conclusion of the tournament. It was no mystery why every town liked to play in Foxholm. Mom had the reputation of serving the best food and the most. One of the players was once overheard saying, "Her cooking could make the lame walk." Many times, she made a big meaty casserole, homemade buns and cake, and other times, it might have been Sloppy Joes, potato salad, pickles and brownies with thick fudge frosting. However, whatever it was, they always went back for seconds.

The old whist players are still laughing about the time Foxholm, during an undefeated hot streak, played Tagus, a town just itching for revenge. After much good-natured bantering, Foxholm lost by a couple of points. Tagus was elated, and Foxholm gamely forked over the bragging rights and their two bucks. The next day, as a couple of guys were "replaying the games," one of them picked up the score sheets that were still lying on the bar and mentally re-added the scores. Something wasn't right. They added them a second time and discovered that Norbert Greman had added incorrectly. Technically, Foxholm remained undefeated. Norbert never did live that one down.

Two locals, Don Streitz and George Gorde, were state champions one year in a tournament sponsored by the Knights of Columbus. They returned home understandably puffed up and full of themselves. After listening for a while, George's brother Elmer and my husband Ray challenged the champions. They may have been state champions in Harvey, but back in Foxholm, they met their match and went down in defeat, three games in a row. You can imagine the razzing they took.

Don Streitz and George Gorde, State Knights of Columbus whist champs

Elmer Gorde and Ray Messer, successful challengers

When I was fourteen, Mom opened a café in the two rear rooms of the bar. Dad did some remodeling, installed a bottle gas stove and refrigerator, a counter, booths and tables, and Miller's Café was in business. Mom was a great cook, and much of her business was from truck drivers who gauged their trips so that they could stop in for meals, especially breakfasts. (Roy, who trucked for the Occident

Flour Company, was a regular for years.) Where else could you get a thick slab of ham that hung over the plate, two eggs, toast and all the coffee you could drink for seventy-five cents? Fat hamburgers on butter-toasted buns sold for twenty-five cents, thick malts with three scoops of ice cream were twenty-five cents, pork chop dinners (two large chops) cost seventy-five cents, hamburger steak dinners were sixty-five cents, T-bone steak dinners were $1.25, pie and ice cream cost fifteen cents, coffee was five cents, and coffee and two donuts cost ten cents. There was a fan above the stove, and whenever Mom made donuts, elevator manager Darrell Rhone would be there in a matter of minutes. When he smelled fresh donuts, it was time for a coffee break, no matter what time of the day it was. He never missed.

During summers, we often fed road crews and railroad bridge gangs. One customer remains in my memory. Old Al was gray haired, thin and stooped but still worked on the bridge gang. Every evening we'd see him come walking up from the bunk car, which stood on the sidetrack. Mom nicknamed him "Hamiltonian" because his flatfoot walk reminded her of the gait of a Hamiltonian Trotter. He never failed to take time to wash up and change into clean bib overalls before coming for supper. His order was the same every night, "Pork chops with plenty of spuds." Mom made sure that his order was filled.

Mom buttering a hamburger bun in the Miller's Café kitchen

One of the easiest and fastest, but certainly not the most popular, sandwiches we made was a raw hamburger mixed with chopped onions and seasoned with plenty of salt and pepper. It was a favorite of Lynn Bryans from Carpio, a frequent customer in both the bar and café.

Lynn would open the door and bellow, "Yabba, dabba doo!" followed by that loud infectious laugh of his. A person couldn't help but laugh with him. His brother Dewey, somewhat quieter but just as crazy, was often with him. I remember the time he came into the café with his arms folded around a large bump under his shirt. Before our very eyes, he opened his shirt and out slithered a large garter snake. The cook and the waitress both left town.

Dewey wasn't the only one who pulled things like that. My mother, unlike Dad and I, loved to play practical jokes. Lois Rademacher stayed with us when she taught school in Foxholm and often helped out in the café. One day as they were working in the kitchen, Mom checked her mousetrap and found that she had caught a nice fat one. As she was carrying it outside, she noticed some dry bread in the garbage pail. Knowing that Lois was skittish when it came to mice, Mom picked up the bread and carefully positioned the dead mouse between the two pieces—the head with its beady eyes sticking out one side and the tail out the other. When Lois turned around, Mom said so innocently, "Here, Lois, I made you a nice sandwich." Lois took one look, let out a scream and was out of there like a shot. Mom giggled about that forever.

Lois Burner (Rademacher) and Edith clowning around in the café kitchen

Edith behind café counter gabbing with customers

Café customers Lawrence and Barbara Esser
Waitress teenage Myrna in background

Our telephone, which was in the café, was the old crank wall phone, sometimes referred to as the "crank and holler" phone. To make a call, one turned the crank and the operator, located in the central office, would answer, "Number please." Our telephone exchange was in Carpio, and Mrs. Bowman was our operator. Bowman's living quarters were in back of the central office, which enabled Mrs. Bowman to be on call twenty-four hours a day, although the switchboard was closed, except for emergencies, from ten at night until eight in the morning.

We were on a party line, which meant that several families were on the same line, with each one having a different ring. Our number was 1603, and our ring was a long and three shorts; my friend Gwen's was 1804, and her ring was a short and a long. Telephone conversations were anything but private as one could listen in on conversations just by lifting up the receiver. This was called "rubbering" and considered very poor manners, but it didn't stop the busybodies. My friend's father was a die-hard "rubbernecker" who even got out of bed to listen if he heard someone's ring. One time when I was staying overnight, the phone rang in the middle of the night and her father, in his haste to "rubber," ran into a piece of furniture and badly bruised his leg. What I couldn't believe was that he wasn't even embarrassed the next morning when he showed us his bruise.

As the telephone operator, Mrs. Bowman was the center for emergency contact. If ever there was a need for an ambulance or the fire department, we would ring her and she would quickly and efficiently dispatch the emergency crew. I timed the Carpio Volunteer Fire Department one time, and it took twelve minutes from the time I put in the call until they were pulling into town, some ten miles away.

Mrs. Bowman's husband Eddie was the repairman for the phone lines. Eddie liked his vodka (without ice) and would stop in every now and then while working for an afternoon pick-me-up. Eddie's black dog Joe always came with him and before ordering his drink, Eddie would go through the bar and into the café where he bought an ice cream cone for Joe. Returning to the bar, Eddie would have his drink, and Joe would lie on the floor next to him and lick his ice cream. When they were at the door ready to leave, Eddie would pause and say to Joe, "Didn't you forget something?" Joe would lower his head as if ashamed and immediately go back and pick up the empty cone. The routine was always the same.

There were times when Mom took care of both places, such as the times Dad coaxed her into watching the bar while he went fishing or to a Minot Mallard's baseball game. Dad loved baseball and had played softball when he was young. In his later years, he umpired local games. He always kept an extra ball in his front pants pocket, and I can still see him pulling it out, and throwing it in. He ripped many a pocket doing this, which didn't set too well with my mother who got the job of mending them.

The Minot Air Base was just over the hill from Foxholm, and many of the airmen found their way to Miller's Bar. Some stopped in for refreshment when they went fishing at Lake Darling, and some came because they were lonesome and our bar felt like home. Mom was "Ma Miller" to them all, and when they were transferred to different bases, many kept in contact with her through cards and letters. When Boeing transferred us to Fort Worth, Texas, our checking account was still in North Dakota. While grocery shopping, we asked if they would take an out-of-state check. When the manager heard it was from North Dakota, she asked where in North Dakota. "A little town right outside of Minot," we told her. The manager was curiously persistent. "What little town?" When we answered Foxholm, her face lit up and she said, "Do you know Ma Miller?" She and her husband had been stationed at the base and had been in Mom's bar many times. It's a small world.

Downtown Foxholm...still hanging on, but barely.

When Dad died in 1962, Mom closed the café and for the next twenty-three years, until she was eighty-seven years old, she ran the bar. Although she was by herself, except for the last couple years when our son Jack lived with her and helped with the business, she was never really alone. She did hire help on special occasions, but many times, customers pitched in and helped. It was not unusual for someone to get up and wait tables or even mix drinks when she got extra busy. Sometimes customers would tend bar just to give her a break. Anna Mae (Ahmann) Plemel, daughter of Dad's old friend Fred, was good at that. Every now and then, she and her husband Tom would drive out from Minot, and Anna Mae, good-hearted to the bone, would see to it that Mom sat on the other side of the bar. Often Mom and Tom would play whist while she poured drinks, opened beers and shot the breeze with the customers, all of which came naturally to her.

Watching out for one another comes with the territory in a small town. If the bar wasn't open by a reasonable time, or if it was closed during the day without a sign on the door, they went to Mom's house to check on her. Occasionally, she would close up and take to bus to Minot to do her business. I remember one time she left and forgot to lock the front door. A man from Carpio stopped in and found the bar wide open and no Ma Miller. He looked everywhere including her house, and after talking it over with another customer who knew Mom well, reasoned that she had gone off to Minot without locking the door. Since it took a key, he couldn't just lock the door and go, so he stayed all-day and tended bar until Mom returned on the four o'clock bus. True to form, she laughed at her goof and jokingly commented that she'd have to do it more often as business was especially good that day.

Most of Mom's customers were regulars, but occasionally someone passing through would stop for a few drinks. My nephew Sam, who had a unique relationship with his grandmother, as did all her big grandsons, tells the story about him and a buddy, who were hot and sweaty after working all day in the blistering summer's heat, stopping in at Grandma's bar on their way home for a cold beer. She was sitting on a stool behind the bar talking on the phone with the receiver in one hand and swatting flies with the other. Two older guys were sipping beer at the other end of the bar. Sam, who's built like a prizefighter with a voice to match, said, "Got any cold beer in this joint?" Mom gestured with the swatter that she'd be right there and continued talking. Pounding on the bar, Sam boomed, "Goddammit, how about a cold beer?" Up jumped the old men, "Who the hell do you think you're talking to?" Mom quickly explained that he was her goofy grandson who, by this time, was laughing his head off. When satisfied that all was okay, they went back to their beers.

Sam Haider

The bar was burglarized several times over the years but only robbed once. It was early evening, and three people were in the bar with Mom— Del Gruber and Pat and Ella Thompson from Burlington. Suddenly, in came a young man brandishing a knife. He quickly grabbed Pat, held the knife at his throat and demanded that Mom hand over the money. Without hesitating, Mom gave him everything in the till, including the checks. After stuffing the money in a bag, he snatched several bottles of liquor. As he was leaving, he turned and ordered Mom to give him cigarettes from the display on the back bar. Out of habit, she asked, "What kind would you like?" and out of habit, he told her, "Camels." With cigarettes in hand, the robber left as quickly as he came. The checks were found along the roadside, and the robber was eventually apprehended, but the money was gone forever

My brother Ralph and Mom behind her bar

The robbery, a rare occurrence in our rural area, made front-page news in the Minot Daily, and Mom's reaction to the robber's request for cigarettes was a source of laughter for a long time. Pat's involvement was also rehashed many times, and people who knew him noted that he had been smart enough not to react as he normally would have.

Pat was a small, wiry man—slight in stature and as feisty as the day is long. He worked hard and played hard, and when he played, he drank—a lot. When he drank a lot, he became akin to a banty rooster. If someone looked at him crossways, he was ready to fight, and the size of his opponent was never a deterrent, with one exception—when the robber's knife was at his throat.

Good-hearted and generous to a fault, Pat had been a good friend of Dad's. He and Ella owned the Idle Hour Lounge in Burlington, and when Dad died, he ordered a truckload of beer and had it delivered to Mom's bar. When Mom tried to thank him, knowing he'd never let her pay him, he brushed it aside saying that it was the very least he could do for a friend. Pat Thompson was a good man.

Over the span of forty-six years in business, thousands of people visited the bar. Many were interesting, some were intriguing, a few were unbelievable, most were trustworthy and some were simply unforgettable.

There was another incident that happened only once in all the years that Mom ran the bar, and many of those years she was a widow. When she was about eighty, she received her one and only proposition. The man was a lifelong acquaintance of hers and had a wife in a nursing home. He was the only one in the bar, and since he wasn't drinking, she decided to close up early. Instead of leaving, he turned to her and asked if she wanted to come home with him. Thinking he was inviting her to play cards with a group of friends, who sometimes got together, she declined, saying that she thought she'd go on home. "Oh, come on," he said, "I'll give you ten dollars." It was then that the light went on, and in no uncertain terms Mom said, "You old fool, go on home and behave yourself." He heeded her words, and there were no more invitations.

Mugs Durbin, one of Dad's out-of-town customers, loved the song "Buttons and Bows", and every time he came in, he'd put money in the nickelodeon, as we called it, and play it over and over. With each beer, he'd become a little happier, and the happier he became, the more he'd sing. One night he treated himself to a good drunk. Concerned for his safety, Dad wouldn't let him drive home, so as he sometimes did with others in the same shape, he brought him home and put him to bed. I heard them coming up the stairs, Mugs stumbling and singing and Dad trying to help and shush him. I don't know if he didn't sleep or if he was singing in his sleep, but into the wee hours of the morning, I heard over and over and over:

"East is east and west is west
And the wrong road I have chose.
Let's go where I'll keep on wearing'
Those frills and flowers and buttons and bows,
Rings and things and buttons and boooooooooooows....
And buttons and boooooooooooows."

Since that memorable night of song, Mugs Durbin and "Buttons and Bows," I've never thought of one without thinking of the other.

One customer that Dad dreaded coming into the bar was his oldest brother's live-in housekeeper. Uncle Ed was a bachelor farmer who lived and farmed near Glenburn. My grandmother lived with him in her later years, and when she passed away, he hired Ella, a good-hearted woman who had been battered around by life, to keep house for him. She also did farm chores and sometimes even worked with Uncle Ed in the field. Hard work was no stranger to her, and neither was beer. When Uncle Ed kept her down on the farm, things went fine, but whenever beer was available, she made up for lost time. They seldom came to Dad's bar, but when they did, it was too often as far as Dad was concerned. When sober, Ella was rather quiet, even subservient, but when she was drunk, she became loud and lusty.

All dressed up in bib overalls and red high heels with anklets, Ella was a comical sight. Her tight corkscrew curls, newly released from thin metal curlers, bounced around a weathered face that was cross-hatched with a million tiny wrinkles from years of sun and smoking. A circle of orange stood out on each thin cheek, and her pursed mouth, which when open, revealed teeth that went off at odd angles, was slashed with bright red lipstick. Often, a smoldering cigarette dangled from her mouth, the curling smoke causing her to squinch up her eyes. After each beer, Ella became a little bawdier. If the jukebox was playing, she'd grab anyone with two legs, give him a lusty pat and dance wildly around the bar. If there was no one to grab, she'd dance by herself, kicking her red heels high in the air. If Dad sat down to visit with Uncle Ed, she'd plop herself down on his lap, throw her skinny arms around his neck, screw up her wrinkled lips, and give him a big boozy kiss on the cheek. Disgusted, Dad would push her away and take refuge behind the bar.

Ella stayed and took care of my uncle until he passed away, and then, she disappeared, without a word to anyone, and was never seen again.

Doctor Lloyd Kjos was our dentist. He and his wife Mae were also Dad's customers. Every now and then, during a drive in the country, they'd stop in Foxholm to enjoy a few drinks with Mom and Dad. More often than not, a few drinks turned into quite a few.

Doc was a small, impeccably dressed man who was always a gentleman, no matter how long they stayed. Mae, flamboyant and gregarious, was nearly a head taller than her husband and built like a canary—a plump upper body and long skinny legs. She loved to wear fancy high-heeled shoes, which made her spindly legs look even thinner. Mae was as outspoken and vocal as Doc was soft-spoken and quiet, and the more she partied, the more evident it was that she was the dominant figure in the family.

Mae took to my mother. Sometimes she, always dressed fit to kill, and a lady friend would drive out during the day to visit over a drink or two. Many times they'd end up visiting the entire afternoon, but somehow, they always made it back to Minot safely. A few times, we visited them at their home. It was during one of these visits that Mae gave me my first pair of Doc's expensive, still-good trousers, which I wore for slacks. They were a perfect fit, and I wore them until I started my growth spurt at about age thirteen.

It was the days that Doc Kjos came in early in the morning that I remember the best. He obviously had been partying somewhere all night and had ended up in Foxholm. The first thing he'd do was call his office and very professionally ask Jo, his long-time nurse/receptionist, to please call and cancel his appointments for the day as he was out of town and had car trouble, or some similar fabrication. Then he'd call Mae with the same story; one could almost see the sparks flying from the receiver. After a minute or two, he'd softly say, "I'll see you soon, honey," and then he'd hang up and order a whiskey.

Dr. Kjos was my dentist for many years, during which time dentists did nothing but fill teeth or pull teeth and fit patients with dentures. I don't remember anyone ever having his or her teeth cleaned.

I was no stranger in Doc Kjos's office, and I remember how glad I was when he got his first new high-speed drill. The suction device, which he used while drilling, never did improve, and the misery it caused was almost worse than the drilling. He'd hook that metal tube over my bottom lip and leave it in the same position until he finished. The longer he drilled, the more it dug into my mouth. It never entered my mind to gesture that it was killing me. I guess I thought it was just another dental misery that had to be endured. After completing his work, he'd squirt a shot of water into my mouth, which I'd spit, after swishing around, into the community bowl, supposedly cleansed by the water running down the sides. I remember the sight well, especially after having a tooth pulled.

Doc and Mae's visits to Dad's bar gradually diminished, I went away to teach and on to new dentists, and Doctor Kjos retired. Our relationship was a thing of the past. However, every now and then when I'm in a dentist chair, surrounded by all the new gadgets, I think about that antiquated suction tube and the miserable old drill, and then I remember Doc Kjos and Mae, their visits to Foxholm and the trousers that were a perfect fit.

George and Sena Sartwell, who once worked in the coalmines, moved their large family to Foxholm where George had gotten a job as a section hand for the Soo Line Railroad. They rented a small house that was just across the railroad tracks from our bar and café. When George worked, he worked hard, and when he played, he played hard, and he liked his liquor. Sena was a good, hard-working woman whose life had clearly not been easy. Her thin, sharp face was etched with premature lines, and her hands spoke of hard, manual labor. Still, she was always pleasant. To help make ends meet, she worked for my mother on dance nights. While she worked, George usually partied in the bar as was the case on this particular summer night. Sena was waiting on tables when George, plastered to the eyeballs, wobbled into the cafe. Mortified, Sena shoved him out the back door, led him home, and put him to bed. For good measure, she hid his shoes before returning to work. A short time later, Mom and Sena heard a strange "Click...thump, click...thump" coming from the back entry landing which was covered with a slab of slate from an old pool table. The screen door opened and in staggered George, grinning like a jackass eating thistles, with a high heel shoe on one foot and nothing on the other. When he couldn't find his own shoes, he had put on Sena's, and as he crossed the tracks, he lost one between the railroad ties.

Old Steve was eighty-five years old but young at heart. He wasn't a homespun Foxholmite, and I don't remember what brought him to town in his later years, but he was an interesting addition. He lived in a small one-room house across the street from Dad's bar, which was convenient for him, as he didn't drive anymore. He liked to visit and could often be found sitting at the bar, wearing his brown felt hat and a tie, drinking a beer and visiting with whomever he found along the bar stools.

Old Steve loved to dance, and whenever we had music in the bar, he was sure to be there. He always dressed up in his Sunday best—suit, white shirt and tie—with his thin white hair combed carefully across his pink head. His brown suit coat, which had once fit perfectly, now hung on his shoulders, and his pants, held up by suspenders, rode high on his belly, which pushed at the buttons of his shirt. His tie was always carefully knotted, but many times the collar points curled up stubbornly.

Waltzes were his favorites, and apparently, I was his favorite waltzing partner. I never had the heart to refuse him when he asked, even though he smelled like a musky old buffalo. "You're sure a good waltzer," he'd say as he circled me around the floor. He was still a surprisingly good dancer, light on his feet, in spite of his stiff joints. I could only hold my breath so long, and then I'd make the excuse that I had to get back to serving drinks.

Occasionally, Old Steve would treat himself to an overnight bus trip into Minot. He never talked about his trips, but it was a known fact that he spent his time in the Torch Light, a strip joint on First Street, watching the show from a ringside seat. Old Steve was, indeed, young at heart.

Many of our customers were from Carpio. Dick, a bachelor farmer who farmed about four miles from town, was one on them. Two things stand out when I think about Dick; he was a two-fisted drinker, and he never bathed. Never! He came in regularly and usually sat on the first bar stool. He was a personable guy, friendly in a quiet way. All visible skin (and no doubt, all that was not visible) was the color of a polished stove pipe—shiny black—and his eyes reminded one of a raccoon. His hair and beard, which were encrusted with field dirt, looked like they had been trimmed with sheep shears. His clothes, including his soft-billed farmer's hat, were monochromatic, dirty. Large teeth, partially hidden by unkempt facial hair, evidenced years of smoking and neglect.

At a later point in life, Dick lost his driver's license and could no longer drive his truck into town for his daily beer. So, his transportation became his small four-cylinder International H tractor. Driving to town in the daylight went quite well, but one night he was caught driving home by the Highway Patrol and told that he could no longer drive it at night because, with no tail lights, he was a hazard on the road. Dick, not to be deterred, rigged up the required lights and continued his journeys. The tractor—still operable, taillights and all—is now owned by Richard Sauer, a farmer who lives near Lake Darling.

Richard Sauer

Thinking of Dick brings to mind the time he fell sick and had to be hospitalized. The day he was released, he and whoever picked him up stopped at the bar for a quick one on the way home. Even though he sat on "his stool," no one recognized him until he spoke. The nurses had soaked him in the tub, scrubbed off all the dirt, shaved him and burned his clothes; he was a different man.

Marvin Walks was a good guy, a good friend of the family and a good customer in the bar. He moved to Foxholm with his son Gary from Wimbleton, North Dakota and quickly became assimilated into the community. Marvin always wore a ball cap with logos—Magic City Oil, Gould Pumps, John Deere, etc. He had one for every occasion, including the one he took to his grave. Marvin helped out in the bar when Dad was sick and then continued to work occasionally for Mom, but most of the time, he'd straddle a bar stool, drink beer and shoot the breeze. Many times he'd suddenly drop off to sleep for a few seconds. (He was later diagnosed with narcolepsy.) On nights we had live music Marvin either worked behind the bar or had a very good time on the other side. He loved to dance, and whether it was a polka, waltz or two-step, he did the same steps and only changed the speed. I remember one night when he had a little too much fun. He got plastered and was falling all over the place. It bothered me to see him making a fool out of himself, and finally I'd had enough. "Come on, Marvin, you're going home," and out the door we went. I helped him across the highway, which was no easy feat, and into the little green house he rented from Dad. I led him to the bed, gave him a nudge and he flopped down like a dead fish. That was the end of his partying for that night.

Another time when he got all boozed up, Alvin and Verlene gave him a ride home. He was then living in our family's picturesque cottage, affectionately called Riverside Mansion, which was nestled in a wooded bend of the Des Lacs River. When he got out of the car, instead of going directly into the house, he braced himself against the car and continued his boozy visiting. After several minutes, he leaned into the open window and said, "Say you folks aren't by chance going uptown, are you? I'd sure like a ride."

Marvin Walks

Ewald Braun was born and raised on a farm near Foxholm. He was raised in a staunch Catholic family and had three sisters who became nuns. One of the sisters, Veronica, stayed in town with us during her freshman year of high school. Ewald bought a farm in a scenic, wooded coulee on the outskirts of Foxholm, married Mary and had one daughter.

Ewald was what you might call stodgy—short, heavily built, slow in movement and stubbornly old-fashioned. He was a nice guy who liked to talk. He spoke slowly and very low so that one had to really listen to understand him, and he always spoke with a wide grin on his face.

He led a simple life, and the world around Foxholm was the only one he really knew. Driving to Minot and around the countryside and stopping to visit was his entertainment. He was a regular at the bar and the kind who took his beer slowly with plenty of talk. One evening, he was visiting down at Gordie's, the other bar in town, and stayed longer and drank more beer than usual, quite a bit more than usual. When he went out and crawled into his car to go home, he couldn't find the steering wheel. Crying, he stumbled back into the bar, "Someone stole my steering wheel!" In his befuddled state, he had gotten into the back seat instead of the front.

Three of Dad's most faithful customers were the Einerson brothers who lived together on a farm near Carpio. They were honest, hard-working bachelor farmers who spoke with unmistakable Norwegian accents. Bennie, tall and lean, had a big shovel of a jaw, a ready grin and a funny, hiccuppy laugh. He had huge, knotty hands, which evidenced years of hard manual labor, and his fingers were heavily stained from nicotine. Sanford, whose stature matched that of his brother's, was crippled and walked with a decided limp. He had two outstanding features, his incredibly long thick eyelashes and his two large, gold, rabbit-like front teeth. He was also a smoker and was seldom seen without a cigarette in his mouth. I remember the time I met them on Main Street in Minot. I can still see them as we talked—Sanford standing so lopsided and smiling so big with his gold teeth protruding and Benny with a cigarette in his wide mouth, grinning from ear to ear. Later, they told Mom how surprised and pleased they were that a young girl would take the time to stop and talk to a couple of old farmers on a busy city street. I didn't think a thing about it at the time, but, as a result, I learned a valuable lesson.

Andy was a big man with a barrel chest and a stomach to match. While all the brothers enjoyed a beer, Andy was the one who could really tie one on. I'll never forget the time he was celebrating and got hungry. This was before Mom opened the café, so he went next door to Bock's Grocery. I just happened to be there, talking to Bonnie when he came staggering in. A large box of cabbage sat in front of the old wooden counter. Andy picked up a huge head and, holding it with both hands, started to chomp away, his round fat face literally hidden by the cabbage. There was a sharp crunch as he bit off a big chunk. With cheeks bulging, Andy stood, chewing like a contented cow with eyes closed and jaws sawing back and forth in perfect rhythm with every bite. When the entire head of cabbage had been eaten, he wobbled out the door and back to the bar.

People react differently to alcohol. Some become belligerent, some melancholy, some giddy and others mellow. Andy was a mellow drunk. When drinking, he was a big ol' teddy bear; he minded his own business and never caused a moment of trouble for anyone. One night when Andy was in town celebrating, along came drunk and feisty Pat Thompson. In the course of a conversation, Andy said something that Pat took as an insult, and up came his fists. It was just comical. There was little banty rooster Pat who barely reached up to Andy's armpits, squaring off with Andy who outweighed him by at least 150 pounds. Andy just brushed him off as if he were an annoying gnat, and the confrontation was over.

The brothers' sister Ann and her husband were also good customers of Dad's. Ann was quiet and very soft spoken, and she liked to have a beer when they stopped in, usually on their way home from Minot. As it will happen, that one beer sometimes turned into a whole evening of beers. With each beer she drank, the quieter she became. She'd just sit there, drink beer and smile that dreamy smile of hers. She'd sit all night on the same bar stool and never move. We used to marvel at her bladder control.

Then came the day when the brothers stopped on their way into Minot to pick up a 7-Up for Andy who was suffering from indigestion. Andy lowered himself into a barrel chair at the card table, and as his drink was being delivered, he slumped over and was gone. Dad was not in the bar when Andy passed away, for which I've always been grateful as Andy was a good friend as well as a good customer.

One can't be in business in a small town for as long as Dad and Mom were and not get to know their regular customers well. I remember one incident, which proves just how well they did get to know their customers. Earl, a young man from Carpio, came in one evening and proceeded to drink all his buddies under the table. The next morning when Dad parked his car in the alley, he noticed that someone had gotten sick the night before, and in the middle of it was an upper plate. Dad knew immediately whose teeth they were just by the shape, and the next time Earl came in, Dad fished in his top drawer, pulled out the false teeth and asked, "Did you, by any chance, lose these?" A sheepish Earl accepted them gratefully, turned around and left without even ordering a drink.

Every town has at least one unfortunate character; ours was the town's wino. He lived with his elderly widowed mother and never worked for as long as I can remember. He lost an eye early in life as a result of smallpox and wore glasses with one smoked lens to hide the sunken socket. Ed alluded to the fact that his eye was the reason for not working, but it was common knowledge that too much wine had become his handicap.

Highly intelligent, Ed read voraciously and was well versed on most subjects. During his more sober conversations, he expressed his opinions very articulately.

Every morning, Ed would walk uptown (he had no car) for a glass of port or muscatel. Some mornings, he had the shakes so bad that he could barely get out his money. He was quiet, almost sullen, until he had his second or third drink, and then he became quite talkative, even jovial. Before leaving, he'd buy a bottle, whatever size he could afford that day, and he wouldn't be seen until the next morning. At times he'd run out of money before his social security check came. Those were the bad days. His poor elderly mother would say, "My Edwin is so sick today." (Obviously, he had tried to hide his addiction from her as some years later when the outhouse was torn down; wine bottles literally filled the hole.) If he could make it uptown, Mom, feeling sorry for him, would give him a bottle, and he'd pay when his check came in. If he couldn't make it, he suffered terribly, which caused his mother untold grief. Dad and Mom had many customers who loved to party and did and some who drank more than they should have, but Ed was the only one who went over the edge, and it was sad to see.

The area in and around Foxholm has been peppered with bachelors throughout its history. John Keller, who was my parents' age, was one of them. He was a neighboring farmer before Mom and Dad moved to town and was often at our house.

John thought he was God's gift to women, but according to the women, that was pure fantasy. He never missed a barn dance and considered himself one of the best dancers in attendance. Dressed in his brown suit, which was highly polished with age, white shirt and tie with his long hair greased straight back, he'd make the rounds to all the ladies. Connie got stuck with him more than once and remembers his dancing well—three quick steps forward and three quick steps back, to every dance whether it was a polka, waltz, or two-step—and instead of circling the dance floor as everyone else did, he'd dance his partner straight across the dance floor, turn (his turns sometimes fouled up his "quick steps") and head straight back. All the while he danced, he would say things like, "Turn a little, it looks better," and he made an obvious, laughable effort to practice what he preached.

In later years, John bought the bar in Carpio and would occasionally stop to brag to Dad about his going business. He prided himself in always looking his best behind the bar and even suggested that Dad wear a white shirt and tie like he did. (Dad wore a shirt and tie every day, but not a white one.)

John did wear a white shirt and tie everyday, but he failed to say that it was the same shirt weeks in a row. Obviously, it was more than his shirts that he didn't change. People still laugh when reminiscing about the time that John got sick and had to go to the hospital. As the story goes, and people swear that it was true, the nurses had to cut off his socks because the hair on his legs had grown through the material, matting them to his legs, much like an unkempt dog.

Many couples came through the door over the years that were forgotten as soon as they left, and then there were those who made an indelible impression. I remember one couple in particular whom we laugh about to this day. They were both about sixty-five. The man, who had a thin salt-and-pepper mustache and bushy eyebrows, wore a green plaid shirt, string tie with a horse emblem on the clasp, green nylon jacket and a baseball cap that said, "Armstrong Tires." His lady friend, who drank whiskey and water, had an owlish, wrinkled face, which was generously rouged and powdered, and dyed-black hair that looked as if it had been combed with a high-speed eggbeater. Perched on top of her head was a small black straw hat with a Minnie Pearl red flower dangling off the side. With heads together, they sat the bar and sipped their drinks. Gazing into her eyes, the old gentleman was overheard saying, "Beautiful women like you just drive men wild."

Another Carpio bachelor was a regular at the bar. Iders Jenson was a farmer—a rich, short, balding farmer—who always wore a black felt cap similar to a baseball cap. Being so short, he obviously couldn't find the right length overalls so he wore pants that were at least six inches too long and solved the problem by rolling them up, way up over his ankles.

Iders was sweet on his petite, attractive neighbor Ella Renz, and he made no bones about it even though he knew that she was happily married to Cecil. When he saw them in the bar, he would buy Ella a drink, but not Cecil, and would figure out a way of sitting next to her. One fall he went so far as giving her several bushels of flax, which was worth a considerable amount of money. Not knowing what to do with grain, which was already unloaded, Ella merely smiled and said, "Thanks." Cecil bought him a drink.

Ella may have come first with Iders, but my sister-in-law Verlene who tended bar on occasion laughed and said that she was his "second best girl," with my mother coming in third. Today, little Iders is gone as is Ella's flax, but memories of Iders with his rolled up pants still bring chuckles.

Norman Moger and his wife Katherine, who lived on a farm west of Foxholm, were frequent visitors to Dad's bar. Norman looked the part of a gentleman farmer; he always wore a dress hat with the brim neatly shaped and a suede leather jacket or dress shirt when he came to town, but he was a working farmer. Katherine, very much a lady, seemed out of her element but actually fit in quite well, drinks and all. Norman, who was highly intelligent, took a liking to my Dad whose personality was very different from his. Norman was a talker; he'd sit for hours and never run out his drinks or conversation. Unlike my mother, Dad was quiet. He spoke with ease to his customers but was not what you'd call a talky bartender. He was more apt to nod a greeting then to call out a "Hello," but he and Norman got along fine. Having been a farmer, Dad understood the farmer's woes and successes, and both he and Norman were avid fishermen. Norman's father had built a dam on a creek on his land, and Norman stocked it with bass and walleye. It was not open to the public, but he'd invite friends to fish. Dad was one of them. Then the State Fish and Game Department stepped in. They told Norman that it was illegal to dam up a creek and that he'd have to open it up to the public. Norman refused, saying he was not going to have the public throwing trash and mucking up his property. The State Game and Fish held firm, so Norman blew up the dam.

Norman, always thinking, thought it would be fun to fly to Africa, so he took flying lessons, became multi-engine rated and bought a twin engine plane. He flew from Minot to South America and then on to Africa. After completing his goal, he sold the plane in Africa, hopped a commercial plane home and never flew again. Mission accomplished.

Pat and Olive Galvin had been good neighbor friends of Mom and Dad's when they were still on the farm, back in the days when they had dances in their big hip roof barn, which was possibly built by my Grandpa Miller, who, with the help of Uncle Ed, built the same type of barns. Retired, the Galvins moved to Minot. They were the type of customers to whom a beer or two was simply a chaser for mellow conversation. With time on their hands, Pat and Olive would dress up and drive out to the bar, buy a quart of beer and hope someone would come to share it with them. When Pat passed away, Olive, lonelier than ever, gamely continued to come. Dressed in a nice dress and makeup, she'd drive by herself, drink her beer and visit for a couple of hours with Mom and whoever happened to be there.

Several of the regular bar customers didn't drink at all. It was merely a social stop for them. They'd order a Coke or 7-Up, play cards or just shoot the breeze. Jack Pritschet was one of the non-drinkers who only drank pop and had as good time if not better than anyone else in the bar.

My mother and dad were raised in a trusting generation. When a person said, "I give you my word," he meant it, and a handshake was as good as a legal document. That's the way they ran their business. If Dad cashed a check for someone, he expected it to be good, and if someone charged, he took their word that he'd pay. I remember young guys who bragged about the big wages they were making doing construction work coming to Dad for a loan "until payday." We used to laugh because Dad couldn't resist giving them a little sermon, "What did you do with all that money you made?" All the while he'd be reaching in his back pocket for his billfold.

My Dad was a man of few words. He said what he meant and meant what he said. We've never forgotten the time someone gave him a bad check. He said nothing to Mom but we found out about it when a note written in Dad's scrawl (Dad was left-handed and forced in school to write with his right hand.) came back in the mail. It said simply, "I've got one guy in jail, and you'll be the next." On the back of it was a note from the errant check writer promising to pay.

Dad kept a simple ledger which listed the bills and receipts and a recipe box filled and cards for the charge accounts. When going through things after Dad's death, we found written on one of the recipe cards, "Fence-post Indian—case of Old Style." It seems there was an Indian who was going around the country selling fence posts, and since he had no money, Dad had let him charge a case of beer. Laughing, Mom wrote it off as a bad debt. About two months later, the man came in, identified himself and paid for his case of beer.

Mom was just as kind-hearted and trusting and always gave people the benefit of the doubt. She, too, used the recipe box, and at times even lent out cash. I remember young Lyle Bock, instead of going to his dad, would come in and borrow five dollars "'until payday," and when pay day came around, he was there with his money.

When Mom passed away, we received a sympathy card, which said, "You don't know me, but when I read your mother's obituary in the paper, I had to write. My husband and I were strangers driving through Foxholm and stopped at her bar for a drink. While we were drinking our beer and visiting with your mother, she suddenly said, 'I have to run to the post office to mail this letter. Would you watch the bar for a minute?' She trusted us and we were perfect strangers." That was my mother, in a nutshell. She trusted everyone, even perfect strangers.

Mom dancing with my brother Francis on her 95th birthday

Mom turns 100! (cake baked and decorated by me and carried on plane from Kansas)

Service Brothers

Alvin, "Boy," as he was called up to this time, graduated from Foxholm High at age fifteen and soon after packed a suitcase and took the train to California where he worked in the shipyards.

In 1944, at age seventeen, he enlisted in the Navy and was shipped to Hawaii where he spent the next two years at Barber's Point as a .45 Caliber Gun instructor. The remainder of his time was spent in the South Pacific aboard the USS Lexington. When his tour ended, he signed up for the Naval Reserves and went home to go on with his life.

In 1950, police action broke out in Korea. The United Nations troops were in bad trouble, and the need for help was urgent and immediate.

The USS Princeton, a brand-new ship that had been put away in mothballs in 1948, was suddenly jolted into action. A hastily assembled crew of twenty-five hundred men, Alvin included, was dragged away from peacetime pursuits. Sullenly eyeing the drab monster that they would be bringing to life and living in, the disgruntled crew set about readying the ship. Few knew what they were fighting for, but all knew that the new war had thrown a monkey wrench into their lives.

Under the expert and understanding guidance of their commander, Captain William Gallery, the crew was changed from a rag-tag group who had only known one another for a few days into a smooth-working precision team. Three months and eight days later, the Princeton launched her first strike off the Korean coast, setting an all-time Navy record for getting a major ship ready for action.

It was common knowledge that Captain Gallery was the secret of the Princeton's success. Because of his encouragement and trust, the men became eager and loyal assistants. (Fifty-five years later, Alvin still spoke highly of "Cap'n Bill.") No idea of his that was sent down to them was considered impossible. After kicking it around for a few hours, the words, "Can do" would make their way back to their captain. As a result of one such suggestion, Alvin, along with four other seamen, received a commendation for devising a way to make the napalm bomb more effective. After analyzing the situation, they came up with the successful idea of adding creosote, a black oily liquid that is normally used as a wood preservative, to napalm powder and gasoline which made the solution gel and thus stick better when the bomb was exploded.

After eight months in the combat zone, the Princeton was sent home to San Diego to rest and recuperate. The city planned a huge two-day homecoming celebration, including a queen and her court, to honor them. The selection of Queen of the Homecoming Ball was left up to the ship's company who passed up eager-beaver starlets in favor of a "Queen Janie," a pretty seventeen-year-old orphan who reigned over her court in a wheelchair. Crippled from birth, Janie was chosen from The Sunshine School for Crippled because of her courage and cheerfulness despite her handicap. Her hard-fought battle for life was symbolic to the hardships the men faced in battle and thus, was a fitting and noble selection. Her maids, each of a different nationality or race whose ages ranged from eight to ten, were chosen from an orphanage. It was predicted by many that this modern "Cinderella Story," made possible by the crew of the USS Princeton, would play a big part in restoring people's faith in the eternal goodness of humanity.

At the time of the Princeton's homecoming, my brother Francis was stationed at Camp Pendleton Marine Base where he was in charge of the Motor Pool. When he heard that Alvin's ship had arrived, he immediately found someone to cover for him; he "borrowed" a military car and went to meet Alvin aboard the USS Princeton. Using government-issued tickets found in the car, he took the ferry to Coronado Island where the ship was docked. Armed with a fifth of whiskey in each hand, he spotted Alvin almost immediately, and the party began. Two days later, bleary-eyed and hung-over, he waved good-bye to his equally bleary-eyed and hung-over brother and drove back to camp. No one had missed him or the car, and outside of a headache, things were back to normal. However, judging by some of my brothers' stories, maybe headaches were not that abnormal.

Francis experienced heavy combat in the South Pacific on Iwa Jima, Okinawa, Bougainville, Guadalcanal and Guam. Only in the most recent years would he talk about any of his war experiences.

On Easter Sunday, April 1, 1945, Francis's Third Division landed on Okinawa. The men were in landing boats heading for shore when it was discovered that the Japs were lying in wait for them. They quickly turned and made their way to the opposite shore. (Francis remembered it as being "the April Fool's joke that backfired.") After a long, hard-fought battle, they took the island, and it turned out to be the final battle of the war; soon after, the atomic bomb was dropped on Hiroshima. It was during this final battle that President Roosevelt suddenly died.

On Friday the thirteenth, the Marines were startled, then grief-stricken to hear the bullhorns of the ships offshore blaring, "Attention! Attention all hands! President Roosevelt is dead! Repeat, our Supreme Commander, President Roosevelt is dead!" (President Franklin D. Roosevelt died the day before at 3:35 p.m. in his small cottage in Warm Springs, Georgia, but communications at that time were slow to be delivered unlike our instant transmissions of today.) Stunned, many cried, but most prayed. Many of the men were too young to have known any other president. They had truly loved him and depended on him. "What do we do now?" was their cry. Everyone at home was asking the same thing.

It was also during this time that renowned war correspondent Ernie Pyle was shot and killed by a sniper on Ise Shima, a small island adjacent to Okinawa.

Ralph on Okinawa and the memorial to Ernie Pyle

Francis and my Army brother Ralph met up on Okinawa. Thinking he was one campaign ahead of Francis, Ralph, on an anti-aircraft mission, had written to Francis telling him that he was on the island and was hoping to meet up with him when his Third Marine Division landed. What he didn't know was that Francis was already there, fighting on the front lines.

As soon as Ralph's letter reached him, Francis—tired, bearded and grimy after a night of heavy combat—made his way to the beach where Ralph was sleeping after his own busy night of fending off enemy aircraft. Ralph was stunned when he awoke to find a grinning Francis standing there in front of him. Ralph often reminisced how Francis hadn't had his combat boots off in three weeks and that he made sure that before Francis left, he had a clean dry pair of socks. After a memorable day together, Francis hitchhiked back to his division. It was an exceptionally hard trip of walking, riding in animal-drawn and even human-drawn carts over difficult terrain. When he finally reached his division, he didn't have the password. In his eagerness to see Ralph, he had left that morning before it had been given out. He came dangerously close to being shot, but by the grace of God, he was able to identify himself before a shot was fired.

Not all of Francis's experiences were so grim. He laughingly recalled that while on the island of Guam, he and his Marine buddies stole an Army jeep. They took it back to their camp, repainted it in navy blue, put on new identification numbers, and presto—they had a new jeep that they used and enjoyed on their ship as well as on the island. He also reminisced about stealing rifles from the Army. During R & R on Guam, they often walked by an Army encampment. There on tripods would be nice, new unattended rifles. The temptation was too great. Quickly, they would snatch the rifles, replace them with their dirty, well-used ones and innocently continue on their way.

Francis reenlisted and in 1952 was sent to Korea. While driving an amphibious truck that was used for an ambulance, he ran over a land mine and was seriously injured. The doctors wanted to amputate his leg, but Francis refused to give his consent. He was put aboard the hospital ship USS Constellation where he spent six months recuperating. He was then put aboard a Red Cross ship. Instead of being sent home as he expected, he was sent back to duty in Korea, both legs intact. He eventually was sent home with the Marines' blessings, the Purple Heart and malaria.

Alvin, Francis, Ralph

.

Happy Days

My childhood home

The toll in broken dreams, physical hunger and hardship during the Depression was immense. Still, people stubbornly held on by carefully managing whatever resources they had, spending carefully and, in some cases, by making a complete change. My dad chose the complete change; he quit farming, and became a business owner.

Shortly after Dad took over the bar, my parents took out a mortgage for fifteen hundred dollars and bought the Frank Lambert house, which was built in 1910 and was located next door to the school in Foxholm. Their mortgage payments were eleven dollars a month. This would be Mom and Dad's last move and the place that I still think of as home.

Our new home, a two-story white clapboard house with a balcony that extended out over the kitchen entrance, was the largest house in town and the only one with two stairways to the upper level. In 1940, in a village even too small to be called a town, it was an impressive structure. A couple years after we moved in, my Aunt Mayme and family who lived in California came to visit. My cousin Ken and I were recently reminiscing about that visit; he told me that he had gone back home and told all his friends that his North Dakota aunt and uncle lived in a big movie star mansion. Laughing, he said that when he returned some sixty years later for my mother's hundredth birthday party, he found that the "big mansion" had shrunk considerably.

The Lambert House, now known as the Miller House, boasted of eleven rooms, six rooms upstairs and five down. (Out of six bedrooms, there were only two tiny built-in closets, as was common in old homes.) There was also a basement under part of the house and an attic.

The basement contained a large concrete cistern, which collected rainwater via a drainpipe from the eaves. (I used climb up this drainpipe to the balcony and then into the house.) Water from this cistern was piped up to the bathroom sink and tub. It bypassed the stool to save on the soft rainwater, which meant that we had to pump water from the well, located about thirty feet from the kitchen door, to flush the toilet. If we used the water, we were expected to refill it for the next person, but many times the pail was empty. "I forgot" didn't go over too well with my mother, and consequently, I made a few extra trips to the pump and back.

Because of the water situation, we used the outhouse except in the very coldest part of the winter, and during the night, we used the slop pail, which brings to mind another of Mom's pranks. My oldest brother Ralph and his wife Edith stayed with us for a short time after they were married, and Edith was as crazy as Mom; the two of them were always playing tricks on one another. Knowing that Edith used the slop pail at night, Mom waited until she went upstairs to bed and then smeared jelly all around the rim. Edith knew immediately who had done it, and the next morning the kitchen rang with loud, good-natured accusations and laughter.

Ralph and Edith

Toilet paper was not readily available, so in the outdoor toilet, we used a Sears and Roebuck catalog. To make the stiff, slick pages more useable, we ruffled the pages back and forth several times. The yellow index pages were softer than the other pages and were always the first to go. During canning season, Dad bought crates of peaches for Mom to make into sauce. The peaches were wrapped individually in squares of soft peach-colored paper, which were a welcome relief from the catalog pages.

Our house had a unique feature. Water from the cistern was pumped from the basement up to the kitchen and into a thirty-gallon holding tank. The water in the tank was heated by its connection to the stove and provided warm water for kitchen cleanup. Pumping the water into the tank took considerable effort because, having no electricity, it had to be done by hand using a push-pull pump. When the heated tank became empty, it made angry hissing, popping sounds which scared me to death. Being a worrywart, I was afraid that it might explode or do something of equal magnitude. When Mom and Dad weren't home, my ornery brothers, who hated the job of pumping, would deliberately ignore the popping noises knowing full well that if they waited long enough, Nervous Nellie would go down and do the pumping. They were right; I did. (Several years later, a gas stove replaced the coal stove, and the worrisome tank was taken out.)

The Monarch kitchen range burned both wood and coal and was used for heating as well as for cooking. Some cold, blustery days, we'd open the oven door to help heat the kitchen, and sometimes we'd sit on the oven door to warm our backsides or pull up a chair and put our feet on the open door, especially after ice skating. The cook stove had a reservoir on the right side, which held a reserve supply of warm water, handy for clean up. During the winter, we filled it with snow. It was time consuming since we had to keep adding snow as it melted, but having that nice soft water was worth the effort.

Old houses lacked adequate insulation, which was a big factor during the long northern winters. Every fall, in an effort to help keep the heat in and the cold out, Dad banked the house. Tarpaper, a heavy paper mixed with tar, which is used as a base in roofing, was wrapped around the house below windowsill level. Dirt, which was hauled in, was then piled up against the tar paper to prevent the cold air from worming its way under the foundation and into the house.

It can be terrifically cold in North Dakota. Temperatures of twenty to thirty below zero are not uncommon, and in 1936, it hit an all-time low of sixty below in nearby Parshall. During extremely cold spells, Mom would hang a blanket over the open doorway between the kitchen and dining room to keep the heat contained in the kitchen. Even with storm windows, the harsh wind bullied its way in around the windows, causing an icy draft. (Thermal panes were yet to be invented.) When this happened, Mom did what she knew best; she got out a paring knife and stuffed rags into the crevices of the window frames.

On those frigid days, the humidity in the kitchen, pushing against the icy cold glass, produced a thick frost, which grew in clusters of crystals, forming designs of lacy ferns and flowers, which shimmered like diamonds in the afternoon sun. I was intrigued and couldn't resist scratching in my own designs. Sometimes I pressed coins into the heavy frost which left perfect prints. Knowing that once the frost melted, the windows would be a mass of smudges, Mom would holler, "Quit smearing up those windows!" I don't think she really cared, though, because it gave me something to do instead of pestering her to play rummy with me.

It was seldom too cold for us to play outside. We'd bundle up in our snowsuits, tie woolen scarves over our noses and mouths, put on two pairs of mittens, and off we'd go. Winter for us meant sliding down the riverbank on pieces of cardboard or participating in our favorite pastime—ice skating, especially on a clear, star-studded night.

We'd clear off the ice with scoop shovels, build a bonfire from the dead branches we found along the river, and skate for hours. There was something magical about a big bonfire on a dark night, with its flames licking upward, spewing showers of reddish gold sparks whenever another log was thrown on. I remember hovering with outstretched arms so close that my exposed face burned from the heat and then turning around to unthaw my backside. Our parents never seemed to worry about us getting burned or the fire getting out of hand, but then, where would a fire go surrounded by ice and snow?

One of the wild and crazy games we played on the ice was crack-the-whip. A good skater would start skating around the ice backwards and be joined by another skater who would hold his hands as they continued to skate. Others would chain onto those skaters by grasping the one ahead around the waist. When the backward skater was skating as fast as he could, he'd make a sharp turn and pull the chain as hard as he could. Often the last two or three skaters would break loose and go flying across the ice, ending up half buried in a snow bank, but that was the fun of it.

I received my first kiss when I was skating. I remember it well. I was fourteen, and the date was December 1st, my mother's birthday, which is why I remember so well. There was a full moon, and the night was clear and crisp. I had skated around the bend, away from the bonfire, and Joe, one of the older boys and my latest crush, gave me a kiss. It was only a mere peck, but at the time, I was starry-eyed and thrilled to pieces. Before he could even think of giving me another, my buddy Phillip whizzed around the corner and spoiled the moment. I still think he meant to do exactly that, but he would never admit it.

On those cold days, Mom often had a big kettle of soup bubbling on the stove, and many times the kitchen was filled with the aroma of freshly baked bread. From part of the dough, she'd make what we called muttzins, which we liked better than the bread. (Some call them dough jacks or elephant ears.) She'd stretch out small pieces of dough and deep-fry them until they were golden brown. Slathered with butter and sprinkled with sugar, they'd disappear as fast as she could fry them.

We had no electricity those first years and thus, no running water. When Grandpa Hoerter built and installed the cupboards, he put the sink in but the drain led to a five-gallon bucket underneath. We washed dishes in the sink, but we used a porcelain-coated dishpan and then emptied the water outside or let it drain into the pail under the sink. (More than once that pail overflowed because we forgot to check it.)

The bathroom was unheated and too cold during the winter to use for bathing. (I remember taking sponge baths in the living room next to the heater.) Not until years later when Dad had a new forced-air furnace put in could we use the bathroom year round. Is it any wonder that full baths were taken only once a week?

Located near the bottom right corner of the kitchen door was a round silver-dollar-sized hole that went all the way through the wood door. This conversation piece had a logical explanation; it was used by Mrs. Lambert and, for a short time, by my mother, to vent the exhaust pipe of the gasoline-powered washing machine. The hole remained in the door, but years later its smooth edges were deeply grooved by a frantic mother. Toots had been accidently shut in the house with her crying babies in the shed. She had tried to get to them by chewing her way through the small hole. Mom had gotten a new electric Maytag wringer machine by this time, and there was no further need for the exhaust hole, so she plugged it with a golf ball, a perfect fit.

Washing clothes in those days was a hard, messy job that took up most of the day. The night before wash day, usually Monday, Mom would see that the big copper boiler was put on the stove and filled with water. In the morning, the machine would be lugged from the unheated entryway (shed, as we called it) into the middle of the kitchen and filled with hot water from the boiler. The galvanized steel rinse tub was also moved in and filled. Bluing, a whitening agent, was added to the unheated rinse water. Mom boiled the heavily soiled white clothes with homemade lye soap that was so acrid it singed one's bronchial tubes for days. I don't remember how she made the soap (with lard and lye somehow), but I remember well the caustic stench as it simmered on the stove. The lye soap was on its way out, thank goodness, and then Mom used P&G's Fels Naptha bar soap, which did its job without sending one into cardiac arrest. Mom used Oxydol in the machine, and I remember that for lightly soiled fine fabrics, she used Dreft, which looked like dry, fluffy snowflakes.

Meanwhile, mounds of dirty clothes, which were sorted into piles according to colors and degrees of soil, made the kitchen floor an obstacle course. All the clothes were washed in the same water, beginning with the white clothes, down to the jeans and lastly, the rugs. (Old habits die hard; I still find myself reaching for the white clothes first.) After rinsing, select pieces such as shirt collars and cuffs and aprons were dipped into a starch solution that Mom made by cooking cornstarch in water. If the aprons could stand alone when dry, Mom knew she had been a bit heavy-handed with the cornstarch.

We had no dryer. The wet clothes were hung outside on the clothesline in a neat and orderly fashion using wooden, non-spring clothespins. Women took pride in their laundry, especially in the white clothes. It was thought that snowy white clothes were a sign of a good housekeeper. To help whiten stained or dingy white clothes, Mom would lay the pieces on the grass and, as the clothes dried the stains miraculously, or so it seemed to me, disappeared. In actuality, it had something to do with the sun interacting with the chlorophyll in the grass that bleached out the stains.

During the winter, Mom hung the dark clothes upstairs on a line that she strung across the big room at the top of the stairs. Except in the most inclement weather, the white clothes were always hung outside to freeze dry—some on the clothesline and others on a wooden collapsible clothes rack, which we set on the back porch. Sometimes they would be as stiff as boards when brought in. With the wet clothes draped around the house, it looked like a Chinese laundry, but the clean, fresh smell was wonderful.

Ironing eventually became my job, and with no wash and wear fabrics or dryers, it was a hard, time-consuming job. Each piece to be ironed, except for the jeans and sheets, was sprinkled with water and tightly rolled, placed into a clothesbasket, and covered with a towel. When opened the next day, each piece was uniformly damp and ready to iron.

When I was about ten, I began my ironing apprenticeship. Using a gasoline iron (the flat irons that Mom heated on the stove were before my ironing days), I started on dish towels and pillow cases that Mom had embroidered and progressed up to her starched cotton housedresses, men's shirts and the heavily starched cotton crisscross dining room curtains. (The curtains looked so nice when they were all done up but were such a pain to iron.) Only on rare occasions did Mom iron, but frequently I'd hear her say, "I rather like to iron." "But when?" I'd mutter under my breath, which came as close to talking back as I ever came. The job of ironing remained mine.

The bathroom could be entered through my parents' bedroom or through a short hall off the kitchen. A door in the bathroom opened to a narrow stairway that led upstairs into the storeroom, which opened to the other rooms. That stairway came in handy many times. We always had someone staying with us. Some of the men were homeless; others boarded with us during the week while working in the area, and over the years, several teachers and schoolgirls who lived on farms stayed with us during the week. All of them used this back stairway at one time or another.

For a while, an old gentleman by the name of Joe Schabel, who had no family and no place to go, stayed with us. He was a little, small-boned, comical-looking man with coarse salt-and-pepper hair (more salt than pepper) that stubbornly stuck straight up in the back. He had a short bristly mustache and wore small, round, wire-rimmed glasses, which gave him an owlish look. Old Joe was quiet, soft-spoken and hard to converse with because of his heavy German accent and pronounced hearing loss. One night, Mom and I had gone up to be with Dad in the bar. It was a slow night, and Dad closed up early. When we opened the kitchen door, there was Old Joe in his long underwear standing in front of the cupboard in the hallway next to the bathroom door with his hand in the cake pan, just about to have a little nighttime snack. He didn't hear us at first, and when he did, there was a moment of startled silence and then a loud, rattling bang as he dropped the tin cake pan cover and bolted for the bathroom stairway. As he flew around the door, the unbuttoned flap of his underwear whipped open, exposing all. It's a good thing Joe was hard of hearing because Mom and I burst out laughing while Dad, with his little half grin, just shook his head.

When Joe left our house, he stayed with Norbert and Darlene Greman. One spring morning, Darlene came into the bar and asked if we'd seen Joe. He had gone up to Walt's Bar to get a haircut from Boss Stach the night before and hadn't returned. Dad's first words were, "Have you checked the creek?" (There was a small creek that flowed underneath the highway between Gremans' house and uptown.) They found him lying face down in the water. Evidently, he had stumbled in the dark, fallen in and was unable to get back up. Dad took care of all the funeral arrangements, making sure that Old Joe had a proper funeral and burial service.

The hidden bathroom stairway drew me like a magnet, as it did all the grandkids who roamed the house throughout the years. When I was little, it had the air of a secret passageway, and when I was a teenager, it was the perfect way to sneak upstairs after coming home late.

As you reached the top of the bathroom stairs, the door to the balcony was immediately ahead. My friend Gwen and I used to play there, pretending to be movie stars looking down from our magnificent castle. We were star-struck pre-teens who read movie magazines with all the latest gossip about the stars and especially about our favorites— Roddy McDowell and Van Johnson. We wrote flattering fan letters to them and were so excited when we received autographed pictures in return, but we were so disappointed that they didn't enclose personal notes. When we weren't reading movie magazines, we read funny books (We didn't call them comic books.), which cost a dime; Archie, Captain Marvel, Superman, Blondie, Katzenjammer Kids and Porky Pig were some of my favorites. We used to trade them with friends. We had an equal-value trading system; those in good shape with covers were traded for others in the same condition, but if they were tattered and coverless, you got the same in return. I also loved Big Little Books, which had flip-action pictures in the upper right corners. As you flipped the pages, the pictures made a motion scene. The Big Little Books featured the same characters as did the funny books, but I didn't trade them as often; maybe it was because they weren't as plentiful as the funny books.

Gwen and I

The dining room had an alcove made up of four bay windows, on which Mom hung those white crisscross curtains that I had to iron. It was my favorite feature of the house, and I've always wanted one in my own home. It was a perfect spot for Mom's houseplants. Even though it was warm and inviting, we never ate in the dining room except on holidays. The rest of the time, Mom battled to keep the table cleared of clutter, as everyone had a bad habit of plopping things on it. It was Mom's pet peeve, and I can still hear her, "I can never see the top of this table. Put this away!" A plate shelf similar to crown molding rimmed the room at the height of approximately six feet. The china that Alvin sent home from Japan when he was in the service was displayed on it. After washing and replacing those dishes so many times, I could still put every piece back in exactly the same position.

There were beautiful hardwood floors in the dining room, as well as in the living room. Mom never used water on them. She cleaned them with a commercial liquid cleaner and then applied a coating of paste wax. To polish them, I'd put on heavy woolen socks and go skating— back and forth and back and forth until they glowed with a lustrous sheen.

Family dinner in the dining room

An open, dark oak stairway led from the living room to the upstairs. Beneath the stairway was an enclosed storage space, which had a four-foot door that opened from the outside only. I clearly remember my two ornery brothers shoving me into it and closing the door. They had buddies over and were probably just being stupid, but I'll never forget those few panicky minutes I spent in that dark, small space. They thought it was funny, of course, and I lived through it without any scars, and most likely, I got even with them.

The upstairs was heated by the open stairway and a fourteen-inch square floor register in the bedroom over the kitchen. I remember lying on my stomach on that register looking down and listening to the adults below when I was supposed to be in bed. Somehow, Mom always knew when I did this, and if she had to come upstairs and help me to bed, which she did a few times, I knew I was in trouble. I think every one of Mom and Dad's grandchild at one time or another spent time on that register doing the same thing that I did. It was irresistible.

Once I was the only one home, Dad would close off the upstairs during the winter and I would sleep on the living room sofa that opened up into a bed. My dog Toots always slept with me, which Mom didn't like but tolerated. In the summertime, she slept on top of the covers but when it was cold, I'd give her the high sign, and she'd creep under the covers and curl up by my feet. Mom acted like she didn't see her and we thought we were really getting away with something. Toots allowed no one to come near my bed except Mom, and she only did so after making the mistake of snapping at her. Just the slightest movement towards me turned my gentle little pet into a ferocious watchdog.

Toots and I

One morning, we were running late. I grabbed a piece of toast and rushed off to school. Dad was already waiting in the car as Mom hurriedly folded up the couch. She was working with Dad that day, so I went directly uptown after school. Mom and I stayed longer than usual, and it was past my bedtime when we got home. Toots wasn't wriggling and dancing at the door like she usually did. I called several times and got no answer. By this time, I was on the verge of tears, but Mom, who was already unfolding the couch, calmly said, "She's around here someplace. Just get to bed; you have school tomorrow." The bed was only half open when out shot Toots. Panting and wild-eyed, she made a beeline for the door and didn't stop running until she got to Dad's bar, something she had never done before or would do ever again. There was a small breathing space where the ends of the mattress folded over, and she had chewed on a little corner trying to free herself, but that was it. She hadn't even wet the bed. For the rest of the winter, she slept on top of my bed, and no amount of coaxing could get her to come under the covers.

Toots had another traumatic experience which affected the whole family. One Sunday afternoon, Ralph and Edith, who were staying with us, decided to go for a ride. The rest of us were gone, and Toots looked at them so longingly that they ended up taking her with them. They ended up in Minot and, on the spur of the moment, went to a movie at the Orpheum Theater, which was located on the north end of Main Street near the Soo Line Depot. They left Toots sleeping in the car, and when they returned, she was gone. Evidently, she had crawled out a window that was left partially open. They looked everywhere, but didn't see Toots. Finally, they had to give up and face telling me that my dog was gone. I was devastated, and Ralph felt worse.

Not a day went by that I didn't think of her. I imagined her cold and starving or lying dead along the roadside. Three months later, Louie Peterson, our Peterson Place neighbor who had since moved to Minot, drove out to tell Dad that he was sure he had seen Toots at a service station down by the Fairgrounds. The next time Dad and Mom went to Minot, Dad made sure to drive to that station to buy gas. He told Mom to get the gas while he looked around out back. A woman came out to help them and, in the process, began to visit with Mom. Suddenly, the screen door flew open and out came Toots. She took a flying leap into Mom's lap, yipped and wiggled and showered her with wet kisses. The lady took one look and said, "Mugs must be your dog." They had found her wandering the streets that afternoon, far from downtown, and had taken her home. Mom and Dad hadn't said a word to me just in case it was a false alarm, so you can imagine my reaction when they carried her into the house. It was one happy reunion.

Toots was with us fifteen years. She gradually turned gray, and her movements became more labored. In those days, one didn't take an aging pet to the vet; we accepted the fact (at least I tried) that she was old, ailing and nearing the end. When the sad day came, she thoughtfully and slowly made her way down to the riverbank at the end of our yard and peacefully went to sleep. My steadfast, loyal companion was gone. I had several dogs after Toots, but none could ever take her place. She remains unforgettable.

An open-covered porch with three wooden pillars supporting the roof ran along the front of the house. Its waist-high, twelve-inch walls were made of native rock and concrete, and the design on the front section included a small archway at floor level. Green climbing vines covered the sides, providing shade during the hot summer afternoons, and purple lilacs, adding their own special touch, flanked the steps. A large picture window in the living room, which had stained glass in the upper section, provided an open view of the porch and the front yard beyond it.

Elm and cottonwood trees formed the dividing line between our yard and the school's. Yellow flowering corrigenda bushes and purple lilacs ran across the back yard along the woven metal fence that rimmed our yard. More trees lined the driveway, which was divided by a giant cottonwood, forming a loop that led back to the entrance of the driveway. Flowerbeds in old tires that were painted white were scattered among the driveway trees.

Everyone had a garden. Produce was very limited in the grocery stores, and in order to do the canning that everyone did, they had to plant their own vegetables. It was also much cheaper, and certainly more convenient. Our garden spot stretched along the south side of our yard. Each spring Dad plowed the large plot and hauled in a load of old barnyard manure, which he worked into the soil. It was Mom's job to plant the garden, which really wasn't a job for her because gardening and growing flowers was her way to relax. Since there were no greenhouses, only seeds were planted. The only plants she had were the tiny seedling tomato plants that she started in the house some weeks before. For some reason unknown to me, everyone planted potatoes on Good Friday, rain or shine. I never could wait until we could pick little new potatoes and fresh peas. Creamed together, they are still one of my very favorite dishes.

At one end of the garden were several thick-stocked rhubarb plants that flourished in North Dakota's cool climate. Strawberry-rhubarb pie was my very favorite and Mom baked many for me. In later years, whenever I came home during the rhubarb season, she always had a pie waiting for me, and no one could bake them like she could.

Although Dad left the farm and continued in the bar business for the rest of his life, I think there was always a little piece of his heart that remained a farmer.

When we moved into town, he brought along several milk cows, a few pigs and chickens, and eventually he added a few sheep. In the backyard, which extended down to the river, we had a barn and a chicken coop, which was nestled in a group of trees. One of my chores was to gather the eggs, which wasn't a bad job until the chickens became infested with mites. You haven't lived until you've had hundreds of microscopic chicken mites running up your arms. Forgetting the eggs, I'd go running into the house in a panic. Mom, who took things in stride, would simply get out the insecticide and sprayer and head for the chicken coop.

The chicken coop doubled as a pigpen. The smelly old sows were anything but cute, but the little pink baby pigs were adorable. I used to visit the pigpen a couple times a day just to watch as the piglets noisily tumbled around on top of one another, making little squealing sounds as they nudged and shoved and pushed their way to their mother's teats. Reaching their nipple (they nursed from the same teat until they were weaned), they sucked greedily, and when their little round tummies were full, they contentedly nestled together to sleep it off.

My friends and I loved to play in the haymow, even though we were told not to. Sometimes we'd jump out of the hay door (about eight feet), and other times we had a good time jumping and rolling around in the hay. The jumping stopped when I landed on a pitchfork that was buried in the hay. A tine stabbed into the side of my left leg, just below the knee. I didn't dare tell my parents how it happened because I knew that we weren't supposed to be in the hayloft. My guardian angel must have been with me because the puncture wound healed without any infection. It did leave me with an oblong scar about the size of a dime—a reminder of my childhood daredevil days.

When I was ten, I joined 4-H. This was not a new concept, given that 4-H groups go back to 1898, but our club was the first in our community. Logically, I should have been in a club that focused on sewing or foods, as raising cattle was not in my future, but this club, made up of farm kids, chose to have beef animals, and it sounded good to me. Furthermore, it hadn't been too long since we had lived on a farm, and my parents still had a few animals, so it was a natural choice. George Eckert was our leader, and Esther Anderson, Gwen's mother, was our associate leader. George was a lifelong cattleman and was managing the Eckert E-7 Ranch on which the family lived, and Esther, along with her husband Frank, owned the Stoney Ridge Shorthorn Ranch. Esther also had many years of office experience, so between the two of them, we had very competent leadership.

Gwen showing her 4-H Shorthorn steer at the Fair

The objective of 4-H, which is a national as well as international organization, is to develop youths to become responsible and productive citizens. Rooted in the rich tradition of American agriculture, 4-H originally focused on the development of skills in farming and homemaking. In order to link home life with school subjects of agriculture and home economics, Iowa county superintendent of schools, O. H. Benson, organized agricultural and home economics clubs, called "four-square education" in all the schools in the county. Benson liked to visit his rural schools. On one such visit, he found the teacher and students out searching for four-leaf clovers. Recognizing the superintendent, the teacher suggested that the children give their good-luck charms to their visitor. Accepting the clovers, Benson told the children that he had been looking for an emblem for the agricultural clubs and that they had just given it to him. From that day in 1911, this universally used emblem, which has a letter H on each leaf (thus the name 4-H) has been the membership badge for every 4-H member.

I was in 4-H for seven years, and each year I had a Hereford steer, which Dad bought from George. We still had our barn, but most of the time, my animal was staked in the yard, and during the summer, we'd move him to the schoolyard where the grass was mowed less frequently.

Showing my Hereford steer at the State Fair in Minot

I was a scrawny kid when I joined 4-H, and as my steer grew, it became increasingly hard to handle him, and more than once, he led me on a merry chase. Dad helped me halter break him, which was not an easy feat as he stubbornly insisted that a halter was not for him. Once he realized that we were just as stubborn, he gave in, and I was able to begin my daily routine of exercise and grooming. I had my toes stepped on several times and suffered many rope burns, but as I became more efficient in my handling, these things happened less and less.

Our monthly meetings, which were held in our homes, were opened with the 4-H pledge lead by our elected president:
"I pledge:
my Head to clearer thinking,
my Heart to greater loyalty,
my Hands to greater service, and
my Health to better living,
for my club, my community, and my country."

The business meeting was run according to Robert's Rules of Order, which all members were required to learn. Esther, with her knowledge of conducting business meetings, was our tutor. One year, I served as president, presiding over the meetings, and another year, I acted as secretary, recording things that we did and discussed during the meetings—all of which were the initial bricks in the foundation of my teaching career.

Every member was required to keep a record book which was signed monthly by our parents and 4-H leaders and turned in to the County Extension Agent at the end of the year. I disliked keeping that record book; it was a chore for me. However, after it was completed, it was fun to look back and see what I had accomplished. The records included things such as the initial cost of my steer, what and how much I fed him, how long it took to halter break him and how many hours I spent grooming. My final entry was to record the amount received from the sale of my animal, subtract all expenses and determine the profit. Even though I didn't like the daily recording stuff, this part I liked. It was exciting to see how my efforts had paid off.

Our meetings were more than business meetings; they were also social gatherings. Growing up in a rural area, we didn't have the social outlets that we do now, so it was a good way to meet people and have fun. While reminiscing about our 4-H days, Marilyn, who lived on the E7 Ranch, talked about how important our meetings were to her. "You lived in the 'city,'" she laughed, "so you got to see people." It was true; I did get to see people on a regular basis, but otherwise, my social outlets were as limited as hers.

4-H was fun, and the Minot State Fair, which later became the North Dakota State Fair, was the most fun of all. All the clubs in the county brought their animals, which would be shown and judged, and settled into the 4-H barn. Being next to the door was the most desirable spot, and we all tried to be the first ones there to claim it. Our club got it more often than not. Maybe we were just lucky, but I think it could have had something to do with the fact that George had shown cattle at the fair for many years and knew his way around. We'd claim our spot by hanging our green and white "Foxholm Better Beef" banner above our area and then smugly greet the other clubs as they settled in around us.

We stayed at the fair all week. It was the first time some of us had ever been away from home on our own for that length of time. We were a little scared and yet excited. We slept on cots and ate our meals in a barracks-type building. I know we had a curfew, but even with no one hovering over us, no one ever broke it. We understood the rule and automatically abided by it. Sometimes we went to the midway after supper, but we always seemed to end up back at the barns where we were sure to meet up with friends.

Bright and early, before breakfast, we washed up, ran a comb through our hair and dashed off to the barn to take care of our animals.

Foxholm Better Beef 4-H Club members at Minot State Fair (L.to R.)
Donny Eckert, Art Rademacher, Robert Laumb, Bud Harmon, Julius
Schaan, Gwen Anderson, and leaders Esther Anderson and George
Eckert

We spent the entire day in the barns going back to the barracks
only for our meals and bedtime. Every day, we cleaned the stalls and
put in fresh straw, and every day we led our animals out in back of the
barns, exercised them and gave them a soapy bath. Using a brush, we
scrubbed every inch, from their heads to their hoofs, and then, using
a hose, we rinsed them several times so their coats would be squeaky
clean and shiny. Many times, someone was "accidentally" sprayed, and
then a water fight was on. The water fights were great fun, but they were
hard on hairdos, especially since there were no hairdryers or curling
irons.

After washing our steers, we groomed them with a brush and curry
comb. To comb the tail, we used a scotch comb. The bushier we could
get it, the better. Since we had no hair spray to keep it stiff and bushy,
we just hoped for the best. We also hoped he wouldn't have a shot of
diarrhea right after we finished.

Striving "To make the best better," as our motto indicated, took hard
work, but we always found time to have fun with the other 4-H kids,
and lasting friendships were made, especially with the Des Lacs Star

Beef kids. Vern Stevick, a Star Beef member, became a good friend of mine, and Marilyn's sister Joyce met her future husband, Bruce Martin, another Star Beef kid, through 4-H. Darrell Sundsbak, Vern and Bruce's buddy, was another popular 4-H'er. (I think every girl in the barn had a crush on him, including me.) Darrell had Black Angus cattle, and one year, his steer had a liking for marshmallows. Watching that black tongue roll out and wrap around the white fluffy treats was comical to see, and often there was a group of kids standing around his stall. I remember buying Campfire Marshmallows, when I got home from the fair and sending them "to the steer" in care of Darrell. (I saw Darrell a couple years ago. He remembered my gift of marshmallows, and we had a good laugh.) Marshmallows, back then, came in a little white box that was covered with a blue and white waxed paper with Campfire Marshmallows lettered in red. There was a layer of waxed paper between the marshmallows, which were softer and stickier than today's, and there was always some white sweet powder in the bottom of the box.

One year, Darrell brought a heifer to the fair, and during the week, she had a baby calf, which caused quite a stir in the barn. One night, our leader and mentor, with the help of Bruce and maybe Vern, snuck the calf and hid it in another barn. When Darrell came into the barn the next morning, his calf was nowhere to be seen. One can only imagine the anxiety he went through before the pranksters, laughing like fools, returned the bawling baby to his mother and agitated owner. Knowing Darrell, I'm sure he immediately began to plot his revenge.

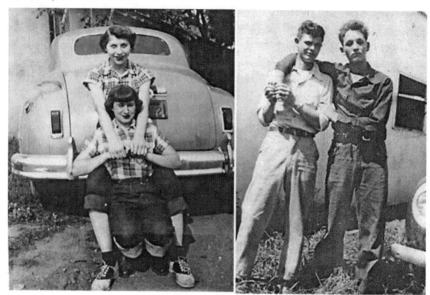

Marilyn Eckert and I and Des Lacs Star Beef members, Darrell Sundsbak and Vern Stevick at the 4-H Barn during the State Fair in Minot

For the judging, we had to train our animals to respond to our commands: how to walk, stop and be set up easily and quickly, which included feet placement. I used hand movements on a halter to do this, but some also used a show stick. When the judges got to us, we held our breaths, praying that our steer would behave and make a good showing. I never did win a purple ribbon, the grand daddy of them all, but I went home with a few blue ribbons which made me proud.

On 4-H Day, we spruced up our animals, attached our ribbons to their halters and paraded them in front of the crowded grandstand. I was always nervous; it wasn't easy keeping a thousand-pound steer under control in the midst of all the noise, people and chaos. I remember the time Darlene's steer spooked and got away from her. Her brother Artie was there to help catch him, but it was a traumatic experience for her—one that she remembers to this day.

It was back to the fair grounds for the Fall Roundup, the culmination of the year for all 4-H'ers, and the time when our steers would be sold. All projects, including our steers, were judged and awarded ribbons. Before the sale, cattle buyers appraised each animal, and it was at this appraised price that the bidding began. Business people from Minot and the surrounding area bought the animals as a community goodwill gesture. With the auctioneer's unique lingo ringing in our ears, we led our steers around the sales ring, trying to remember everything we learned to make one last, good showing. With a sharp rap of the gavel and resounding "Sold!" from the auctioneer, it was all over for another year. I remember the excitement I felt when I was given my check. I also remember trying to hide my tears as I turned and walked quickly away.

Today, when Ray and I attend the State Fair in Hutchinson, our first stop is the cattle barns. When I enter the barns, I am overwhelmed with familiar scents which trigger a wave of nostalgia; I'm fourteen again, back in the 4-H Barn at the Minot State Fair. I shut my eyes and see George, our leader, sitting on a bale of hay by the door, cowboy hat at a jaunty angle, western boots showing signs of mucking out stalls and, as always, his infectious grin. I see our 4-H steers with their carefully groomed tails lazily swishing away the pestering flies and hear the sound of adolescent laughter echoing throughout the barn.

Eventually, the cows were sold, and the barn was torn down and replaced with a garage. Dad did keep the sheep, a few pigs for butchering and the chickens, which provided fresh eggs and Sunday dinners. Mom was the one who killed the chickens, but Toots was the one who caught them. All Mom had to do was to point out the chicken she wanted and Toots would chase it, weaving in and out among the other chickens, until she ran it down, and then held it between her front paws until Mom got there to ring its neck. By rights, it should have caused her to kill chickens, but she never did. She was, indeed, a special dog.

Mom still had the sheep, which continued to pay their way by keeping down the weeds on the riverbank, when Ray and I and our little boys lived with her. One rainy, miserably cold spring day, a ewe gave birth to twins. The mother, as ewes will do sometimes, refused to take the smaller one. Mom wrapped the cold, wet "bum" lamb in a warm blanket, and laid him in a cardboard box, which she put on the bathroom floor register. Mom had gone to open the bar, and I, busy with the house and kids, forgot all about the little orphan. Suddenly, I heard a "Baa!" and out wobbled the tiny lamb. From that moment on, Baby was a member of the family, and I became her caretaker. I warmed the milk, and instead of using a bottle with a nipple, I encouraged her to drink by putting my hand into the milk and letting her suck on my finger. "Sluuurp!" The milk slowly disappeared. The lamb flourished like no lamb ever had, and before we knew it, our scrawny little bum lamb had become a big, fat, contented sheep and was still sucking on my finger. One day it dawned on me, "Why am I still feeding this big lug?" From then on, Baby was on her own.

My little boys Jack, Mike and Jeff

Summertime came, and the boys were forever in and out of the house, and many times, the screen door was left ajar. More than once, when I turned around, there would be three full-grown sheep, Baby and her pals, George and Charlie, standing in the middle of the kitchen, looking at me as if to say, "Well, here we are."

The phone rang one day, and our neighbor, Madeline Larson, who lived across the highway and down the road a little way, called to tell me that the sheep, all ten of them, were near her house. I grabbed a little bucket of grain and hurried down the road calling, "Come, Baby; come, Baby." Up came her head, and she immediately made her way toward me. Soon we were all headed home, Baby following me and the others trailing along behind. Later Madeline, who had been watching the entire episode, laughingly commented that our sheep minded better then her kids. I could have added a similar comment.

Jack was about three when we had those sheep. He loved to play outside, and every time he went out, one frisky young buck would come up behind him and give him a playful butt, knocking him to the ground. Finally, Jack got smart. From then on, whenever he went outside, he'd put on his floppy, old hat and grab for his plastic bat. It didn't take long for the mischievous sheep to get the message. A couple good whacks over the head cured him, and Jack continued to play happily.

Mom kept the sheep for a long time, but slowly, they began to shrink in number. Some were sold, and at least two died. Baby's buddies, George and Charlie, got into the corn and over-ate, causing severe bloating. Mom treated them with a shot of Peppermint Schnapps, one of her favorite home remedies, but she couldn't save them. "Well," she quipped, "at least they went happy."

When the sheep left in the 1970's, the last visible trace of the farm went with them; there were no more animals, the chicken coop was empty, the black cast-iron butchering kettle lay forgotten in the trees, and even the garden spot lay fallow. Change is many times hard and always inevitable, but my mother never dwelled on such things. She lived in the present and planned for the future up to the very end.

School Days

Foxholm School-home of happy memories

I was six years old in 1939 and couldn't wait to start school. I was ready. After having kids at home for twenty-two years straight, I'm sure my mother was also ready for me to go. The only one who wasn't happy was my dog, Toots.

I had been an "afterthought." Actually, I had been given no thought at all; I was a complete surprise. It's not that all my siblings weren't surprises, you understand. None of us were planned or unplanned; we all came when we came, but after six years of no babies, Mom and Dad had thought their family was complete.

Everyone else was in school by the time I came along, which left me at home with only Toots for a playmate. We were inseparable and drove my mother to distraction with all our noisy shenanigans. Therefore, when I abandoned her each morning, Toots was mad. In a fit of anger, she chewed a pair of my shoes to bits. Mom convinced her that it was not the thing to do, and after pouting a few days, she finally accepted the inevitable

Montez Sanders, who lived several miles from town, was staying with us and going to high school. It was not uncommon for farm kids to do this. Montez was an experienced seamstress, and one day when Mom went to town, she gave Montez the job of stitching up the red dress that she had cut out for my first day of school. For some reason, Montez couldn't find the pattern, and she screwed up while sewing it. Mom wasn't too happy with the goof-up, and Montez wasn't too happy that she didn't have the pattern. At any rate, she wasn't asked to redo it, and no one remembers whether or not it was ever finished. I like to think that Mom did finish it and that I wore it proudly as I excitedly entered my new world.

Our school had four classrooms and a science lab. For many years, all the classrooms were utilized. By the time I started school, enrollment warranted only two classrooms, one for high school and one for the lower grades. In essence, I spent my primary years in a one-room school.

My first grade teacher was Mrs. Tate. Her husband, Tom, was teaching in the high school at that same time and was my brother Francis's teacher. Being a typical first grader, I thought Mrs. Tate, with her ready smile and warm hugs, was the nicest teacher in the whole world. I don't remember very much about that first year, but I do remember the list of vocabulary words that was posted in the back of the room. Phonics was not being taught at this time; memorization was the "in" thing. Memorizing was easy for me, and I quickly learned all the words. I can still recite part of that list: cow, cat, dog, was, were, hen, here, her. I loved learning to read. "Dick and Jane" opened a new world for me and began a lifelong love for books.

We had a very limited library in our school and none in our small town. The nearest library was in Minot, and no one that I knew, much less my parents, ever drove into town to go to a library. Using such a facility was not in Mom and Dad's experiences. In all probability, they had never been in a public library in their entire lives. I'm sure had I known enough to ask, Dad would have taken me, but no one ever suggested it. Consequently, I grew up without ever experiencing the wonders of a well-stocked library. However, having inherited my Grandpa Hoerter's love for reading, I eagerly devoured the books that were available to me.

First Grader progresses to Grade Two

In one corner of our classroom, there was a small light blue wooden table and four matching little chairs. In the center of the table sat a bright blue, rectangular tin box that held a set of colorful books. I loved those books and couldn't wait to finish my work so I could dig into them. One of my very favorites was Little Black Sambo. I reread it many times and never grew tired of it. Today that book is banned from public school libraries. They say it's racist; I say they're crazy.

I have one other memory from that first year of school. It's been sixty-five years, but I still remember the embarrassment I felt. I even remember where I was sitting in the classroom when it happened. I had waited too long to ask permission to leave the room, and as I raised my hand, I knew it was too late. I looked down, and there on the floor under my seat was a telltale puddle. I was mortified. I remember Mrs. Tate discretely taking me out of the room through the door, which luckily was close to my desk, but I don't remember if Mom came to get me or if Mrs. Tate waved her magic wand. At any rate, I did survive and went on to the second grade in spite of it all.

Margie Skarsgard and students

Marjorie Skarsgard, my second and third grade teacher, was young, had Little Orphan Annie curls and fat cheeks and wore round wire-rimmed glasses. Up to this point, we had only learned to print our letters. Now was the time to begin writing. (The word "cursive" was never used. Neither was "lower case.") We were taught the Palmer Method style of writing with all its characteristic curlicues, peaks and loops. Penmanship was taught in a class period much the same as spelling, and we received a letter grade. It was one class in which I always made an A. We also received a letter grade for Deportment (conduct), but for some reason, I never made more than a C. It seems I couldn't keep my mouth shut.

(L.to R.) lst row—Raymond Stack Frankie Lauinger, Clarence Christenson, Clayton Rostad 2nd row-Maurie Fuller, Kenny Harmon, Calvin Troxel, Glen Rostad 3rd row Ilene Rostad, Lois Karlsen, Evelyn DeGree, Marlyn Rostad, Donna Karlsen 4th row Gwen Anderson, Darlene Rademacher, Myrna, Rose Mary Lauinger, Clara Karlsen

Violet Houston from Burlington was my teacher for five consecutive years, the fourth though the eighth grade. While she was my teacher, Miss Houston married George Gorde from Foxholm and became Mrs. Gorde, a permanent resident of Foxholm.

Miss Violet Houston becomes Mrs. George Gorde

Darlene Rademacher, Clara Karlson, and Calvin Troxell were my classmates. Darlene and I remain close friends even though our lives took separate paths, but Clara and Calvin gradually drifted away, never to return, leaving us with only faded memories.

Clara was a whiz in school, and my competitive spirit continually spurred me to outdo her. She was part of a large, hardworking, protestant family who lived where the Keller family lives today. At times, she had to stay home from school to help with her younger siblings and rarely was she able to join us in play after school.

Clara's father Einar, a sharp-face little man, owned a small old truck with a wooden box that he used for his coal-hauling business. He'd pick up coal at the local mines and haul it to homes in the community. I can see him still as he putted along at a rousing thirty-five miles per hour. He'd hunch his back and lean towards the steering wheel, which he clutched with both hands. He wore his work cap pulled down low on his forehead with the bill all but covering his eyes, which stared straight ahead.

The Karlsons didn't socialize with the townspeople, but the times I went there to see Clara or to buy cream for Mom (They milked cows to supplement their income.), they always went out of their way to make me feel welcome. Many times when I came, Clara would be washing dishes in a dishpan with no running water and dirty pots and pans stacked two feet high. There she'd be, just scraping away on those stubborn pots with a single-edged razor blade. For some reason that bit of ingenuity impressed me, and to this day, Clara occasionally comes to mind when I'm scrubbing away on my own pots.

Instead of going to Carpio High when our two schools consolidated, Clara chose to attend Minot High, and after that, our paths seldom crossed. When her family moved to Oregon, our ties were completely severed.

I don't remember many details about Calvin except that he looked much like Dennis the Menace with glasses. He wore bib overalls, had sandy blonde hair that flopped down over his forehead and an infectious, mischievous grin that stretched all the way up to his chipmunk cheeks. He loved to tease his classmates, and as I think back, he probably did it in self-defense. I do remember that we liked Calvin, and most likely, we enjoyed the bantering more than he did. I haven't seen him in so many years, but I know I'd still recognize that smile.

Darlene is my second cousin, but better than that, she was, and still is, my very good friend. One of our notorious feats was our success at winning three-legged races, which were popular recess competitions. Both of us were very competitive and both tomboys, so this was right up our alley. The race required the couple to tie two of their legs together (We usually used a headscarf.), which left us to run on "three." We constantly worked to improve our speed and had our synchronized movements down pat, which proved to be a winning combination. Surely, our undefeated record remains unequaled.

Darlene's study habits were better than mine. The minute she got home from school, she sat down and did her homework, while I dilly-dallied around until after supper and then suffered through it when I would rather have listened to The Green Hornet. When I think of homework, arithmetic comes to mind. (The word math was never used.) It seemed like we had ten rows of long division or three-digit multiplication problems to do every night. The written problems were often skipped. We were so glad because word problems were much harder for us to figure out than multiplication or division problems. I had no algebra at all in the seventh or eighth grade and not even in my freshman and sophomore years. Years later, the lack of a good math foundation would come back to haunt me.

Lloyd Kluver was the principal of the school when we were in grade school. He had a daughter named Gladys who was a year younger than Darlene and me. There was constant friction between us. We thought that she was a brat who threw her weight around because she was the principal's daughter. One day at recess, something was said, and Gladys stuck out her tongue at us. I can still see it all so plainly. She raised her head defiantly, screwed up her chubby face, closed her eyes and stuck out her tongue as far as she could. Instinctively, Darlene raised her hand and slapped her across the face. Believe me; Gladys's tongue went in faster than it came out, and she ran into the school to her father even faster. The next thing we knew, Darlene and I were in the office, where each of us received a good swat on the seat of our pants, no explanations accepted. To add salt to our wounds, when we came out of the office, there stood Gladys with a big fat smirk on her face. If that wasn't enough, we had to sit in the high school room where he was teaching for the remaining recess period. Then, I had to face my mother when I got home. That was not one of my better school days.

Darlene married Bob Berry from Lone Tree, a neighboring town that had the distinction of being smaller than Foxholm, and moved to Sebeka, Minnesota where they continue to live. We drove through Minnesota recently and stopped in to see them. Had you been within four city blocks, you would have heard Darlene and I laughing over some of the crazy things we did way back when we still had all of our original body parts.

Memorizing poems was a big part of our language class. I was good at this, and it was easy for me to stand in front of the class and recite them. When I was in the fifth grade, we had to memorize "The Table and the Chair," a nonsensical poem by Edward Lear. I wrote the poem in a booklet form and drew a picture on the front cover which I remember very clearly—a table who appeared to be stressed out talking to a chair who seemed equally so. If you are familiar with the poem, you'll know that they are stressed "from the heat and from chilblains on my feet." I loved that poem, and to this day I remember every word of it. When I taught school, I acted it out for every class I ever had. The younger grades were mesmerized, and even my big eighth graders got a kick out of it.

We had art every Friday afternoon after recess. I looked forward to it. We never did anything creative or different, as Mrs. Gorde had no training in that area and no special art supplies, but I always enjoyed the things we did, however simple.

Some of my fondest and most vivid school memories are of the parties and programs that we had. Valentine's Day and the Christmas program were very important occasions, and our carnivals served a two-fold purpose.

Valentine's Day hasn't changed much over the years except, perhaps, for the cards themselves. We always had a big party with special treats and the exchange of valentines. We each made our own valentine box.

Some were elaborately decorated and some merely served the purpose. As you might guess, I worked hard on mine. I cut every red heart with great care and labored over pasting them in exactly the right place. Sometimes I added crepe paper ruffles. (Crepe paper, which came in two-inch rolls in all colors, was popular back then.) When I finished, I thought it was "Just perfect!" as my granddaughter Allie would say.

Writing out valentines was not an easy task. I would painstakingly go through all of them, searching for exactly the right one for each of my schoolmates. When the time finally came to open mine, I eagerly looked to see who had sent me a special one, which sometimes was a big surprise. I received many special valentines during those happy years, but none could compare with the one I received from Otto Stach.

Otto was one of the older boys, and I had a big second-grader's crush on him. He wore his hair parted in the middle, which made him look very sophisticated, and when he smiled, I compared him to Van Johnson, my very favorite movie star. He'd tease me and send me little notes that I thought surely must be love notes. He occasionally came to our house with my brothers, and sometimes they would play Monopoly. I remember sneaking him extra money when no one was looking. When I found his valentine in my box, I was thrilled to pieces. I just knew that I must be his special valentine. I nearly wore it out looking at it, so I remember it clearly. On the valentine was a smiling clown dressed in an orange clown suit that had a wide white collar, long full sleeves and baggy pants. He had Harpo Marx hair, wore a cone hat and held a large hoop through which a black Scotty dog was jumping. The verse said, "I would jump through hoops for you. Be my valentine."

Valentine's Day was great, but a teacher was not considered worth her salt unless she could produce a good Christmas program, which was the social highlight of the school year.

During the pre-World War II days, social events in rural North Dakota centered on family and community. Roads, vehicles and communication were a far cry from the norm of the twenty-first century. The narrow two-lane roads were mostly dirt or gravel, cars were not suited for the cold, snowy winters and there certainly were no cell phones to use in case of an emergency. Therefore, when an event such as the school's Christmas program was held, the entire community attended.

The Christmas festivity, which was held in the school gymnasium the night before the beginning of our two-week break, consisted of a program with recitations, singing of carols, a gift exchange, bags of candy and of course, Santa. A new holiday outfit was a must. Mom, no amateur when it came to sewing, always made mine. The most memorable was my eighth grade Christmas dress. It was a two-piece red corduroy suit with a straight skirt and a jacket with a peplum, which had four large round silver buttons down the front. With it, I wore silk stockings with seams (attached to a garter belt) and my new black patent leather shoes.

Besides the short recitations and singing, it was traditional to put on a play, which took a considerable amount of time. During the final days before the program, we practiced every day, all but forgetting our lessons, which delighted us to no end. Everyone participated. I could memorize quickly, and had a flair for acting; I loved it. I usually knew everyone's part and would coach the younger ones when they forgot a word. Doris Ann Schmitz was one of those younger ones, and I still hear her shyly reciting:

"I have some gay wed bells
All fastened to a stwing,
And if you don't believe it,
I'll let you hear them wing."

She then proceeded to "wing" the bells, which she clutched in her hands. I recently saw her when we were back in North Dakota, and I asked if she remembered that little Christmas program poem. I was disappointed and little surprised when she said, "No." How could she forget such a big, important thing that happened sixty years ago? After all, I remember it clearly.

Doris Ann Schmitz

When the program was over, Santa made his "surprise" entrance. Down the stairs he'd come with jiggling bells and a hardy "Ho-Ho-Ho." Even when we were old enough to know the difference, we still looked forward to his appearance. After distributing the candy which came in brown bags that were folded over on top (no staples in those days), he passed out gifts, which had been placed under the huge, gaily trimmed, fresh Christmas tree. (Artificial trees were a long time coming.) Names had been drawn so all the students received a gift. Teachers, highly respected, were also remembered with tokens of appreciation. Often Santa stayed long enough to mingle and have cake and coffee before disappearing into the night. His departure was a signal that the party was over and that this special evening would soon be just another of our cherished childhood memories.

All the small schools in our area had an annual carnival. Besides being another social event, carnivals were moneymaking projects. The proceeds went into a fund for things that the school budget didn't cover—playground equipment, classroom supplies and athletic equipment. (Our school's "athletic equipment" consisted of softballs and bats, basketballs and volleyballs.) The carnival was held in the gymnasium, on Johnny's polished gym floor. Volunteers and high school boys put up a wooden framework for the individual booths, and bed sheets or strips of white butcher paper were used to make the partitions.

The types of carnival games were very similar to those of today—baseball throw, fishpond, basketball toss, make-up booth, ring the bottle, dart throw, cakewalk, etc. Bingo, whose prizes local merchants donated, was a favorite of the older people, and one part of the gym was sectioned off for this purpose. The prizes for the carnival games were purchased in bulk from companies who sold such novelties. There was no handling of money. Tickets, valued at five cents each, were sold and used for all the activities.

The food and refreshments center was also a good moneymaker. Usually it was set up on the gym floor near the Bingo tables. Coney Islands, hot dogs with chili on top, were a favorite. This was a place for people to sit, visit and enjoy a piece of cake and coffee. These were the days before people worried about calories and cholesterol.

Another way of making money was the Carnival Queen competition. The community voted for their choice by donating money. Cans for the donations were decorated, labeled with the candidates' names and placed in the business places. The candidate who received the most money won the honor and was crowned during the carnival. When I was a second grader, my sister Evie, who was a senior, was chosen to be queen. Mom sewed a beautiful peach formal gown, and I knew she would be Foxholm's prettiest queen ever. All was in readiness. Her gown was finished, her jewelry chosen, her white shoes ready and her hair stylishly cut by Lillian, who owned Lillian's Beauty Shop in Minot. (Mom's haircut just wouldn't do for this special occasion.) The only thing that she lacked was a pair of silk stockings. A few days before the big day, Evie rode into Minot with a neighbor in his Model A Ford to shop for her stockings. On the way home, Mike lost control when he swerved to miss a deer that bounded onto the highway and crashed into the ditch, hitting a culvert. Evie received a huge gash in her leg and had to be rushed to the emergency room for multiple stitches. It was a traumatic experience that left her weak and unable to walk.

News of the accident spread quickly throughout the school. The teachers hurriedly met to discuss the dilemma. If the queen wasn't able to attend, should the coronation ceremony be cancelled? If not, what was the alternative? Finally, a decision was made. If Evie couldn't be there to accept the crown, she would still be the reigning queen, but I would take her place at the actual crowning ceremony. I felt sorry for my sister, but I was also excited. Mom hurriedly sewed me a new long dress that was very similar to the one she made for Evie. I practiced with the queen's court and knew just what to do. I felt a twinge of guilt when I thought of how sad and disappointed Evie would be, but it quickly vanished.

The day of the carnival finally arrived. I could hardly contain my excitement as I raced off to school. Right after our lunch hour, a high school teacher came to get me. Instead of the usual practice session, I was told that my sister had sent word that she was feeling well enough to take part in the crowning ceremony. Disappointment shot through me. My chance to be a queen was gone. (Eight years later I received my own crown and reigned over the carnival.) As it turned out, I was not forgotten.

That evening, dressed in her new gown and one silk stocking, Evie was carried onto the stage and placed on the queen's throne. Amid much applause, she was crowned Foxholm's Carnival Queen, and I was right there by her side in my new peach gown. They had given me the honor of carrying the crown, which I proudly placed on my sister's head.

Evie-Carnival Queen

Being in a one-room school setting proved to be beneficial in more ways than one. Some of the older boys taught us a lot. Dave Gorde was one of them.

Dave, three years older than I, was a big kid who had a large head, which earned him the nickname Jughead. He was easygoing and took the kidding in stride. Dave was smart. His vocabulary was such that one nearly had to take out a dictionary to understand what he was saying, but the talent that really impressed us was his ability to eat an apple, core and all, in just two bites or less. I can see him still; he'd take a good bite, and his cheeks would be pouched so full that he'd look like a chipmunk. After chomping away, he'd stuff in the other half, seeds and all. Every time he did this, we couldn't help but laugh, which is probably why he continued to do it.

Another crazy thing that Dave did was drink ink, or at least lead us to believe he did. There were no ballpoint pens; we used fountain pens that were filled from a bottle of ink. He'd open his bottle, tip it up and seemingly guzzle it down, and then he'd grin at us with blue teeth and mouth. We reacted with mock horror, of course, which made his day. Dave is now a retired dentist. I wonder if he ever thinks back on the "blue teeth days" of his youth. I have an idea that this was one stunt that his children would never have gotten away with.

Dave "Jughead" Gorde

Because we didn't have enough kids for two softball teams, we played a game called Work Up. The players started at certain positions, such as fielder or first base, and "worked ourselves up" to home plate. When the batter made an out, everyone would move up one position, and the batter had to go back to the field and start over. We'd barrel out of the school during our recesses and noon hour yelling, "Pitcher!", "Catcher!", "Batter!" (We also played this in the school yard at night, when we had even less kids.) The older boys were strong and could throw and run much better than the rest of us, but we girls weren't milquetoast, by any means, and through pure grit and determination, we became quite good in our own right. I was very competitive and would rather have died than duck one of those whizzing "bullets" and miss making an out. We had no ball gloves, and I got many black and blue marks proving my skill, or was it courage? Stupidity? Whatever it was, I loved every minute of it, black and blue marks and all and would do it all again in a heartbeat. Foxholm, like many small towns in our area, was never big enough to field a football team; therefore, basketball reigned. Foxholm had some pretty impressive teams in its day. When Evie was a senior in high school, her team took a State Championship.

We grew up with a basketball in our hands. Every chance we got, we scrimmaged, played Horse or just shot baskets. When I was a freshman, it took all of the girls we had to make up a team. For uniforms, we enlisted our mothers to sew the blue shorts that we wore with white blouses. One team that we played was a team from Minot High. I'm sure that big city team wondered what hills we hailed from when we came out in our homemade uniforms, but, when the game was over, we had earned their respect. We played on the basketball court as we did on the softball field—with great tenacity. When I recently visited Darlene, we were reminiscing about our basketball days and how good our little team had been. "We must have been good," she laughed. "When we got to that big school in Carpio, we were immediately on the starting lineup." (When our two schools consolidated, the high school enrollment was fifty-six.)

During the winter or when it was raining and we couldn't go out for recess, we played games in the gym such as Red Rover, which was a contact sport. The players formed two lines facing each another about ten feet apart. Each line would grip hands and take turns calling to the other side, "Red Rover, Red Rover, send Phillip (or Darlene or whoever) right over." The one called would begin a headlong rush for the other side. The goal was to break through the line by overpowering the kids' hold on each other. If Phillip broke through, he would choose one person from the opposing team to join his line. If he didn't break through, he had to become part of their team. They would keep alternating calling players until one team had all the people and became the winner.

Captain, May I was another game that we played. The players formed a line in front of the one who was it. "It" would tell each player in turn to move forward. "Evelyn, take one giant step," or "Gwen, take two baby steps." If the player moved before saying, "Captain, May I," he would lose a turn. The first one to get to "it," was the winner and became "it" for the next round.

I was only eight when The United States entered World War II, and even though I bought defense stamps in school with my dimes, which I pasted in a book and later redeemed for a war bond, I didn't fully understand the impact of it. I began to understand a lot better when the news came that Homer Johanness, our neighbor's son, had gone down with his ship, the Oklahoma. Two more young men from Foxholm were killed in action, Manfred Moe, husband of Lois Bly, and Francis Clouse, son of William and Julia Clouse. Francis served aboard the USN Hadley and was killed during the invasion of Okinawa and buried at sea. All of my brothers were serving in the South Pacific, and the fear I felt for their safety increased ten-fold with each of these deaths.

Teresa Mayhew, Evie's future sister-in-law, was the only woman from our town who served in the armed forces. She was in the Women's Army Corps (WAC), and I remember how awed I was when she came home in her uniform. She taught JoAnn Bock and I how to salute, let us march around wearing her hat and told us stories about her experiences. We were fascinated and decided then and there that we were going to join the service when we graduated from high school.

Darlene and I

When I graduated from the eighth grade in 1948, an eighth grade graduation was still a big community event. Donald Thorson, the Ward County Superintendent of Schools, was among the dignitaries who attended our commencement exercise, and it was he who introduced me when I gave my valedictory speech. I remember sitting on the stage, which was flanked by big bouquets of lilacs that bloomed profusely every spring, and how nervous I was until I actually reached the podium. I laugh recalling how I vowed that I was ready and willing to meet the challenges of tomorrow, when, being a typical fourteen-year old, I really had no concept of what those challenges might be. Being valedictorian in a class of four was small potatoes when compared to a class with any size, but it never occurred to me that it was no big deal. To me, it was a big deal, and I was very proud.

When I entered ninth grade, there were only a handful of students in the whole high school. It was obvious that changes were in the not too distant future.

Teresa Mayhew

The academic part of my freshman and sophomore years escapes me, but I do remember taking those dreaded state exams. The State Board of Education determined the course of study used by our teachers and the office of the Ward County Superintendent of Schools sent out the exams. Just the thought of having to pass state exams in order to advance to the next grade was very scary, but they certainly motivated us. Ardis Fuchs, a farm girl who stayed with us during the week, and I studied like mad when we knew they were coming up.

Esther Pike from Minot, a teacher in our school, also roomed with us during the winter months. With the roads and cars being what they were, seventeen miles in wintry weather was a long way to travel.

Mrs. Pike was unforgettable. She was intelligent, witty and stylish in her own way, and she had a knack for story telling. She could make cleaning toilets sound like an enviable adventure.

Mrs. Pike was short in stature with a thick upper body and thin legs. She had a rather large face with great cheekbones that were dusted with sandy freckles and a unique jaw structure not unlike a walleye. False teeth made the unusual shape even more prominent.

Mrs. Pike took pride in her appearance. She wore her hair in an upsweep, and on the top of her head was a pile of curls, haphazardly anchored with bobby pins. She also had a complete set of Merle Norman cosmetics, including powder that was mixed especially for her, and she used it religiously every day. I was so impressed—powder mixed just for her! I can still see her standing in the kitchen in front of the mirror on the medicine cabinet carefully applying each cosmetic and then giving her orange-rouged cheeks one last generous fluff with her powder puff. Imagine, powder mixed especially for her! (My mother used Ponds Cold Cream, Blue Waltz powder, Maybelline lipstick and a generic rouge, all purchased at Woolworth's.)

In those days, teachers always dressed up for school, and slacks were definitely not allowed. Mrs. Pike often wore a tailored suit. I can still see her as she went from our house into the adjoining schoolyard. She walked slightly hunched forward, took short, quick steps, and always had her large pocketbook tucked securely under her arm.

Teachers were highly respected, and it was understood that they would act appropriately. When Mrs. Pike was with us in the evening, things were more relaxed, but we were still very aware that she was a teacher in our school, and I'm sure she was, too. Still, suppertime at our house was very relaxed, and comfortable conversation flowed freely. I remember the night Mom made vegetable soup and Mrs. Pike had just taken a big spoonful when Mom, always a card, said something that tickled her. She busted out laughing, spewing vegetables in all directions and nearly losing her false teeth. Taken by surprise, we all busted out laughing, including poor embarrassed Mrs. Pike.

Mrs. Pike and her husband Clarence had only one son. She spoke proudly of his accomplishments, including his job of writing for The Stars and Stripes while serving in World War II. With our limited exposure to things outside our immediate area, we didn't fully understand or appreciate those accomplishments. Some fifty years later, I realized that Mrs. Pike did, indeed, have reason to feel proud of her son.

Douglas, her son, who died in 2002 at age seventy-seven, was one of the nation's leading Vietnam scholars. He compiled over seven million pages of documents on the country, in addition to writing eight novels and hundreds of articles on the Viet Cong and Southeast Asia. He had accrued the largest non-governmental archive of material about the Vietnam War, which is still used as a resource for diplomats, journalists and academics. Sadly enough, having died in 1953 of a lingering illness, Mrs. Pike didn't live long enough to see all of his prestigious accomplishments.

In the spring of our freshman year, all eight of us high school students along with our principal, Oscar Anderson, and the other high school teacher, Mrs. Peterson, went on a "skip day" to Bismarck. I had only been that far from home on one other occasion—a 4-H trip to Williston earlier that same year. I feel quite sure that the rest had about as much travel experience as I did, so you can imagine our anticipation. We toured the new, impressive state capitol building, which is known as the "Sky Scraper of the Prairie." (The old capitol building burned in 1930 and was rebuilt in 1934.) It had nineteen stories, and I remember the thrill of riding in the elevator all the way to the top floor. (The only elevator I had ever ridden in was the one in Ellison's Department Store in Minot. An elevator attendant manually opened and closed the door and then spirited the patrons to the upper level, one story up.)

We also visited the State Penitentiary in Bismarck. To this day, I can hear the sound of that heavy iron prison door as it slammed shut behind us and feel the eeriness that permeated the secured area. As we nervously walked down the long corridor with our guide, fierce-looking inmates clutching the bars like gorillas leered at us as we passed their cells. I imagined them ripping apart the bars and attacking us all. It was a relief when the tour was completed and we, once again, heard the heavy door slamming shut behind us. Had I been on the road to becoming a juvenile delinquent, believe me, this experience would have straightened me out in a hurry.

Another highlight of our day was an airplane ride over the city of Bismarck. Mr. Anderson had arranged for each of us to have a short ride in a small, two-passenger plane. Twenty years later I boarded a commercial plane in Denver for my second flight. I have to admit that I was nervous and even excited, but it couldn't compare to that memorable ten-minute ride during our school trip to the capitol city.

We went to Carpio for our last two years of high school. Carpio's school burned in its entirety shortly before the consolidation of our schools, and a new building was in the process of being built. In the meantime, the old hotel building was utilized, as were the fire hall and the town hall building.

The hotel building was the main school facility. The seventh and eighth grade classrooms were on one side of the building, and the high school rooms were on the other. The superintendent, Tom Bosworth, and his family lived in the apartment upstairs.

The fifty-six high school students were confined to only two rooms, and one was half the size of the other. To help alleviate the overcrowding, classes were held next door in the fire hall which housed the volunteer fire department's fire trucks. (My typing class was in that building. I could have reached out and touched the fire truck as I typed.) Bathroom facilities were limited to one indoor chemical toilet, which was used mostly by the faculty. We students were asked to use the outhouse behind the building except in the most inclement weather.

The old town hall building, located several blocks from the school, was used for basketball, school plays, school dances and all other extracurricular activities. It consisted of a gym floor, stage, small balcony and a small room off the entryway. There was no running water and, therefore, no bathroom facilities. (There was one unheated, two-hole, indoor-outhouse.) The gym floor was much smaller than today's gymnasiums. The ceiling was so low that when shooting, the ball would sometimes hit the lights. Platforms, that were raised about two inches off the floor, lined both sides of the gym floor. It was just wide enough to accommodate a single row of folding chairs that were lined up on this elevated section. The out-of-bounds lines for the basketball court were painted directly in front of this platform which resulted in occasional spectator participation. We cheerleaders had no place to lead the cheers except on the basketball court when the ball was not in play.

Basketball team (L. to R.) Delores Erickson, Leona Lemke, Myrna, Darlene Rademacher, Betty Lemke, Phyllis Dahle and Coach Patterson's sister Helen Haaland in front of the Town Hall gym.

Girls' basketball was big during this time, and I lived for our games. I was a scrapper and what I lacked in skill, I made up for with pure grit and determination.

I was always too nervous to eat before a game, but once on that court, all butterflies were gone. I was a forward, and because I was tall and springy, I jumped center and many times got the tip. Darlene, a strong athlete, was usually waiting to receive it, and away we'd go.

Huddle during tournament game in Stanley. Two of our players
injured...we lost.

Unlike today, our basketball was played with a team consisting of
six players—three guards and three forwards. We played on half of the
court—three guards on one side of the centerline and three forwards
on the other. Neither the guard nor the forwards could cross the line,
and only the forwards could shoot. We were not allowed to take more
than one bounce to move the ball down the court. Later, the rules were
changed allowing us to take two bounces when dribbling the ball. The
reasoning behind these absurd rules was that it would be too strenuous
for girls to dribble the length of the floor as did the boys. Another rule
stated that no one could reach in and touch the ball when it was in
possession of a player. Any slapping or stealing of the ball resulted in
a personal foul. Our coach was Fern Patterson, the seventh and eighth
grade teacher, and her husband Girdell was her unofficial assistant. Our
practices and pre-game warm-ups consisted of us running the length of
the floor a few times, scrimmaging and doing basket-shooting drills—a
far cry from the intensive training and warm-ups today's athletes are
trained to do.

Coach Fern Patterson and "Assistant Coach" Girdell

Basketball team at tournament in Newburg (stayed in private home)
(L.to R.) Verna Burner, Judy Cunningham, Darlene Rademacher,
Betty Lemke, Myrna and Leona Lemke. Lost in final game 16-14.

Carpio Carnival Queen Judy Cunningham and her court
(L. to R.) Clarice Sandberg, Elaine Sandberg , Queen Judy, Gloria
Carson and Margaret Anderson

Carpio is ten miles from Foxholm. In 1949, that was a very long way. Daily commuting was not even considered; we would stay in Carpio during the week and go home on weekends. Marilyn Eckert and I rented a room in the home of a widow by the name of Mrs. Skarsbo. It was not a match made in heaven. We used too much water and too much toilet tissue. We were highly indignant because, after all, we had paid for it. We made too much noise climbing the stairs to our room, and we slammed the door when we got there. Everything we did irritated her. Miserable, we left after a couple months and lived happily in the Francis Hansen home for the reminder of the school year.

During my senior year of high school, Darlene and I rented an upstairs room in Helen Asbe's home. She was not our housemother. We had no curfew and were not supervised, and yet, we never skipped school nor were we ever late. Our responsibility was understood, and it never occurred to us to act differently.

Our stay with Mrs. Asbe was a test of endurance. Our room was so small that there was only room for a tiny table and two chairs, one washstand, which held a washbasin and water pail complete with a dipper, and a three-quarter-size bed. There was no chest of drawers and no closet and only a few hooks to use for hanging garments. We kept our underwear in our suitcases, which we stuffed under the bed.

Our wardrobe was simple. Basically, we wore blue jeans that we rolled up three turns, black and white saddle shoes and white anklets, white short-sleeved blouses and our cardinal red sweater with black letters. When we cooked, which we did every evening, we used a hot plate that we placed on the table. During the winter months, the room was so cold that the water froze in the pail, the floor so cold that we had to sit on the bed to prevent frostbitten toes and the window so heavily covered with frost that we could barely see out. Needless to say, we didn't need a refrigerator. We simply put our perishables out in the hallway at the top of the stairs. Finally, our parents bought us a small oil space heater. Darlene's dad, a farmer, brought a small barrel from the farm, set it up in the back yard, and filled it with fuel oil. It was our responsibility to keep our heater filled. (It was a wonder that we didn't burn down the house.) I remember the time Darlene was filling the can and the hose on the tank got away from her, spraying fuel oil all over her brown winter coat. Her parents had no telephone, and Darlene had to call a neighbor to get word to them that she needed another coat. (I remember her new coat very well. It was a fashionable maroon quilted storm coat with a tie belt and a mouton "fur" collar. I was so envious.) We had no indoor bathroom and had to use the outhouse in the back yard. During the cold winter months, we used a slop jar that sat out in the hall and then fought over whose turn it was to empty it.

It was customary for the seniors to go on a senior skip day. We felt so fortunate to be able to travel to the Twin Cities, St. Paul and Minneapolis. Tom Rossiaky and Orville Schultz were our chaperones and drivers. It was here that I saw my first television, which was on display at the Home Show. We had such fun, saw and did so many things that we had never experienced (I saw my first armored car and ate my first spaghetti.), but loving to dance as I did, the one thing that I enjoyed the most was the Prom Ball Room where we danced to Frankie Carl and his orchestra. As an added bonus, we saw the Andrew Sisters, a singing group who were popular at that time. It was an unforgettable experience.

Class of 1951

Carpio High "Fire Hall" Graduates

Class of '51 fifty years later

We had no counselors in high school to advise us. Therefore, after graduating in 1951, I had no idea of what I wanted to do. During the summer, a recruiter from the Minot Business College came into my mother's café and convinced me to enter their program. In September, both Darlene and I became business school students. Darlene only lasted a few weeks, but I didn't come to my senses for nine months and even then not without the urging of my brother Ralph who witnessed the tearing of hair and gnashing of teeth that I went through daily. I then enrolled at Minot State Teachers' College and found my niche in life. I also found my lifelong friend, Kathy Kremer.

Two days before I entered MST, I turned my head and hit the bone above my left eye brow on the tall refrigerator in my mother's café. A bump the size of a chicken egg immediately appeared and signs of a possible black eye emerged. Being my first experience as such, I didn't realize that this was just the beginning. On Monday morning, I had the blackest eye—then purple, then green, and finally, yellow—you've ever seen plus a very bloodshot eyeball. This was the topic of a future A+ paper, "A Green Freshman with a Black Eye." I found out later that I was known as "the one with the black eye." ("Do you know Myrna Miller? You know—the one with the black eye.") It was not exactly the ideal way for a nervous college freshman to make her debut, but I must admit, I did stand out among the six hundred students.

There's a very good chance that my infamous black eye saved my life. There was a dance in the neighboring town of Donnybrook the night I hit my eye. Don Jensen, a young college guy and friend of Dave Gorde's, was on his way to the dance and had stopped at Dad's bar to pick him up. Dave was a little late because he had been harvesting with his dad all day, but they still played a game of whist with my brother Ralph and his partner before heading out to the dance. As they were leaving, Dave invited me to go with them. Under normal circumstances, I would never have turned down a chance to go dancing, but I had that huge, angry, still-throbbing bump on my eye, so I declined. On their way to Donnybrook, a car came out from a side road and crashed into them. Don was killed on impact, and Dave, who was thrown from the car, was gravely injured. No doubt, I would have been sitting between the two, which would have afforded me little chance of survival. Ralph had left before I made the decision not to go, so you can imagine his fright the next morning when he heard on the six o'clock news that someone (The name had not yet been released.) had been killed the night before in a fiery car accident on Highway 52, near Donnybrook.

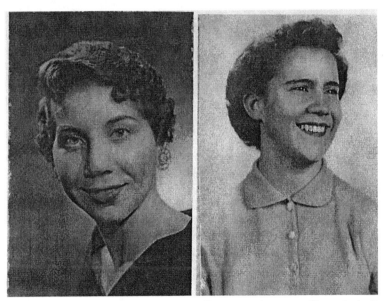

Myrna Miller and Kathy Kremer, college graduates, off to their first teachings jobs in Crosby, N. Dak.

I completed my two-year Standard Teaching Certificate in 1954 and made my way with Kathy to Crosby, North Dakota, where we began our career in teaching. I taught sixth grade, and it's amazing that I didn't quit teaching after that first year. Out of thirty-six students, one-fourth of them had been retained at one time or another. I now realize that one of my students had a classic learning disability, but at the time, such students were not identified and, therefore, did not receive the special help that they so desperately needed.

Danny was a handsome, young boy, already two years older than his classmates. He couldn't read, and looking back, I'm sure he had other processing problems, as well. In order to survive, Danny had adopted a nonchalant "I don't care" attitude, but it didn't take a specialist to see that this was only a cover-up. My heart went out to him, but try as I may; he needed more than a regular classroom teacher with thirty-five other students could give. He dropped out of school as soon as he could and fell in with the wrong crowd. The last I heard, he was serving time in prison.

I never forgot that experience with Danny. Thirty-five years later, I attended Wichita State University in Kansas where I took courses in special education while getting my Bachelor of Arts degree. It was too late to help Danny, but hopefully, I have helped others like him realize their potential and go on to live productive lives.

After our first year of teaching, Kathy married Bob Steen, traded teaching for motherhood and settled down in Crosby. I went on to Williston, North Dakota where I taught sixth grade for the next four years. One of my students was a long and lanky kid who loved to shoot hoops at recess time. I was playing on a city basketball league at that time, so I often shot baskets with him and the other kids. This young man's name was Phil Jackson, and he played college basketball at the University of North Dakota and went on to play professionally with the New York Knicks. During Phil's coaching career, he coached the Chicago Bulls to six NBA titles. He retired after being coach of the year in 1997 and returned in 1999 to coach the Los Angeles Lakers to three more NBA titles. After reading his book, "Sacred Hoops" and watching the Lakers win another NBA title; I wrote him a note of congratulations. I was surprised to receive a personal handwritten thank-you note, which included reminiscences about being my sixth-grade student.

I met Ray when I was teaching in Williston. Once again, I was dancing at the American Legion Club when a fellow asked me to dance. He introduced himself as Archie Bartosh and said that he was in town working on a Mobil Oil seismograph crew. During the waltz, he asked where I was from and I told him Minot and then corrected myself by saying, "Well, actually I'm from a town near Minot, but it's so small that you wouldn't have heard of it." "What small town?" he persisted. When I told him Foxholm, a look of amazement crossed his face. "I work with a woman named Val who's from Foxholm," he said. I knew everyone in and around my hometown and told him quite emphatically that he must be mistaken because there was no one by that name. When he kept insisting, it finally dawned on me that he was talking about

Valetta Ahmann, who had married Ken Tate, an engineer with Mobil Oil. The very next dance, Archie's buddy and co-worker, Ray, curious to meet someone who knew Val came and asked me to dance. That was the beginning of our forty-eight-years-and-still-blooming romance. We married in June of 1958 and moved to Sheridan, Wyoming where I substituted in the rural schools. When our first son, Mike, was born, I quit teaching full time, and worked as a long-term substitute at Washington Grade School in Minot and then as Mike's kindergarten teacher in Carpio. When Mike was in the first grade, we began our gypsy life with the Boeing Company. Traveling to the different Air Force missile bases in the Midwest, we moved twenty-three times in twenty years, making it impossible for me to continue teaching.

Ray and I meet

...and marry on June 30, 1958 in St. Mary's Catholic Church in Foxholm

...and 48 years later

In 1980, Ray was transferred by Boeing to Wichita, Kansas, and we moved to Derby. With my last two boys in school, I went back to substituting. Having only my two-year associate degree, I could not sign a contract for a regular teaching position, so when the teacher I was subbing for decided not to return; I was unable to apply for the job. When I left, the principal said, "When are you going back to school so I can hire you?" It was the push I needed. I gathered up all my courage (It took every ounce I had.) and enrolled in Wichita State University. Entering college at the junior level after a thirty-one-year-hiatus was not easy; it was rewarding, but definitely not easy. However, I had two good study buddies—a strawberry blonde and a black, both twenty-one years old. Together we waded through. I graduated with honors two years later and couldn't have been more proud. True to his word, the principal at the middle school called and offered me a teaching position. I happily accepted and taught eighth grade social studies until I retired in 1995.

Back to college and studying….and studying

I did it! WSU Graduate at age 54

The Borger Family

P.P. Borgers, Foxholm's longtime rural mail carrier, lived at the Cashman Hotel. His wife and family lived in the family home, just down the road from our house. To my knowledge, the cause of the estrangement was unknown which, in a town where everyone knew the name of every dog in town and could recite people's license tag numbers from memory, this had to be the favorite dinner topic for sometime.

The Borger Family basically kept to themselves. They never invited any of their neighbors to their home, nor did they go out to visit. Their religious beliefs were different from anyone in town, so they didn't even have that common bond with the community. They were not unfriendly; they just chose not to mingle socially with one exception. Bill and Franceen Glick were their next-door neighbors, and friendly Franceen loved to mingle and was good at it, so mingle she did. Delia, one of the Borger girls, and she became friends. Not shopping or coffee buddies but comfortable neighbor friends.

Mr. Borgers was known to be highly intelligent (It was rumored that he was rewriting the Bible.) but not always the smartest. Jack Pritschet had a good laugh when he recalled the story about his brother Frank and a couple of other teenagers (most likely my brother Alvin) going to the hotel to ask Mr. Borgers for help solving a difficult math problem. Mr. Borgers obviously was an aficionado of alarm clocks as he had many of them sitting around in his room. While he was helping them, one of the boys set each alarm to go off at a different hour. The next day, Mr. Borgers was heard telling about the weird experience he had had the previous night. With a mystified expression on his face, he explained how all his alarm clocks had gone off intermittently throughout the entire night.

Even though Mr. Borgers didn't live at home, his role in the family remained unchanged. Daily, he returned to help with the farm chores, which included caring for the many cows that had to be milked—come rain or shine, hell or high water—every morning and night. As did other farmers, they sold milk and cream to supplement their income. In addition, they farmed, and son Roy, an auto mechanic, had an auto repair business in the back yard.

Occasionally, Mom would send me down to their house with a quart jar to buy cream, which was always thick and rich, just what Mom needed for her caramel rolls. (It was also very good on bread with brown sugar sprinkled on top.) The hand-cranked DeLaval separator, which took a strong arm and endurance to run, sat in the entryway of the kitchen, which most likely accounted for the smell of sour milk that lingered in their house. The separator, which worked on centrifugal force, was used to separate the cream from the milk. The machine consisted of a large bowl, two long spouts and two round discs on which to set milk pails. The milk was poured into the bowl at the top of the machine. A pail was placed under each spout, and as the crank was turned, the cream magically (as far as I was concerned) ran into one pail and the milk in the other.

Delia most often filled my quart jar. I remember her as a pleasant young woman who wore no make-up, matronly flowered housedresses and serviceable brown oxfords. She wore her reddish-blonde hair in two fat braids, which she carefully wound over her ears. (I remember wondering how she could hear with all that hair over her ears.) The thing I remember the best about Delia, though, was her laugh, almost a nervous laugh, as I recall. Her conversations were peppered with them, and whenever she laughed, her nose (with its freckles) would wrinkle up, which made me think of a bulldog. It never failed to tickle me, and I'd laugh right along with her.

Delia wrote the Foxholm news for the *Ward County Independent* for quite some time. The news consisted mostly of reports of day-to-day activities, such as "Mr. and Mrs. Balzer Stach motored into Minot where they spent the afternoon shopping...." How she came by all this news, which she reported with surprising accuracy, was a mystery considering she was so seldom seen about town, but evidently she had her pipeline because no one ever sued her for slander.

Roy moved his business uptown to a large garage next door to Dad's bar. He was a nice, quiet man who met Catherine, Father Kopp's housekeeper, turned Catholic (which probably curled a few toes) and married her. It was an unlikely match, to say the least, but a good one.

After their marriage, Roy sold the garage, and they moved to Minot where he resumed his mechanic work with his brother Paul, and the lovely Katherine became a sales lady at Ellison's Department Store.

Clyde, another of the Borger brothers, was our postmaster for several years. (This was years after his father retired from his postal job.) The post office was housed in the grocery store of which he took possession when he became postmaster. Therefore, in addition to being the postmaster, he was also a storekeeper. Clyde was an intelligent man of few words, but if he did become engaged in a conversation, he made well thought-out, concise statements that were not open to discussion. He did have one vice that was well suited to him—chess. He and Freddie Sauer played the game of skill for hours on end (Neither it nor the post office kept him too busy.) without saying more than two words between them.

Mr. Borgers moved back home when the hotel closed, and there he stayed until he passed away. The family home is now empty, the barn silent, the garden neglected. Time has taken its toll.

Lauingers

Annie and Mike Lauinger and their children, Rose Mary, who was a year older than I, and Frankie, who was a year younger, were part of my "Foxholm family" when I was growing up. Mike and Annie were not original Foxholmites. Both were raised in German communities near Anamoose, North Dakota. Mike knew Boss Stach because of their German heritage ties, and a job opportunity drew them to Foxholm where he worked on the section crew with Boss.

Mike was a character, especially when he had a few beers. You always heard his laugh before you saw him. It was very loud, very distinctive and made a person want to laugh with him. Mike would have fit very nicely into a character role for the movies. He was not a big man, I'd say maybe five feet, eight inches tall, but his girth made up for it. His hair, which he wore quite short, was a mass of very tight, wiry, salt-and-pepper curls that fell down onto his forehead, which was marked with a raised scar shaped like a rope of fat teardrops. His eyes were small, and he had deep squint lines that were accentuated by working out in the sun. His plump cheeks tapered down to full lips that stuck out reminiscent of a pig's snout. He used snuff and usually had a lump tucked inside his lower lip. I can still see him taking out his round snuffbox, tapping on the metal lid and then taking a large pinch.

Mike wore blue bib overalls for work and around home, but when he dressed up, he wore nicely starched white shirts and dress pants, which often came just to the ankles. Instead of a belt, he wore suspenders, and one knew at a glance that they were not just for decoration. He had a comical, stiff-legged walk—feet pointed outwards, his shoulders held slightly back and his stomach thrust forward giving him a slightly backward slant. Occasionally, on a busy Saturday night, he would help out in Dad's bar. A beer now and then was part of the bargain, and before the night was over, he was having as much fun as the customers.

Annie was such a nice lady, a little "dutchy" (a German expression meaning someone who is not real stylish), but it only added to her charm. She was a happy-go-lucky person and as German as they come. I can still hear her saying in her thick German accent, "Aye, aye, aye" when she heard something she couldn't quite believe. I can also hear her say to Mike when he did something goofy (usually when he had those beers), "Miiiiike, shame yourself!" Both she and Mike had a minimal education and could read very little. She used to have her children, especially Frankie who was quite sharp, read things of importance to her.

Annie Lauinger

Annie was a good mother, a spic-and-span housekeeper, a loyal friend and a first-rate practical joker. She and my mother made a good pair; maybe that's why they were such good friends. One Saturday night, there was a masquerade party in Dad's bar. Dad hired Mike to help tend bar, and Mom and Annie put on costumes, unbeknown to their husbands, and not only did they join in the fun, but they helped create it. Mom dressed as a man. She wore big bib overalls that she padded with pillows, an old plaid shirt, work gloves, men's old work shoes, a floppy black hat that she pulled way down and a funny mask of some kind. Annie went as her partner. She was quite slim and wore an oversized, gaudy housedress with the bosom padded to rival that of Dolly's, high heeled white shoes with red anklets and white gloves, and she carried an oversized purse. A long blonde wig and a painted-lady mask completed her costume. They never spoke, of course, but their actions made up for it. At one point, they went up to the bar to order drinks. Mom pounded obnoxiously to get Dad's attention and then ordered by pantomiming. It took awhile to figure out what these two characters wanted, and Dad being very busy, was getting more frustrated by the minute. When they finally got their drinks, they made motions that they had no money to pay. Annie went behind the bar and attempted to give Dad a hug in lieu of money. Meanwhile, people were impatiently waiting to be served. Finally, Dad told them to just take the drinks and go. In gratitude, Annie gave him a big bear hug and kiss, Mom pumped his arm, and off they went, laughing like crazy, to circulate among the other masqueraders. When the time to unmask came, Dad, who was a man of few words, just shook his head.

Annie and Mom weren't the only jokesters in town. My sister-in-law, Edith, was one of the best. We are still laughing about the time she, Mom and Evie had just gotten into the car behind the bar when Annie darted out in front of them and ran down the alley toward home. Edith laughingly said, "There goes Annie, running like a striped-assed ape." Ralph and Edith had the Speedway Bar west of Minot for twenty-five years, and I'm sure their customers are still smiling at all the jokes, surely a truckload, that she told over the years. It is said that laughter is the best medicine and with these three women it was certainly true.

Ray and Odelia

Ray and Odelia

Ray Sauer and his wife Odelia added spark to the Foxholm community. Nothing much went on in our little village, so a spark now and then was most welcome. Ray was a native of the Foxholm area. His father John, a schoolteacher, was one of the earliest pioneers in this area. Odelia came with her family when her father, Andrew Orchard, became the manager of the Foxholm Grain Elevator.

Ray was a tall, raw-boned young man with a long angular face, a prominent nose and chin and a large, wide mouth that literally stretched from ear to ear when he smiled. His hair was quite long on top and artfully slicked straight back with Brylcreem, which made his face appear even longer. Ray played the piano and the accordion, and his music livened up many a party in our small community. Instead of cash tips, his tall whiskey glass was often replenished. If he missed a beat or two after several tips, no one seemed to care or even notice.

Odelia was short and pleasingly plump. She loved a good joke, and her ample bosom shook with each peal of laughter. She had candy-apple cheeks, a square jaw and a small broad nose dusted with freckles. She wore her hair pulled back on the sides and swept up high from the forehead over a roll made of tightly woven horsehair to create a stylish pompadour.

Ray and Odelia bought the defunct dance hall that was located across the street from Mom and Dad's bar and made it into a café, the "The Duck Inn." Thoughts of that old dance hall bring back a mountain of memories.

Dance nights were busy times in Dad's bar, and Mom had to work with him. They thought nothing of me being in the dance hall without their supervision. Most of the people were neighbors and friends, and my big brothers were always there to keep an eye on me. (As it turned out, I had to keep an eye on them.) I can still hear the band as they tuned their instruments and then broke into a lively tune that brought the dancers to their feet. Sometimes the music was corny, and sometimes it was pretty good, but always, it was live music, never D.J.'s and records. The Huizenga family, who were neighbors of my family before I was born, was a popular local band. I remember Mom telling about how their father Art, also a musician, was a stern taskmaster when it came to practicing. Every evening after supper, come rain or shine, all would gather around the piano with Alice at the keyboard, May on the bass, Bob on the saxophone and Orrie on the drums. His discipline paid off. All of them became accomplished musicians and played together for many years.

In those days, it was common for women to dance together. My friends and I did it all the time. Oftentimes, guys would come out onto the floor and cut in. Sometimes, we hooked good dance partners and other times not so good ones, but we never refused to dance with them, as it would have been considered rude.

At midnight, the band would take its customary thirty-minute break and then continue on until two a.m. when they closed with "Good Night Sweetheart" or "Show Me the Way to Go Home." Everyone danced with everyone throughout the evening, but when the last dance came, the husbands were expected to find their wives. It was also a time for the single guy to ask his favorite gal to dance, which many times led to giving her a ride home.

Dancing came as natural to me as breathing. I don't know who taught me; I think I was born dancing. When I was barely six, my brother Alvin and I used to dance the schottische around the kitchen table. (We'd practice up for the big dance that night.) By the time he came home from the Navy, I was old enough for him to dance with in public. (Or maybe it was he who was old enough to dance with his little sister in public.) At any rate, it was the days of the jitterbug, and jitterbug we did! Even when we waltzed, we added a jitterbug swing. Those were the good old days, the days before Celebrex, Ibuprofen and heating pads

Alvin and I jitterbugging

I was about thirteen when they quit having dances in the Foxholm Dance Hall. I remember feeling sad. No more town dances? I couldn't imagine it. (Years later, this dance hall was moved to Minot and made into a private residence. The last time I was in Minot, I drove by it and marveled at how much smaller the building had gotten during the past fifty-some years.) By then, I was considered to be old enough to go to neighboring town dances with older friends. Frequently, I went with Joe and Carol Brunner, a young couple who lived in town. Joe, who worked on the Soo Line Railroad section crew, was my polka partner, and I could always count on him seeking me out when the band swung into the "Beer Barrel Polka." They didn't come much better than him when it came doing the polka and we burned up the dance floor many times. It's one of my fondest memories.

Ray and Odelia, who lived in the apartment in the back of the café, threw themselves into the café business. Ray did much of the cooking, and Odelia worked the front. She loved to socialize with people, and when visiting with a customer, she had the habit of leaning over and resting her arms on the counter. She was completely oblivious to the fact that this was not exactly the most flattering pose for one so endowed, especially since she often wore low V-neck dresses.

Odelia loved to dance and was surprisingly light on her feet for being as heavy as she was. Sometimes, when business was slow, Ray would bring out his accordion or we'd put a quarter in the jukebox, and away we'd go. Odelia was a strong leader, and being a lightweight, I had to be on my toes so I wouldn't end up across the room when she swung me out. It's funny how I still remember the jazzy bounce she had and the little extra step she squeezed in before twirling me around. Fast dancing with Odelia was fun, but being crushed against those sofa-pillow-bosoms during the slow dances made me slightly uncomfortable.

Odelia, with her bubbly personality and her infectious laugh, was well liked, and Ray was obviously very proud of her. One of the popular songs of the day was "Too Fat Polka," which Ray would play and sing to her:

"Oh, I don't want her, you can have her,
She's too fat for me, she's too fat for me,
She's too fat for me.
Oh, I don't want her, you can have her,
She's too fat for me, she's too fat,
She's too fat, she's too fat for me!
I get dizzy, I get numbo
When I'm dancing with
With my Jum-Jum-Jumbo
Oh, I don't want her......"

The song continued to describe how fat she was with each stanza ending, "But she's just right for me!"

Ray would smile widely as he sang, and Odelia fairly beamed. People roared with laughter which didn't seem to bother them at all.

Odelia and Ray were the affectionate type and often called each other "honey" or "sweetheart." Many of the old Germans, my dad, included, were not accustomed to expressing themselves as such and were certainly not comfortable doing so in public. Therefore, the couple's sweet talk stuck out like a sore thumb, sometimes to the point of irritating. One day when their "sweetheart" and "honey" was extra thick, Old Joe Haider, whose everyday language was peppered with curse words, snorted, "Gotdammit! Why don't you just call her 'seerup?'" This became a favorite story and the expression "honey and seerup" brought forth laughs for a long time

Old Joe Haider

Ray's parents, John and Rose Sauer, who were considerably older than my parents, were our next-door neighbors in Foxholm. In fact, they lived in the very house that we happened to buy so many years later. I was young when they passed away, but the thing I remember about Mrs. Sauer was her talent with a pair of scissors. She took plain brown paper or sometimes newspaper, folded it and then cut out designs. When it was unfolded, she had a beautiful length of paper that she tacked up for window shades. These hung in the entryway, and I was always fascinated and very impressed by their intricate patterns. Little did I know that one day I would be putting shades on those same windows. Unfortunately, they were neither intricate nor unique.

I remember old John Sauer as being a tall, quiet, reserved man who peered at people over his glasses. I had a hard time picturing him as a teacher except for that over—the-glasses look of his; maybe it was because I had never known a man of his age who had gone to college. When John first migrated here from St. Cloud, Minnesota, he worked on the railroad. He then attended college in Devil's Lake, North Dakota and taught school southeast of Foxholm. Later, he married Rose Schneider, who had been one of his students, and moved to Foxholm.

Sometimes during the winter, Mom and I would ford the snow banks between our houses to play whist, which was a popular pastime, especially during the long North Dakota winters. I was only about twelve years old at the time but had been playing whist since I was old enough to hold the cards. Therefore, in spite of my young age, I was considered to be a viable partner. John played quite passively until he took a crucial trick, and then, he'd slap down the card and say with emphasis, "How do you like them apples?" This phrase became part of our whist vernacular, and to this day, when we're in the middle of a hot whist game, someone will invariably say, "How do you like them apples?" It was a happy time in our lives, in spite of the four-foot snow banks.

Odelia had a blind brother named Bobby who was several years older than me. He was a bright young man who didn't let his handicap interfere with living life to its fullest. As I recall, Bobby, before moving to Foxholm, had received his education in Bathgate, North Dakota at the State School for the Blind. He was an avid reader and often read to us from one of his Braille books. He even took time to give us a few lessons in Braille, but I don't think we ever advanced further than the first half of the alphabet.

To make a little money and give him something to do, Bobby set up a workshop in one of the elevators that his father managed. He made craft items plus different tooled leather goods including belts and purses, all of which he sold in the local businesses. When walking around town, sometimes delivering these craft items, he always strode at a brisk pace with his head held high, and as he walked, he often snapped his fingers. Curious, we asked, "Why?" He explained that when he snapped he was listening for an echo, which told him when something was in his way. This intrigued us and for the next few days we walked with our eyes closed, snapping our fingers and listening intently for an echo. We never heard any echoes. Hearing our frustration, he explained that since he lacked the sense of sight, he was blessed with an extra good sense of hearing which made it possible for him to hear things that we couldn't. Satisfied, we were happy to leave the finger snapping to him.

There were no minorities in our rural community, just Germans with a few Norwegians and a couple of Irish thrown in the mix. Dee Dee Goven and Saul Davis, Minot's Third Street celebrities, were practically the only blacks in the area. Since we didn't patronize their businesses, we never saw them. No one even spoke about racial discrimination around us. Bobby was the closest thing we had to someone being "different," and we innocently accepted him without even realizing that we were learning a valuable life's lesson.

The Stach Family

The Stach family was an integral part of my community family during my childhood and teenage years in the tiny village of Foxholm. Balzer, a German from Russia, worked for the Soo Line Railroad as a section foreman, which earned him the nickname "Boss." It was the job of the section crew to keep the railroad tracks in perfect condition. Boss's workday started at the depot in Foxholm where he and his crew picked up the speeder, a four-man, open rail cart that they used to travel on the rails. We didn't need an alarm clock; the railroad tracks ran right past our house, and every morning at eight o'clock, we awoke to the distinctive putt-putt-putt of the two-cylinder speeder as Boss and his crew started out to check the track

Railroad speeder

Boss was a lean, wiry man with muscles honed from years of hard physical labor. He walked, often with his hand on his right hip, with his head tilted slightly back and his back ramrod straight (due to back problems). He had a heavy German accent and often spoke with spit flying. Although he laughed easily and often, the old German autocratic trait flowed through his veins; he was the boss!

Bearing children, cooking and keeping house were not thought to be noteworthy accomplishments, but they fixed a woman's place in the German-Russian family. Worn down by hard work and by repeated child bearing ("Another baby every nine months and three minutes," some said.), wives commonly died before husbands, often while still young. It was not uncommon, therefore, for a German-Russian man to marry more than once and to have children by more than one wife. Boss was such an example. His wife died at an early age leaving him with five young children. He soon remarried and sired two more.

Available women were limited in our rural community, so when Boss heard about a German-Russian widow in Canada who was also looking for a mate, he made the trip and a few days later came home with his bride, Wilhelmina Vetter, and her seven-year-old son Phillip. What courage it must have taken for Minnie, as she was called, to leave behind all that was familiar and follow a new husband, a man she didn't even know, into a different country to become an instant mother of six!

Minnie came from a humble background, and her life experiences had centered on her family and immediate surroundings. She had little formal education and was unable to read or write. Her children attempted to help her, but since German was her primary language and she had little time for book learning, she never became fluent in either German or English.

However uneducated, Minnie was not a stranger to hard work. She took on her new country and family with energy and enthusiasm and was soon a well-liked, productive member of the community. Boss and Minnie had two sons, Raymond and Ollie, which brought their family to a total of eight children.

Minnie and three of her sons, (L. to R.) Raymond, Ollie and Charlie

Minnie was big, solidly built and strong as an ox. She had a square face with a bulbous nose and a mouth that was made for laughing. She laughed loudly and often, and when she did, it exposed a gap on the lower right side where a tooth had long since been extracted. Minnie wore glasses that slightly magnified her eyes calling attention to the sprig of white eyelashes on her upper right eyelid. Mascara would have easily remedied the imperfection, but Minnie wasn't into mascara. A fluff of white powder and a touch of rouge were all she needed. She liked her heavy black hair tightly permed—the tighter the better. (If her permanents, as they were called, didn't come out in tight little spirals, she felt she didn't get her money's worth.) When she washed her hair, usually on Saturday as most women did, she didn't set it on metals curlers or in pin curls, she'd just comb through it and let it dry naturally which resulted in tight little corkscrew curls.

The new bride had good heart and a quick hand when it came to disciplining her newly acquired brood, all of whom called her Ma. In no time she earned their respect and then, their love. She ran a tight ship. Everyone was expected to help. They had no running water and had a coal cook stove and heater. It was the boys' job to bring in the water from the outside pump and coal from the coal bin. "Chonny, make some wood and lay the coal down," she'd say in her German accent. "Mach schnell!" If Johnny didn't "make hurry," there'd be a cuff on the ear.

The old house that the Soo Line provided the Stach family had never been so clean. Minnie wiped and scrubbed and waxed until everything gleamed like a bright new penny. The standard floor covering of the time was linoleum that was sold by the roll at Sears and Roebuck, Montgomery Ward or even the Gambles store, a popular hardware chain. It could also be ordered through the catalog, which was a staple in every home.

Minnie had a unique way of cleaning the floor; she'd sweep a little area, then stop and scrub—sweep a little more, then stop and scrub again. She repeated this until the entire floor was finished, and every time she scrubbed, she'd take out the can of liquid floor wax and give it a good coating which eventually created a build-up of wax around the heavily traveled areas. When that happened, it took a lot of elbow grease to restore the linoleum to its original color as there were no commercial wax removers available.

After heating and cooking with coal all winter, a thorough spring cleaning was a common practice. Minnie tore into it like a whirlwind. She cleaned everything from the curtains to the bedsprings, and she always gave the walls a fresh coat or two of paint, whether they needed it or not. If someone happened to paint their walls in the fall, she'd follow suit and give hers another coat. There must have been at an inch of paint built up on those old walls during Minnie's reign.

Minnie was a fast worker which left her with time on her hands. Since she couldn't read and there was no television, she'd take her crocheting and head for the neighbors'. Few people in town had telephones, and even if they did, it was customary for visitors to drop in unannounced, which Minnie often did. To get to our house, she would take the shortcut through the schoolyard, and we could see her coming. She did everything in a hurry, and walking was no exception. Carrying her crocheting, she'd come charging through the trees like a linebacker. She always looked neat; every day she'd wear a nicely starched and ironed cotton dress which, due to her bulk, hiked up slightly in the back and black oxfords with no socks. Mom never had as much time for visiting as did Minnie, but she would automatically stop what she was doing, put on the coffee pot and get out the cookies. If it was an afternoon visit, the two of them would sit at the oilcloth-covered kitchen table and crochet while listening to the soap operas.

Soap operas, radio daytime serial stories, were very popular through World War II. They were aimed at housewives who often listened while doing laundry or other chores and were sponsored by soap-powder and detergent manufactures. Characters in the soaps were similar to ordinary people on the street but, of course, more handsome, seductive and richer than the typical person listening. Their ongoing melodramatic episodes provided entertainment and a chance for the listening audience to escape the drudgery of daily chores and hardships for at least a few minutes of the day.

Mom and Minnie listened to several fifteen-minute serials, but Ma Perkins was a favorite, one they could relate to and understand. (Ma Perkins aired twenty-seven consecutive years and paved the way for modern soap operas.) It moved at the slow deliberate pace which typified life in a small town and "Ma" was the woman next door—a kind, trusting, middle-aged widow who owned and operated a lumber yard in Rushville Center with the help of her son-in-law Willie. Mom and Minnie would listen with interest as "Ma" offered sage advice to her children and grandchildren. Minnie's loud and infectious laugh often rang throughout the house as she added a little sage advice of her own.

Crocheted fancywork was very popular in those days. Minnie was good at it, and it gave her something to do when she finished her housework. Minnie's pieces didn't go into a drawer; she proudly displayed them on all possible surfaces—on every table, on the backs and arms of the sofa and chairs, under the battery radio and she even over the floor lamp. (When I dusted the furniture at home, I would take off the doilies and put them away, so you can imagine my reaction when I saw the one drooped over the lamp.) Minnie's living room with all its doilies was off-limits for everyday use, as was the custom of many old German Russians. The house was quite small for such a large family, and without the use of the living room, they were even more cramped, but the rule "for special use only" held firm.

Not only were they friends of the family, but Boss and Minnie also worked on and off for Mom and Dad. Minnie helped in the café during the busy times, and occasionally, Mom would hire her to help with spring house cleaning, (Lord knows she was an expert at painting and cleaning!) Boss helped Dad in the bar on party nights or whenever Dad needed someone to fill in. Boss always looked so fresh and nice behind the bar with his sparkling white shirt and suspenders; Minnie saw to it.

I was eight years old when Minnie was pregnant with Ollie and my knowledge of pregnancy was next to nothing. In those days, being pregnant was a very private matter. It was not considered a suitable topic for mixed company and certainly was never discussed with or in front of children. If ever it was mentioned, the word pregnant was never used. An expectant mother was referred to as being "p.g." or "in the family way" which is what Mom told me about Minnie. (How it came about was a mystery to me, and it remained a mystery for a good long time.)

Foxholm was too small to have its own doctor, and everyone had to travel the seventeen miles to Minot for any medical attention. When Minnie's due date neared, she had her bag packed and plans made for her long stay in the hospital. Things, however, didn't go exactly as planned.

It was December 24, 1941, a typical Christmas Eve in North Dakota—cold, very cold. It was so cold that the snow crunched and crackled when you walked, glistening ice crystals hung in the air, and it was so still that smoke from the chimneys rose lazily, creating spirals that went straight up. My entire family was home for our usual raucous Christmas celebration. We had opened gifts and were basking in the afterglow, waiting to go to Midnight Mass. Unfortunately, Mom was getting one of her migraine headaches and was resting on the bed. The tranquility was broken by a sudden impatient knocking on the kitchen door. Minnie's son Phillip, wild-eyed and frenzied, stood in the doorway. Minnie's labor had started suddenly and was proceeding rapidly. Considering the circumstances, St. Joseph's Hospital was out of the question, and Boss had sent for my mother.

In spite of her migraine, Mom hurriedly grabbed her coat, and they left as quickly as Phillip had come. She returned home early Christmas morning, sick as a dog, but with the happy news that she had delivered a big, healthy boy—a wonderful Christmas present for the entire Stach family.

Later that day, with Mom in bed and the stuffed turkey in the oven, my sisters ventured out in the frigid weather to see the new baby whom Mom described as being perfectly beautiful. Naturally, I tagged along. We found Minnie, tired but happy, cozily tucked into an over-stuffed chair in the doily-bedecked living room and Boss nervously holding the squalling newborn who was completely naked, wrapped only in a little receiving blanket. The look of relief on Boss's face when we walked in was actually comical. He quickly thrust the baby into Connie's arms and poured himself a double shot of whiskey.

Mom and Dad were chosen to be the baby's godparents, and my dad was given the honor of having the baby named after him.

When Ollie was thirteen, he was riding his bike on Highway 52, which was the main street of Foxholm, and was struck and severely injured by a car that was speeding through town. The sound of impact was horrifying, and the sight of Ollie, twisted and bleeding, haunted my dreams for a long time. I ran to call for the ambulance, a voluntary service from Carpio, which was ten miles down the road. Mom rushed to the scene and found Minnie screaming hysterically as she hovered over her son who lay entangled in his crumpled bicycle, his leg twisted into a grotesque shape. Mom forced Minnie back, knowing that her hysteria would only make things worse and then gently took Ollie's head and cradled it in her lap, calmly soothing and reassuring him until the ambulance arrived.

Young Ollie grows up

I recently spoke with Ollie about that accident. He told me that when he was lying severely injured on the highway, he heard voices calling to him, urging him to come, and he knew that he was dying. Suddenly the sky lightened, and a stairway wreathed in fluffy white clouds descended. On the stairway sat an a little old woman who resembled an old Russian peasant with a babushka on her head and a shawl wrapped around her shoulders. Her face, creased and worn, was radiant. She had no wings, but he knew that she was an angel. She didn't speak, but her soft gaze reached out and held him gently in her arms. A sense of peace flowed through him, and when the ethereal stairway moved up through the clouds and disappeared, Ollie knew that he would make it. That angel on the stairway, he realized, had been my mother, his godmother, and he firmly believes to this day that it is because of her that he is alive today.

Occasionally, on Saturday nights, Dad would have a party in the dance hall behind the bar. (My friends nicknamed that hall "The Blue Moon.")The hall, a twenty-four-foot by forty-foot frame building with open rafters, had a raised platform that comfortably held four musicians, stationary benches along the outside walls (where women sat waiting for a man's invitation to dance) and a pine dance floor. Spangles Dance Wax, which looked like white fluffy soap flakes, was sprinkled on the floor to enable the dancers to glide across the floor. If we ran out of the dance wax, we reverted to the old remedy—cornmeal—which really worked quite well. The hall was unheated and only used during the summer months. Two doors and four small windows provided the only ventilation, and when it was full of happy dancers, there was a lot of fanning going on. The men often stepped outside to soak up the delicious coolness of a North Dakota evening and, on occasion, have a little nip from a bottle that was passed around.

On special occasions, we would decorate the hall with colorful strips of crepe paper which, with the help of thumbtacks, we draped from the center rafters to either side of the hall forming a festive canopy. One such occasion merited a few extra streamers. After a courtship of thirty-two years, Johnny Haider and Clara Sartwell, a native of Burlington, were married in St. Mary's Catholic Church. A rousing celebration filled with dining, drinking and dancing followed the long-anticipated ceremony. According to my sister Connie, Johnny, in his youth, had been a fox on the dance floor. She said she can still see him doing the jaunty, strutting Lambeth Walk.

Dad often hired Boss's sons to provide the music; Balzer played the accordion and piano, and Charlie accompanied him on the banjo. Boss really enjoyed these parties and never failed to entertain us with his Russian dance. I can still hear him laughing as he, with arms folded, agilely squatted down and expertly kicked his legs straight out in front of him, never missing a beat. He was naturally limber, but after a few beers, he became a real showman. It was obvious that the musicians were very proud of their father, and when he danced, they played especially for him. Boss loved it, and with the bystanders circled around him, clapping in time to the music, he danced with an enthusiasm that would've made any Russian proud.

The entertaining music makers-Charlie and Balzer Stach

Boss cooling off after his Russian dance

Minnie enjoyed these parties, too. Always fun loving, she'd have a couple drinks and be the life of the party. Occasionally, in her silk navy blue party dress and her sturdy navy Sunday shoes, she'd get down beside Boss and try to do the Russian dance with him. With Ma and Pa both on the dance floor, Balzar and Charlie, with grins a foot wide, would pick up the tempo. Minnie tried to keep up, but lacking her husband's agility, she would give a few kicks with her stout legs and end sitting on the floor, which sent up a wave of laughter, hers being the loudest of all.

Boss's son Raymond carries on in his dad's footsteps. He looks a lot like his dad, and I understand that he acts even more like him, especially when he does his Russian dance. I don't know if Boss ever got to see Raymond dance, but I hope so. I know he would have been very proud and happy to see the tradition live on.

Johnny Vicha, Minnie's reluctant dance partner, and her son
Raymond who is following in his dad's footsteps

I danced with Minnie many times. She'd grab me, and away we'd
go. She was, as I said, strong as an ox, and I'd have to watch that she
didn't swing me off my feet when we went around the corners. It makes
me think of the time she grabbed Johnny Vicha, a shy non-dancing
bachelor farmer who was standing complacently on the sidelines
watching the dancing. She pulled him out on the dance floor and
whirled him around and around. He was a slight man, and before he
knew it, she had swung him completely off his feet. Everyone roared
with laughter. Johnny turned beet red but gamely laughed with them.
Boss was proud of his Mina, as he called her, and would stand with his
hands on his hips, watching and laughing with them. Minnie could also
swing Boss around the floor. She'd grab him around the neck, and away
they'd go. When they did the polka, it was almost dangerous to be near
them. She was a powerful force when under full steam, and a good fast
German polka generated a lot of steam.

Those fun times in the old dance hall are a thing of the past. Nothing
remains, not even the building, only memories. Some memories make
me laugh, some bring tears, but all are significant parts of the youth I
left behind.

Minnie never forgot my birthday. Every year without fail she gave me
a quarter. I grew to expect it and anxiously waited for it. One could buy
a lot for one cent in those days—Tootsie Rolls, huge jawbreakers (I loved
the black ones that made my mouth and teeth black.), Tootsie Pops,

bubble gum, penny candy bars and more. The path we took to walk to uptown went through the school yard, over the railroad tracks and through Stach's yard. I made sure I walked that path on my birthday because I knew Minnie would come out and give me my present. It wasn't like I never had money for candy, but Minnie's gift was special, and it remains one of my fondest childhood memories.

Many years later, I sent Minnie a birthday card and letter. In my reminiscing with her, I mentioned my birthday quarter and how much her thoughtfulness had meant to me. Three years later, I received a letter from her son Otto. (The same one I had a crush on when I was a second-grader.) He lived in California and had gone to Seattle to help move Minnie into a nursing home. When going through her things, they found the letter that I had written. Minnie had carefully saved it all those years and asked Otto to answer it for her. I was so touched and so sorry I hadn't written many more. Minnie didn't live too much longer after that, and even though she hadn't been part of my life for many, many years, I missed her and still do.

It is customary for German-Russian Catholics to celebrate their "Name's Day" which is a day set aside to honor the saint whose name they share. The German-Russian Catholics were sociable, church-going people who were always ready for a good time, and this occasion was the ideal opportunity. Boss loved to celebrate this special day, and celebrate they did. The preparations took days. Minnie would cook and bake and clean like crazy (including the company living room), and the amount of food she prepared was enough for a small army. There were always huge bowls of potato salad, baked beans, hams and dozens of homemade buns, and there were always dill pickles that were flavored with garlic. (The German Russians love their garlic.) The party wouldn't have been complete without a little hooch, and Boss always made sure he had plenty on hand. A sixteen-gallon keg of beer plus whiskey was the usual fare, and sometimes he passed around a shot glass and a bottle of Red Eye, a potent brew made of 190 proof alcohol mixed with a little grenadine and a flavored liqueur, which was served at weddings or other special occasions. (It made for a good polka.)

Their German friends from Karlsruhe, North Dakota were the first to arrive and the last to leave. The German Russians are notoriously good polka dancers, and these friends of his were some of the best. I remember one in particular. Leo Nice was one of the best polka dancers I've ever danced with, and I've danced with many. He was as light on his feet as a feather, and when we danced, our feet hardly touched the floor. Recently, Jack, who lives in Minot, met Leo in one of the local bars. During the course of the conversation, he discovered that Jack was my son. On impulse, Jack called me and put Leo on the line. We had a good time reminiscing, and we agreed that, in spite of our gray hair and creaky joints, we'd still be able to show 'em how to do a good old-fashioned polka or die trying.

Boss was a jack of all trades. With so many boys in one house, the cost of haircuts can add up. Furthermore, there no longer was a barber in town, which meant they had to drive into Minot. Consequently, Boss became a barber. He bought a pair of hand clippers (and a bowl, we jokingly said), and he was in business. When the weather was nice, he'd take a kitchen stool and one of Minnie's old sheets and set up shop in the front yard. I can still see him. After draping his customer, he'd straighten his shoulders, and like a maestro conducting his orchestra, raise his hands with a comb in one hand and the scissor in the other, pause, and then with a flourish, begin his cutting.

As Boss's barbering reputation spread, he attracted a few of the locals whose satisfaction was influenced by the price—free—and perhaps by a beer at the local bar. From his back yard, Boss progressed to the backroom of Walt's Bar where he set up shop. He still couldn't charge because he had no barber's license, but his customers knew how much of a good-will offering was expected, and everyone was satisfied. Eventually, the road to Minot became shorter, and Boss's sideline trickled away.

Boss called me Worna and my sister-in-law, Worlene. I knew it was because of his German accent that Verlene came out as Worlene, but I was puzzled why I was Worna. The mystery was solved when we received a Christmas card written by Boss and addressed to Mr. and Mrs. Ollie Miller and Verna. I never did correct Boss, and I remained Worna to him forever. Verlene and I still have a good laugh when we reminisce about that. Just last Christmas, I addressed her card as Worlene Miller and, of course, signed it, "Worna."

Verlene Miller

Since Minnie could barely write, it was Boss's job to take care of the correspondence. When she did make the attempt, she wrote the words as they sounded. Since she pronounced many words with a German accent, it took a lot of thought to decipher what she had written. Actually, it was kind of fun. I remember reading a letter that Mom had gotten from her after they moved to Washington, and it was like reading a complicated code. We loved it.

Phillip and I were great pals for as long as I can remember. He was three years older than me, but that never made a difference. I had always been a regular tomboy (With three older brothers to battle, I learned to hold my own.), so we got along well. I prided myself in being as tough as him and proved it many times. Then, something happened; he suddenly became much stronger and faster, and I could no longer throw as hard, bat as far or run as fast as him. This bugged me to no end. There was one consolation; I could still beat him in card games.

Growing up in a town that was even too small to be called a town forced us either to sit home and be bored or to use our imaginations; we chose to use our imaginations.

One of our favorite pastimes was playing cowboys and Indians. I remember making a fort out of old boards that we scavenged. Armed with a hammer and nails, we spent the entire day constructing our fortress which served us for a long time. What fun we had! Everyone had a gun and holster set and did his share of "killing", and yet not one of us grew up to be a serial killer.

Climbing trees was another great pastime. We had some big cottonwoods in our backyard that became an African jungle, home of Tarzan. Phillip had the privilege of being Tarzan because he was the oldest and biggest, I was Jane and Frankie Lauinger, being the youngest, was Boy. Phillip would give the Tarzan yell and swing from one branch or tree to another, and Frankie and I followed suit. It's a wonder we never fell and broke our necks, but luckily, the only thing we broke was an occasional tree limb.

There were no organized sports in our town and no place for us to even congregate and talk. We had no television, and the radio batteries were dead half the time, so we had to make our own fun. We often played workup in the schoolyard. If we couldn't find enough players for that, we played catch. Phillip had a strong arm, and that ball would come at me like a bullet! Even if it killed me, I never would have flinched or backed away. One day, when we were tossing the ball, he threw an exceptionally fast fastball. I put my hand out to catch it, and it hit the tip of my ring finger. I looked down and my finger was bent straight up at the first joint! I must have yelled because Phillip was beside me in a minute. He took one look, grabbed my finger and gave a hard yank. It slid right back into place, and except for being black and blue and sore as the devil, it was as good as new. Phillip made one mistake, though; he laughed as he was doing it. When I think back, I'm sure the laugh was out of nervousness, but at the time, the fight was on. Of course, I didn't win. He merely laughed some more and held my hands so I couldn't swing at him. I'm sure that, eventually, I did get even with him. If I didn't, it wasn't for the lack of trying.

School was hard for Phillip, and after struggling through eight years, he quit and went to work for his dad as a section hand. His school days were over but not our friendship.

I was fourteen when Mom opened our café, which was in the same building as Dad's bar, and Phillip was a frequent customer. He did hard, dirty manual labor, but when he came uptown at the end of the day, he was always shiny clean and smelling of lava soap. He was such a good guy and always a good friend, but occasionally we'd have our fights. When he didn't show up for a few days, Mom would know that a feud was brewing, and invariably, she'd take his side, which really made me mad. I never could stay mad at him for very long, and then we'd be back to our normal picking on each other.

Phillip had his own car, and occasionally he'd take a friend and me to a movie in Minot or to dance in neighboring town. I loved to dance and had danced since I was able to walk. Phillip had never learned, but I was determined that he would, so the lessons began. We played the jukebox in our café every night and practiced by the hour. Over and over, I showed him the dance steps. He was a willing student, but bless his heart, it was like leading around a plug horse. He had a goofy laugh, much like a snort, and I can still hear him laughing when he clumsily stepped on my toes for the umpteenth time. Eventually, he did learn to two-step, waltz and even polka, but I never could accomplish my goal to instill in him a sense of rhythm. He remained a plug horse on the dance floor forever.

Phillip eventually married Shirley Zuzulin from Minot. I think Shirley was a little jealous of me when they were first married, which made me laugh, but she got over it. They settled in Foxholm and had several children. I'm sad to say that Phillip was stricken with a rare disease and died at a very young age. Shirley moved her family to Minot, and I never got to see his children grow up. His oldest son, Phillip Jr., still lives in Minot. I understand that he looks and acts a lot like his dad. I look forward to meeting him one day. Boy, do I have some stories for him!

My pal Phillip

Freddie

Fred and Fronnie

I knew Fred and Veronica Sauer well, and I knew their son Frederick even better. Frederick was sometimes entertaining and most of the time exasperating, but there were so few young people in town that, like family, we just naturally accepted one another, faults and all.

Fred was short and stubby, easy-going and likeable. His sharply chiseled facial features, which gave him a hawk-like appearance, were softened by his ready smile. He had a noticeable gap between large front teeth and a dimple in his check that deepened when he smiled. His eyes were small and squinty, and when he laughed, they all but closed.

Fred was most often seen wearing blue bib overalls and a railroad engineer's cap. For Sunday Mass, he traded his overalls and cap for a brown suit and a wide-brimmed fedora, which he wore at a jaunty angle. Whether in his overalls or suit, Fred had a cigarette either between his fingers, which were permanently stained a dark yellowish-brown, or dangling from his mouth.

Unlike Fred, Fronnie, as Veronica was called, was anything but easy-going. High-strung and vocal but good-hearted in her own way, she was definitely the dominant force in the family.

Don Streitz, a Foxholm native and friend, laughed as he recalled the summer afternoon he visited Freddie on their farm just outside of Foxholm. It was during World War II, and thoughts of the war were never far away. Don and Freddie were sitting on the front porch, dangling their feet and idly chatting. Fronnie was busy in the house, and Fred, with a team of horses and his old mower, was mowing some tall weeds out near the barn. Suddenly, there was a flurry of flapping wings and loud, raucous squawking as chickens with severed legs came flopping out of the weeds. The noisy commotion brought Fronnie on the run. She took one look and screamed, "Fred! What are you doing? Stop! Stop! You're killing my chickens! You Hitler, you!" Don said Freddie leaned over to him and calmly said, "You know, if they ever got into a downright fight, I think Ma could take Dad."

Freddie

Fronnie doted on their only child. She waited on him hand and foot, smothering him with attention, which carried over into adulthood. This obsessive babying caused him to become self-centered and spoiled.

Weekends found Freddie out partying with the boys, which many times left him with a whopping hangover. Fronnie worried herself sick over these recurring "illnesses." Julius Schaan, a buddy who hoisted his share with Freddie, laughed about the morning he went to pick up him up after one of their nights on the town. A distraught Fronnie met him at the door with rosary beads in her hands. Seeing his questioning look, she explained that Frederick was having another of his terrible sick spells and she was praying for his recovery.

There was very little for us to do in our small town, and getting to Minot or other towns was no easy feat when one didn't drive. Even after I got my driver's license, I didn't have a car, and since my family only had one car, I knew better than to ask to use it. Sometimes Phillip and Freddie, who were older and owned their own cars, would give Darlene and me a ride to a dance in Carpio or Berthold and occasionally to a movie in Minot, but these were never actual dates. One particular Sunday, the four of us piled into Phillip's car and headed out for a Sunday movie. On the way home, I somehow ended up in the back seat with Freddie. I don't know if the guys had gotten their heads together and planned this, but this seemed a little suspicious to me, so I was on the alert. Sure enough, he slowly began moving closer, and the next thing I knew, he was all hands. When he wouldn't stop, I picked up the floor mat and hit him over the head. I can still hear the "whomp" and see the stunned look on his face as he brushed the dust from his new jacket. (I remember that jacket so clearly. It was a shiny, light pearl-gray, military-style Eisenhower jacket that was popular in 1945.) With his ardor cooled, he rode the rest of the way home in a huffy silence. Darlene and I recently reminisced about that car mat episode and laughed as hard as ever

Fronnie was careful not to serve Freddie hot food. Even after he was married, she was ever vigilant of his welfare. Don tells about the time he was at Freddie and Arlene's and was invited to stay for lunch. When Arlene served the food, she happened to set the pot of hot chili in front of Freddie. Visibly upset, Fronnie quickly grabbed the chili and lashed out at her daughter-in-law. "Don't you know you can't set hot food in front of Frederick? He could have burned his mouth!" Many years have passed since then, and it's still one of our favorite, "Do you remember when..." stories.

While Freddie inherited his looks from his father, he got his frugality from his mother. He was more than frugal; he was just plain tight. It was a well-known fact that he had his bladder trained much like Pavlov's dog. Whenever the bill for a round of drinks or the hamburgers came, he had to make a trip to the bathroom, whether or not he had a date with him. The guys would rib him about it and sometimes even come right out and insist that he pay his share, but the next time, it was the same old story. He never changed.

Remembering the floor mat episode and understanding that I would not be his date, Freddie still asked me to do things with him. Being obnoxiously persistent, he'd occasionally wear me down, and I'd go. I'll never forget when he talked me into going to a class play in Carpio.

The junior and senior classes at my high school put on annual plays to make money for various projects. This particular time, it was the juniors' play. On the night of the performance, Freddie stopped at our café and asked me to go with him and his parents. I had already seen it and told him so, but as usual, he wouldn't take no for an answer. He kept begging and whining about how he didn't want to go alone with his folks and kept rambling on and on and on. Finally, Mom said, "Just go along. You don't have to marry him," which was one of her favorite sayings. Finally, I said okay. I was already out the door when I realized I hadn't any money, so I quickly ran back. When we got to Carpio, Fred and Fronnie paid their admission and went on in. Freddie, without a backwards glance, nicely followed suit. Obviously, I was expected to buy my own ticket to sit through a play that I had already seen just so it would look like Freddie had a date. Freddie's date? In his dreams! I ignored him and the seat he was so thoughtfully saving, and sat three rows down. It was a quiet road home.

There was another time when I stupidly let myself get talked into going with Freddie—this time to a dance in Burlington. Today I laugh about it, but at the time, I definitely was not laughing. I remember telling him no several times, but Freddie was relentless when it came to getting his own way. I think that this time it was the lure of the dance (the Wagon Masters, a talented country band was playing), that persuaded me. At any rate, I went. I wouldn't have minded half as much if he had escorted me to the door and then left me, but, when we arrived, he immediately jumped out of the car and without a word of explanation, disappeared into Vance Remington's bar. The dance hall was above the bar, and bar patrons could get in free through an inside stairway. Of course, Freddie knew this. He also knew that I wasn't old enough to go into the bar. Once again, if I had not had money, I would have had to sit in the car until two a.m. when the dance was over. This time I learned my lesson; it was the last time I went anywhere with tightwad Freddie.

Freddie had occasional dates but was never too successful in snagging a steady girlfriend, and when he did, he immediately wanted her to marry him. Janet, my classmate, went out with him a couple times, and before she knew it, he was offering her an engagement ring. Needless to say, they didn't become engaged. In fact, it was their last date. He eventually married Arlene Skaufel, a nice country girl who was considerably younger than him. It was a short engagement, as I remember. I think he hurried her along before she could change her mind.

Freddie was very competitive and liked to win at all costs, especially when there was money involved. Our community was big on playing cards, and during the winter with little else to do, we would have progressive whist tournaments with a small monetary prize for the winners. The men's organization at St. Mary's Church usually sponsored one that was held in the church basement. There were several tables, and the winners of each game would move up toward the head table. Once there, the winning partners stayed, and the losers went back so square one. The winners at the head table at the end of the evening won the prize. This was serious business to Freddie, and he played to win. One time when I was at his table, I caught him fudging on the score. Of course, when I brought the error to his attention, it had been just an honest mistake.

Another time, several of us, including Freddie, were playing a friendly game of poker at my brother's house. Freddie was not having any luck at hooking jokers. Frustrated, he slipped them out of the deck, and slid them under a big ashtray. (If he couldn't get a joker, no one else would either.) It didn't work; I saw him do it. I was sitting directly to his left, and when I dealt the next hand, I just reached over and nicely put them back into the deck. He pretended not to notice, but I couldn't resist needling him with a little knowing smile.

Freddie drove me crazy at times, but, inspite of it all he was a good guy—a tightwad for sure, but still a good guy. Just think of all the laughs we would have missed out on had he been any different.

Fred and his wife bought the Joe Haider filling station and retired from farming. Eventually, they bought a little house, moved it in next door to the station and became full-time city folks. (At the time, Foxholm had about eighty hardy people.)

It was a small old-time station with a canopy and a gas pump, which was topped with a white glass globe bearing the name Standard. Originally, this pump was a visible gasoline pump, which was used in filling stations after 1915. This eye-measurement style allowed the customer to see the fuel they were buying and verify that the amount paid for was actually delivered. Since there was no electricity, the gas was pumped manually from an underground storage tank into the exposed glass holding tank. At the release of a gate valve, the gasoline was gravity fed through the hose and nozzle and into the automobile's tank.

The station had the eye-measurement pump when Joe Haider owned it. Joe and Mrs. Haider were my sister Evie's in-laws, and my nieces and nephews laughingly recall how Grandma Haider kept tabs on the filling station. The Haiders lived a short way down the road from the station, and she used to sit at the kitchen table and watch how many times the gasoline pump was emptied and refilled during the day. Every night Joe would give her a percentage of the day's take, and she wanted to make sure she got her fair share, which she stashed away in her brown leather coin purse. Sadly, Joe was killed in 1952 at age seventy-eight when he was struck by a car as he crossed the highway on his way home from the service station.

Mrs. Haider and her husband Joe dragging the air hose to service a customer at the gas station

Like all stations at that time, Fred's station was full service. The customer pulled up to the pump, and Fred did the rest. He pumped the gas, checked the oil, washed the windows and aired up the tires, all for the price of the gas. Besides all this service, the customer also received the latest town news.

When the position of postmaster opened up, Fronnie applied and got the job. The post office was a small, eight-foot by eight-foot structure that was built adjacent to the filling station. It only held a few boxes and the service window. Our box number was forty-five, and although I could no longer tell you the combination, I could still open it.

The location of the post office was perfect for Fronnie. When she wasn't sorting mail, she was in the station. Often, potential customers would have to go next door looking for her. It was common knowledge that she did this so she could keep an eye on Fred, who might let a bottle of pop leave the premises without the nickel deposit.

Foxholm's population slowly dwindled, and when it was no longer economically viable, the post office became nothing more than a memory and the village became part of a rural route. It was a sad day when my hometown's address changed from Foxholm to Berthold—a very sad day.

Fronnie, who was becoming more eccentric with each passing day, now devoted all of her time to their business. She sold pop and candy, pumped gas, added oil and often sent her customers away shaking their heads over the latest Fronnie story. For some reason, she felt that she had a special rapport with wild animals. She told the following story over and over to anyone and everyone. Fronnie often scouted the coulees for seasonal berries. On one of her early morning outings for Juneberries, she found a tree that was loaded with plump berries, but the branches were out of reach. Luckily, she said, there was a huge rock below the tree. Absorbed in her picking, she thought she felt a slight movement under her feet. Glancing down, she discovered, to her amazement, that the "rock" she was standing on was, in fact, a large deer. The animal supposedly lifted his head, gave her a big knowing wink and settled back down.

Fronnie and Fred literally lived in their little filling station. It had no modern conveniences except electricity, not even running water, but that didn't seem to be a problem. They brought in a two-burner hot plate and a dishpan and carried in water by the pail. The only time they really used their house was when it was time to go to bed. In fact, it was said that they never even fully unpacked

Fred's Standard Station

In between customers, Fronnie would do her domestic chores. She even butchered chickens in the station—scalding them in water heated on the hot plate before plucking and degutting them—all in the small area in which their business was conducted. You can imagine the stench and the unsuspecting customers' reactions when they walked in the door.

She also canned vegetables from her garden and made jellies from the fruit she picked in the coulees. My niece Debi laughs remembering one year when the plums were exceptionally plentiful. Fronnie had gone out picking at the crack of dawn and returned a short time later with several pails of fat, juicy plums. She immediately began the jelly-making process. She had to carry water from the well, and heat it on the hot plate to sterilize her jars before she could start cooking the berries. This was a lot of work, which could have been easier if she would have made the jelly in their house. However, had she done it the easier way, she wouldn't have been able to keep watch on those pop bottles. Debi happened to be one of their customers that afternoon, and when she saw all the jars of jelly lined up next to a pyramid of oil cans, she commented on how good the jelly looked with its nice clear red color. "Do you like plums?" Fronie asked. When Debi said she did, Fronnie quickly turned and disappeared into the back room, returning with a large, heavy-looking brown grocery bag. Already visualizing her own sparkling jars of jelly, Debi expressed her thanks and happily peeked into the bag. Lo and behold, instead of plums, she had a sack full of pits; all she had to do was plant them.

Maybe Fronnie's eccentric ways were contagious, or perhaps Fred had acquired a uniqueness of his own. At any rate, he did his share to add flavor to the community. I remember the time he broke his glasses. For quite some time, he went about wearing them with one shattered lens. It looked like a rock had hit the direct center of the lens causing dozens of fine cracks to radiate from the point of contact. The cracked lens was the topic of conversation at more than one dinner table. "Fred still hasn't had his lens replaced. Is he getting a little senile, or won't frugal Fronnie let him spend the money?" Finally, one of the locals came right out and asked him. Fred didn't answer; he just smiled and kept on pumping gas. Then one day, to everyone's relief, new glasses appeared. As it turns out, they had belonged to Joe Haider and had been left behind when Fred and Fronnie bought the station.

When reminiscing, people often mention Fred's pet gopher. Fred had encountered many ground squirrels during a lifetime of living on the prairie but never, so he said, one like Stripey. Fred loved to tell the story about how he first noticed the gopher as he was walking behind the station on his way to the outhouse. It stood up and intently watched Fred and then scampered back to his gopher hole. The next day, the curious gopher was there again, and once more, he seemed to be watching Fred. During the following days, the gopher, getting smarter and smarter, waited daily for the Corn Curl that Fred threw to him. Then came the day when Stripey boldly made his way into the station and inched his way toward the enticing Corn Curl that Fred held. From then on, the famous gopher came daily for his treat. He ignored Fred's customers who watched with amused fascination as he boldly took the cheese curls from Fred's outstretched hand. I don't know what happened to Stripey; perhaps he fell in love and left for greener pastures. I do know that while he was there, he made headline news in Foxholm.

Time went on, and Fronnie became even more eccentric. She did all kinds of bizarre things that implied extreme poverty, which was not the case by any means. She refused to hook up the hot water heater in the house and continued to heat water on the hot plate in the station. She began to wear what looked like Salvation Army rejects—baggy old pants, men's jackets that hung off her shoulders, work shoes that were beyond their better days—and many times, she wore a pair of panty hose, with the legs cut off at the knees, pulled down over her head like an aviator's cap. The remaining portion of the legs flopped in the breeze as she went about serving their customers. She also wore her "cap" when she worked in the garden. She swore it was the best mosquito deterrent she'd ever had.

Fronnie seemingly became more and more obsessed with saving

money. Later on, knowing that aluminum pop cans could be sold in Minot for a small amount of money, she collected them as if her next meal depended on it. Nary a discarded can escaped her. The station was the only place in town where kids could buy pop and candy. My great-nephew Kyle tells the story about how his babysitter used to take him there to buy a Pepsi and how Fronnie wouldn't let him take it out of the station. She made him sit on an old metal kitchen stool to drink it so she could add the empty can to her savored stash.

Fronnie's eccentric behavior led to rumors about her squirreling away money in fruit jars and coffee cans. Fred seemed to be unaware of his wife's dotty antics and the gossip it generated. Perhaps he had grown so accustomed to her actions that he no longer noticed, or it could have been due to his increasing ill health.

When traveling to appointments became too difficult for Fred, they closed the station and moved into Minot where they would be near his doctors and to Freddie and their grandchildren.

Once an integral part of the community's fabric, the old filling station now sits alone, silent and forlorn. Mice roam through crumbling walls that once stood proud and resilient. Sunshine filters through dirty, cracked windows illuminating the abandoned, empty interior that once housed jars of plum jelly, cans of motor oil and Milky Way candy bars.

There are no more Fronnie stories, no more village gossip and no more laughter—only silence and memories.

The Haider Filling Station, a Ward County Historical Landmark

The Gremans

Norbert (Nobs) and Darlene

The Norbert Greman family added their own special touch to the character of Foxholm. Norbert, son of Martin and Mary Greman, spent his entire life in the Foxholm area. Born on the family farm, he never strayed much further except for the time he spent in the army in World War II.

Norbert, who worked for the State Highway Department as a road maintenance man, was the town's version of Icabod Crane. He was tall, thin and knobby which earned him the fitting nickname "Nobs." Weathered from working a lifetime outdoors, his long bony face bore deep vertical creases that outlined his cheeks. His drab green Eisenhower-style jacket was not put away in mothballs; he wore it forever. His reasoning was, "Why spend good money when it isn't necessary?" Darlene got a taste of this reasoning early in their relationship.

Darlene moved into the area when her stepfather, Elmer Richwalski, was transferred to the Upper Souris National Wildlife Refuge. She lived with her parents at the Refuge, which meant that Norbert had to drive fourteen miles round trip whenever he went to see her. After a brief courtship, Norbert analyzed the situation and came up with what he thought was the most logical solution—marriage. His proposal, as Darlene told it, went like this, "This driving back and forth is costing a lot of gas money. We might as well get married."

Norbert was very well read and, consequently, quite knowledgeable in spite of his lack of formal education. He savored a philosophical conversation and could keep up with the best of them. When in a conversation, he'd listen intently, head tilted slightly downward, and say with a sense of wonder, "Noooooo."

Norbert and Darlene were as different as two people can be. thirteen years younger, Darlene was much slower intellectually and talked very little in public. She was also as heavy as Norbert was lean. Pillowed in fat, she hung over a chair on all sides and literally swallowed up a bar stool.

As a young girl, Darlene was a pretty blond with large, round, blue eyes. Tall, big-boned and shy, she stumbled through her school years. The schools back then did not offer programs to help students with special needs. Frustrated, Darlene dropped out of school, got married, stayed at home and had babies. Over the years, she became obese and slovenly.

As she gained weight, Darlene masked her feelings with humor. When she became too heavy for a bathroom scale, she freely admitted that she weighed herself at the grain elevator on the small platform scale. She wore housedresses, and when she needed a new dress, she would jokingly say that it was time to "go to the parachute store." She laughed about not being able to bend down to tie her shoes and how she solved the problem by wearing slip-ons that became broken down from shoving her feet in.

Darlene had an inferiority complex, which is understandable when you consider how she must have felt, day after day, in a regular classroom setting. She was very shy and mostly just sat and listened when in a group of people. Only with her closest friends was she less introverted. Her shyness, however, lessened with a few beers, and when she had more than a few, she became a totally different person. Gone were her inhibitions. Loud and obnoxious, she would greet any stranger as her long-lost twin. Bellied up to the bar with a quart of beer in front of her (a Norwegian Pony, as she called it), she'd tell raunchy stories and then laugh lustily. Batting her blue eyes, she'd sidle up to a man and teasingly address him as "my sexy butterfly," "poopsie" or "baby doll". The locals humored her, and strangers didn't know quite what to think. When she finally left to continue her fun at Walt's Bar, we all breathed a sigh of relief, especially my dad who used to say, "I'd take ten drunken men over one drunken woman any day of the week."

Walt's Place (L. to R.) Walt and Alpha Black (bar owners) and Boss Stach

Even though the locals shook their heads at her antics, Darlene's behavior was accepted without judgment. People knew she was a good person who did stupid things when she drank. That's just the way it was.

Darlene didn't bother with housekeeping. It was obvious that the entire family adopted her attitude because they lived in surroundings that would have been intolerable to most people. Still, if a friend would have asked for her help with something such as wallpapering or painting or even raking the yard, she would have been there in minutes.

The Greman children, three boys and one girl, were likeable, robust and resilient little urchins. I can still see them when they were little— hair sticking up every which way, smudged faces, grubby callused bare feet, and the boys went without T-shirts with their bib overalls hinged up by only one strap. It was not uncommon to see them during the cold North Dakota winters running outside without a coat and barefooted, and yet, they never got sick. My husband Ray tells about the time he drove with our son Mike up to Dad's bar. It was cold and blustery, and the ground was dusted with snow. Just as they pulled up, two of the Greman boys, with nothing on but their underpants, darted out in front of the car. Like startled deer caught in a car's headlight, they stood for a moment, wide-eyed and staring, and then bolted for home. Mike, who was not yet three, cried, "Step on it, Dad. You can get both of them." (He didn't learn it from me.)

When Mike was in kindergarten, Willie Sauer, Superintendent of the Carpio Public Schools, called and offered me the job of teaching Mike's class. It sounded good, but who would take care of our preschool boys? In our small town, services such as daycare were nonexistent, and it would have been out of the question to take them out of town. I thought of Darlene. Since Norbert was very tight-fisted, she might like to earn a little money of her own. The deal was made. She would come to our house and bring her daughter Sissy with her. It worked out to be a viable deal; the boys were well taken care of and she was happy to receive what were probably her first and only paychecks.

Norbert, in his army jacket, often stopped at Dad's bar on his way home from work to have a beer and shoot the breeze for a few minutes before going home. (I can still see him taking out his little, well-worn coin purse and digging out change with one finger.) On one occasion, he evidently had a few more beers than usual and stayed much longer. When he finally did get home, hours late for supper, he had the audacity to complain about it being cold. That was the final straw. Darlene, who was already aggravated, grabbed the cast iron frying pan off the stove and hit him over the head. He crumpled to the floor like a rag doll and was out like a light. Frantically, Darlene called Alvin and Verlene, "Come quick! I think I killed Norbert!" When they got there, they found Norbert on the floor with potatoes and cabbage splattered everywhere and Darlene hovering over him crying, "Is he dead?" When she realized that he was only knocked out, she shrieked, "How dare you scare me like that!" and let him have it again. Later she told Verlene, "You know, that was the last time Norbert ever complained about his supper."

Years later, Norbert, by then a widower, made it a Sunday ritual to drop in to see my mother who was nearing one hundred. Many times, he'd bring a pair of pants or a shirt for her to mend. If it was beyond patching, as it often was, Mom would tell him straight out, "Throw it away and get yourself a new one. Spend a little of that money you've been hoarding." He never took offense, but I doubt if he ever bought a new one.

During these years, Norbert also spent a lot of time with my brother, who had become disabled. Alvin no longer drove a car, so Norbert chauffeured him to Minot to shop for groceries, go to doctor appointments, etc., and on the way home it was a must that they stop at Speedway for a couple of beers. Alvin, a survivor of throat cancer, used to laugh and say that the reason he and Norbert, who was hard of hearing, got along so well was because he couldn't talk and Norbert couldn't hear.

Many Sundays, Norbert would pick up Alvin, and the two of them would drive over to Mom's. Connie and my sister-in-law Edith were often there, and as soon as Norbert walked in, out came the cards for a hot whist game. Mom and Norbert were always partners and were hard to beat. Friendly noisy bantering was part of the game, and it was not unusual to hear, "Do you think you're playing with kids?" or "How do you like them apples?" as they laughingly slapped down a card and raked in the trick. These whist games with Norbert livened up many afternoons for my elderly mother, and it was a sad day when he fell sick and passed away a short time after he was hospitalized. Sunday afternoons at Mom's were never quite the same. He was sorely missed.

Norbert's children had all gone their different ways, so when Norbert died, another pioneer family of the community was gone. Only laughable memories of splattered potatoes and cabbage, "sexy butterfly" and Norbert's famed "noooooo" remain.

The Glicks

The Rawleigh Man and his first route truck complete with chicken crates

Dick Glick was well known in Foxholm and the widespread surrounding areas as the Rawleigh Man. He was also well known in the livestock world.

Dick grew up in Roseglen, North Dakota near the Indian reservation. As a young man, he broke horses for the Indians, which began a lifetime of working with cattle and horses. He met and married Margaret Hall, an area schoolteacher, and had four children, three girls and a son, Bill. In 1928, when Bill was two years old, the Glick family moved to Foxholm where they became active and longtime members of the community.

Dick, tall and imposing with a bullhorn voice, was a personable man who dealt easily with the public. He loved his cigars and was often seen with one clenched between his teeth.

Dick and Marge, Frank and Esther Anderson and my parents often got together on Sunday nights for a friendly game of poker. Dick's loud, friendly banter kept the game interesting, and the blue haze of his cigars lent a slight atmospheric resemblance to the poker games in an old Wild-West saloon. His hands were very large, and he had one stub finger as a result of a gone-awry steer-roping episode. Consequently, he wore his impressive gold ring on his middle finger. I remember that ring because it represented an organization that was not found in our Catholic community. I grew up knowing nothing about the Masons except that it was a forbidden subject for Catholics; therefore, Dick being a Mason piqued my interest. I never heard Dick discuss his affiliation with the Masons, but I knew that he occasionally motored to Minot to attend different functions. In my mind, that placed him a little higher up on Foxholm's social ladder.

For at least 50 years, Dick sold Rawleigh products. The motto of this company is: "Rawleigh, a Friend of the Family Since 1889."

The Rawleigh Man and his products truly were "friends of the family" in the days before cars and good roads were commonplace. The Rawleigh dealer traveled to the farmers and their wives with a myriad of products that included everything from household cleaning products and pudding and pie mixes to home remedies. His visit meant more than just restocking your shelves. It was a diversion from the daily grind, a chance to hear news from the surrounding community. The kids also looked forward to his visit knowing that before he left, there would be a piece of candy or gum for them.

Dick's first Rawleigh vehicle was the very popular Model A Ford which he customized a bit to accommodate chicken crates. Many times in the 1930's, his customers didn't have the money to buy his products, so they would barter for them—often with live chickens. I can still see him coming down the road, kicking up a regular dust storm as he whizzed along at thirty-five miles per hour. As he drew near, we could hear the loud squawking of chickens that nearly drowned out the sound of the Model A's four-cylinder motor.

Carbolic salve, commonly known as cow salve, was a staple in all households, and Mom made sure that we were never without it. It came in a yellow, round tin box with red trim and lettering and had W.T. Rawleigh's picture on the top. The advertisement boasted: "Fit for Man or Beast, excludes and destroys germs and protects wounds from dirt and air. Softens, lubricates, and soothes skin and helps to reduce inflammation and soreness."

And it really, truly did! It was rubbed on the cow's teats to heal them when they became cracked and sore, on chapped hands and on scrapes and skins. It was the miracle salve of all time, and it still is. Other Rawleigh best sellers were nectar, vanilla, pie fillings and red liniment. One of my favorites was the lemon pie filling which came in powdered form in a tall, tin can. It had just the right amount of tang, not overly sweet and not too tart, and when poured into one of Mom's piecrusts, it couldn't be beat. She made the best piecrusts. Her technique plus the use of lard, the shortening of those days, resulted in a crust so flaky that it would crumble when touched with a fork. Of course, the pie had to have meringue, and Mom's was always high and fluffy with just the right tinge of golden brown. Lemon pie is still one of my favorites, only now I make it from scratch as the Rawleigh Man is long gone from my life. I did inherit Mom's touch in making the crust, but I use Crisco instead of lard, which has now become out of favor.

Nectar was very popular with the old as well as young. There were neither soft-drink machines nor soda fountains in our rural area, and pop was not on the grocery list, so this was the drink that found its way from the supper table out to the fields during harvest time. It came in a concentrated liquid form in a bottle similar to a large bottle of vanilla. There were several flavors, but orange was always my favorite; cherry was my least.

Rawleigh's peppermint extract is another thing that I recall. I conjured up many stomachaches knowing that Mom would make me a hot, sweet, peppermint drink, which miraculously cured it every time. I was always sure that my act was convincing, but as I look back, I know that I hadn't fooled her for a minute.

Rawleigh didn't offer S&H Green Stamps or dishes in their oatmeal, but it did have its own sales gimmick. My sister Connie recalls choosing a pink-checkered dress with a little white collar and cuffs for her daughter Sharon as a premium for having purchased a certain amount of Rawleigh products.

Greg Ulberg, my niece Renee's husband who grew up on a farm near Berthold, was part of a later generation who waited for the Rawleigh Man. They could see Dick's panel truck (minus the chicken crates) when he left their neighbor's farm about half a mile away. He'd purposely hang around the house until the transaction was completed so he wouldn't miss out when Dick asked, "You kids want a treat?" I laughed when Greg told me that because I could just see Dick looking over his glasses and asking me the same question. Greg said he most often chose the little package of gum because there were two pieces in it, and he could make it last longer then the candy. As for me, I always went for the candy.

Greg Ulberg (my whist partner)

While on his Rawleigh route, Dick made a lot of cattle deals that benefited both the rancher and Dick. He would buy good young bulls without pedigrees and then would loan them to area ranchers to use for a year or two. The bulls were returned to Dick all fattened up and ready for market. Gradually, he worked his way into a successful business of buying and selling cattle. The cattle were held in the stockyards in Foxholm and then shipped by rail to the meat packing plants in South St. Paul, Minnesota. It was necessary that someone accompany the cattle, which was time consuming and inconvenient. Therefore, in 1950, Dick's son Bill, who was working in Chicago, came home with his wife Franceen and his two daughters to go into the trucking business. Instead of shipping, Bill trucked his father's cattle to Fargo as well as South St. Paul. This was the beginning of his own very successful career in the trucking and cattle business which evolved into part ownership of Minot Livestock, an auction sales ring, and Dakota Meats, a packing plant.

Bill was a big, broad-shouldered man with rugged good looks. He had a shock of dark brown hair that appeared almost black when he applied his Brylcreem, expressive eyes accentuated with a mass of laugh lines and beautiful white teeth. He was an outdoorsman and during the summer always had a dark suntan that made his smile all the more dazzling. Bill, who only had an eighth-grade education, was highly intelligent and an astute businessman. He could look at a pen full of cattle, estimate the weight, make an offer and show a profit for the cattle owner and himself. He acquired many of these skills from working with his father, but he quickly learned and applied new and improved business tactics.

Not only did Bill work for himself, he also worked for his community. Bill's business brought him in contact with many people with whom he became very well acquainted. His honesty and directness earned him great respect. When he decided to run for Ward County Commissioner, he won by a landslide and went on to prove that the voters had made a good choice.

Bill met Franceen in New York when he was in the service. He and a buddy had gone to Coney Island to wile away a Sunday afternoon when he spotted an attractive girl who was drinking from a water fountain. Bill couldn't resist. He leaned over, placed his finger on the waterspout and squirted her smack in the face. That was the beginning of a lifelong love affair between the six-foot-two farm boy and the five-foot-two city gal.

Franceen and Bill

Franceen was a city girl through and through. She was born in Austria to Jewish parents, Leon and Adela Kornbluh, and moved with her family to Montreal, Canada when she was three years old.

The city of Montreal offered a variety of interesting and fun activities for all ages. Winter was a time for skiing on the nearby slopes and ice-skating on the huge outdoor rink at the foot of Mt. Royal. Since their father was a tailor, Franceen and her siblings were the best-dressed kids on the block. She fondly recalls an ice-skating outfit that he made for her—a dark purple circular velvet skirt and a white turtleneck sweater that complimented her white figure skates. She tells about the Royal Canadian Hockey team that practiced on a nearby rink and how she and her friends would stand and watch, hoping to learn a few pointers. Kids in Canada grow up on the ice and play hockey at a very young age. Franceen was no different. She, however, played hockey in the street with the neighborhood boys and proved herself to be a formidable player. For this sport, Franceen's father fashioned a rust-colored pants suit that sported a short jacket with a mink collar and cuffs. The matching fur-lined, Dutch-style cap tied under her chin emphasizing her Liz Taylor eyes, classic high cheekbones and her prominent Jewish nose that only added to her charm.

Franceen loved to dance and, at age seventeen, frequently went to a pavilion in Montreal that was equivalent to the American USO Club. Her Jewish parents were very strict, but because the club's policy forbade any girl to leave the pavilion with a serviceman, they allowed her to go. It was here that she met a sailor who was a master of Latin dance, and they became a favorite couple on the dance floor. When Franceen danced, she was very expressive; when she moved, everything moved! Her long black hair became a mass of riotous natural curls as she whirled around the floor. Franceen loved reminiscing about these dancing days and was known to break into a tango to demonstrate how she and the sailor stole the show as they glided and dipped their way across the large dance floor.

When she was eighteen, Franceen and her family moved to the Bronx, New York. They attended the Synagogue regularly and observed all High Holidays and other religious traditions.

Life was good for Franceen. She worked as a bookkeeper and wore designer clothes made especially for her by her father. Wool coats lined with fur, matching hats, and trim for her snow boots (sometimes wool and sometimes fur) were only some of the creations that bespoke his talents. She frequented art museums, dined in elegant restaurants, played handball in the park, visited the Bronx Park Zoo with her grandmother and often took the subway to Coney Island. It was on one of these excursions that she met Bill at the drinking fountain, and the rest is history.

Bill and Franceen's wedding was storybook material. Bill wore a black tuxedo and top hat that accentuated his natural good looks. Franceen was a lovely bride in an elegant white gown that was designed and sewn especially for her. Dancing followed the reception, and although Bill was more at home on a horse than on a dance floor, he gamely gave it a try. After the wedding, they moved to Chicago. Franceen was right at home in the cosmopolitan city, but Bill felt the pull of the country, and when the opportunity to move back to his roots arose, he jumped at the chance. Franceen, always ready for a new challenge, gathered up their two small children, donned her dark turquoise wool coat with its generous amount of grey Persian lamb trim, her matching pillbox hat (also trimmed in Persian lamb) and her three inch high heel boots (also trimmed in fur) and followed her husband. One can only imagine the culture shock that she experienced upon her arrival to what would be her home for the rest of her life.

Franceen's immediate impression of her new home on the Midwest prairie was one of amazement. "It's so vacant! Why on earth don't some of the people who are crowded into New York move out here?" As she shook her head in wonderment she added, "Whoever thought there was so much available land and so few people living on it?"

Suddenly, the big city girl was living in a rural North Dakota community of less than a hundred people. They bought the Nick Johannes house that was just down the gravel road, about two city blocks from our house. I would make many trips down that road in the years to come, as Franceen and I became very good friends.

After living all her years with only having to turn on a faucet, Franceen now had no running water and no indoor plumbing. I can still hear her laugh as she said, "We've got running water. We run out to the well, pump a pail of water and run back into the house." Baths were taken in a large tin tub that was hauled into the kitchen on Saturday nights. It didn't take her long to figure out that she had to make sure she closed the curtain on the window in the kitchen door before climbing into the tub.

The coal cooking range was a particular challenge for this prairie pioneer. Until she walked into her new kitchen, she had never even seen such a stove, much less try to use one. She laughed as she recalled how long it took for her to figure out how to cook a meal in a reasonable length of time without it being raw in the inside and burnt on the outside.

Minot, the nearest and largest city, boasting of a population of about eighteen thousand, was seventeen miles away. Having never learned to drive, it was difficult for Franceen to attend the Synagogue, which, if she remembered correctly, only observed the High Holidays. Eventually, Franceen gave up her Jewish religion entirely, and she and her children were baptized in the Lutheran Church in Carpio.

Franceen slowly became acclimated to her new environment, and things became a little easier for her. Water was piped in from the cistern for kitchen use but not for drinking. She could tolerate hauling in drinking water, but the outhouse was a continual irritation. Still, she was a trouper and gave it all she had. One day, her brother Harvey, who was staying with them and working for Crane and Ordway, a plumbing supplies store in Minot, brought home a real find—two cracked, blue wooden toilet seats that were headed for the dump.

Franceen immediately got out her tool kit and headed for the outhouse. She positioned the toilet seats over the holes and nailed them in place. Next, she purchased blue checkered gingham and sewed a curtain for the window. She gave the white painted walls another routine washing with Rawleigh sheep dip to help mask the odor and stood back to survey her handiwork. With the electric light bulb and the redecorating, it was a downright work of art! However, the inconvenience of no bathroom remained. The children used a chamber pot in the upstairs bedrooms during the night. Franceen told about the time she fell down the stairs carrying a full pot. Pregnant and big as a house, she had only taken a few steps when she slipped and lost her balance. The pot flew out of her hand, splattering its contents in every direction. Her first thought was of the baby. When she was sure that the baby was fine, she sat and cried. Finally, crawling on hands and knees with her big belly barely clearing the floor, she managed, with a help of a generous amount of Pine Sol, to get everything cleaned up and back to normal.

Franceen was an animal lover. One day when Bill was out in the country, he discovered five crying baby raccoons and their dead mother in an old threshing machine. When Bill came in for lunch that day, he happened to mention the raccoons. Franceen immediately rushed to the rescue. She took a chicken hook, which is a staff with a hook on the end, and painstakingly fished them out one by one. She bottle-fed and nurtured them until they were old enough to be weaned. The little bandits romped and played like kittens and grew bigger and bigger. The day came, as fate would have it, when they disappeared over the riverbank. Time passed and Franceen and her children, who now numbered five, knew they had to accept the inevitable; their pets had gone back to their natural habitat. One day to their surprise and delight, the raccoons were back, but they were not alone. They had brought their families. The Glicks admired the new members, wished them well and waved goodbye one last time.

After the raccoons, Franceen cared for skunks. A young skunk came wandering in one day, and Franceen enticed him to stay. She had him descented, and Barney became a house pet. By this time, Bill was used to Fran's pets—but a skunk? Barney stayed. Then came the day when he, too, disappeared over the riverbank. It seemed he fell in love, and he later brought his mate home for their approval. The mate promptly sprayed, and the Glick-Skunk relationship was severed forever.

One of the stockyards in Fargo received a small Mexican burro along with a truckload of cattle. He was rather cute, but who wants a burro? Glick's name was mentioned, and there were grins and nods. A conspiracy was formed, and when Bill came in with a load of cattle, they were waiting for him with a convincing story about why he should have this premium burro. Bill ended up taking the burro home and gave him to Franceen for Mother's Day. Pedro loved his new home and became a wonderful pet. He followed Franceen around like a puppy dog. If the door was left open, Pedro would trot right into the kitchen where he'd stand and wait for a treat and maybe a scratch behind his long, floppy ears. When she went to the neighbors for coffee, Pedro would follow and wait at the gate for her. If Franceen visited a little longer than usual, they'd hear "Eeee Ahh, Eeee Ahh" as if to say, "I'm tired; I wanna go home." When Franceen walked past the schoolhouse, Pedro tailing behind, all the kids jumped up and ran to the window. Mrs. Ahmann laughingly gave up and let the kids go outside to greet the obliging animal. No doubt about it, Pedro became the most famous "kid" in town. It was a sad day, indeed, when he was found dead in the garden. I don't remember the cause of death, but I do remember that the little stockyard orphan was fondly remembered for a long time.

Eventually, Franceen and Bill did get running water and indoor plumbing. She did learn to drive, to cultivate a garden, to fish and to work cattle, but more importantly, she learned to adapt and enjoy a completely different way of life. Garage sales finds took the place of custom-made clothes, and spike heels and silks were replaced with loafers and jeans. The big city slowly faded away and was replaced by the serenity, simplicity and intimacy of small town living.

Bill, I'm sad to say, is gone as are his parents, but Franceen still lives in their home in Minot. I'm happy to say that she is as adventurous and outgoing as ever. Adella, their daughter, is the only one of the Glicks left in Foxholm. She lives with her husband in her Grandpa and Grandma Glick's home and has a pet forty-pound lynx. The acorn didn't fall far from the tree.

Franceen today...She hasn't changed a bit.

Epilogue

The Foxholm I knew is gone. The ghost-town gods are smiling, ready to claim it as their very own.

The mechanization of farming and the lack of job and entertainment opportunities have sent Foxholm's young people scurrying off to the cities, never to return. I was one of those who left, and although I treasure my rural roots and often long for the simplicity, the peacefulness, the closeness that would await me, I, too, will never return.

I wanted to believe that the town whose traditional values were sewn into the fabric of my very soul, the small town to which my heartstrings remain tethered, could somehow survive this exodus, but it was not meant to be. Foxholm, a community which once evidenced the robustness of rural America, is worn out, blowing to dust. The only things remaining are a cluster of homes, the Catholic church that is stubbornly hanging on by its fingernails and one bar that clings to the dream of a miraculous resurgence.

I am glad that I was born soon enough to have seen our small town, if not at its height, at least in the early stages of decline and to have experienced the strong sense of togetherness, the nurturing and protecting that ran throughout the community, forming bonds that have lasted a lifetime.

It is my hope that you have enjoyed this book—that it evoked happy memories, historically enlightened and brought back to life, if only for a moment, a town that was.

Foxholm today
Photo by Patty Erickson

Sources

The incidents and stories, all of which are true, have been taken from family records and personal memories. The historical information was taken from "Why Not Minot" found in Minot Public Library, Minot State University Library, North Dakota Archives, Historical Research Library, Ward County Courthouse, and the Minot Daily New's 1992 annual magazine "Home Town".